TOWARD A DANGEROUS WORLD

U.S. National Security Strategy for the Coming Turbulence

Richard L. Kugler

Prepared for the Joint Staff

Approved for public release;
distribution unlimited

National Defense Research Institute

RAND

This report is the final product of RAND'S two-year National Defense Research Institute (NDRI) project on future U.S. military strategy for the twenty-first century. The project's first report dealt with U.S. conventional-force planning methodology for the post–Cold War era. A second report dealt with future trends in American military strategy as a function of U.S. interests and goals, alternative international security systems, technological changes, and military trends. Building on those efforts, this report focuses on one particular challenge of the future: the possibility that the current international system will give way to something far more dangerous. The need to prepare for this possibility is growing because negative trends have emerged in international politics (e.g., stagnating world economy, turmoil in formerly communist countries, cultural antagonism) since the optimistic aftermath of the fall of the Berlin Wall. If such trends gather force, they could confront the United States with a need to rethink its national security policy, military strategy, and force planning.

This report was prepared for the Department of Defense. The research for it was carried out within the International Security and Defense Policy Center, a component of RAND's NDRI. NDRI is a federally funded research and development center sponsored by the Office of the Secretary of Defense, the Joint Staff, and the defense agencies.

The material presented here is intended to be helpful to U.S. government officials who deal with national security policy, military strategy, and forces. It also will be of interest to other analysts who deal with these issues.

CONTENTS

TABLES

This study examines the foreign policy and national security implications of a single dominant hypothesis: that a dangerous world may lie ahead, a world of greater turbulence than today's. Immediately after the Cold War ended, many observers felt optimistic that an enduring era of peace lay ahead, and the generally tranquil situation gave them reasons for thinking so. The past months, however, have brought troubling events abroad and mounting worry among governments and security experts everywhere. Only a year ago, the prevailing mood was optimism, but pessimism is now starting to take hold. Nobody can pretend to have a crystal ball. Yet the time is fast arriving when the United States and its allies will need to take stock of the negative trends that are unfolding, determine what those trends mean for Western security interests, and decide how to respond.

Surveying the current trends, this study offers scenarios of how those trends may play out and puts forth ideas about how U.S. and Western policies will need to be altered over the coming decade or two. But its message is more fundamental than that of endorsing any single, inevitably controversial scenario or policy response: It asserts that a dangerous world will be far more complex than the very menacing but comfortingly clear-cut situation faced by the Western world during the Cold War. The United States will no longer confront a single hegemonic threat in a bipolar setting with many close allies at its side. Indeed, the era ahead may offer precisely the opposite of all these features. The United States will need to learn not only how to act differently than during the Cold War but how to *think* very differently as well.

Many of the security premises and precepts inherited from the Cold War are today buried so deeply in the "subconscious" of U.S. strategic doctrine that policymakers and strategists are scarcely aware of their existence. Most will have to be uprooted and replaced by something new. During the nineteenth century, Britain—then a global superpower—developed a capacity to react flexibly and adaptively, and to juggle many "security balls" in an ever-changing and turbulent international setting. The United States will not have to repeat Britain's performance, for the twenty-first century will be very different from the nineteenth century, and U.S. values are different from imperial Britain's. But if a dangerous world evolves, U.S. policymakers may have to acquire some of Britain's core strategic skills. Thus, the looming prospect of a dangerous world means that before the United States starts to act, it had best think deeply about exactly what confronts it, what options are at its disposal, and what it is trying to achieve.[1]

TRENDS: TOWARD A DANGEROUS WORLD?

Any attempt to grapple with a dangerous world should begin by acknowledging that the heady optimism of the immediate post–Cold War years was premature, as the survey of the literature of optimism in Chapter Two demonstrates. The end of the Cold War did not itself mean the onset of permanent tranquility, and the downfall of European communism did not mean that peaceful, market democracy[2] was on the verge of spreading everywhere. Today's mounting pessimism thus is partly the product of exaggerated expectations suffering inevitable disappointment.

Yet more is involved than readjusting U.S. hopes downward, for international events appear to be sliding downhill: Democratic reforms are faltering in Russia, and the Bosnian crisis continues. The underlying causes go far beyond these two events, however. If the

---

[1]For an assessment of changes in U.S. policy and strategy if the international system becomes more stable than now, see Richard L. Kugler, *U.S. Military Strategy and Force Posture in the 21st Century: Capabilities and Requirements*, Santa Monica, Calif.: RAND, MR-328-JS, 1994.

[2]A *market democracy* is a country that has a democratic political system and a capitalist, free-enterprise economic system.

newly published academic literature of international pessimism surveyed in Chapter Three is correct, many powerful factors are at work, and they are interacting in ways that magnify their negative consequences. Moreover, not just one region is being affected. In varying ways and with varying magnitudes, nearly all regions are being affected, and trends in a separate region are influencing those in other regions. The result is a global drift toward instability that is taking place silently, unobserved, below the surface—but one that is real nonetheless.

This drift is being caused by many factors working together, some old and some new. They include the rise of angry ethnicity, resurgent nationalism, cultural antagonism, and anti-Western ideologies. Also important are rising expectations amid deepening poverty, turmoil in former communist countries, a stagnating world economy, and growing economic competition that is threatening to bring about a return to autarchy and mercantilism. Faced with these negative trends, governments everywhere seem to be losing not only the willingness to cooperate with each other but also the ability to shape their own destinies. To top this list are destabilizing geopolitical dynamics reminiscent of bygone eras: explosive power vacuums,[3] mounting fears that give rise to imprudent conduct, the reappearance of old rivalries, and the replacement of stable bipolarity with unstable multipolarity—dynamics that are magnifying the incentives for nuclear proliferation while posing an equal risk of the spread of modern conventional weapons. The consequence is not only a growing capacity to wage war but also the emergence of military imbalances of power that further weaken global stability.

Where will all these trends lead? If the worst does transpire, the world could combine the negative features of nineteenth-century geopolitics, twentieth-century political passions, and twenty-first-century technology: a chronically turbulent world of unstable multipolarity, atavistic nationalism, and modern armaments. Yet the future is unknowable. The "tectonic plates" of international politics are shifting in profound ways, and because we do not grasp the complex causal dynamics at work, we are unable to predict the

---

[3]A *power vaccum* is a situation in which security guarantees are absent and imbalances in physical resources—especially military resources—invite aggressive conduct.

outcome. To the extent that destabilizing dynamics take hold, tomorrow's world may well be more dangerous than today's, not only in the magnitude of the dangers but in the types of dangers.

SCENARIOS FOR A DANGEROUS WORLD

In an effort to forge conceptual order out of confusion, this study points to three variables as being critical to the future: Western relations with Russia and China; the magnitude of regional tensions in Europe, Asia, and the Middle East/Persian Gulf; and the status of the Western Alliance. These variables will not control all dimensions of the future, but they will play influential roles in shaping the all-important structural features of the international security system: As they go, so will go the world.

Chapter Four describes 28 different ways in which these variables could interact. It points to one scenario as being the most probable, or at least as best representing a host of similar outcomes: traditional geopolitical rivalry of the West with Russia and China; heightened tensions in Europe, Asia, and the Middle East/Persian Gulf; and a still-cohesive Western Alliance, but with an uncertain capacity to address problems beyond its borders. If this scenario hints at the future, it offers some comfort, for it is not a worst-case outcome. Western geopolitical rivalry with Russia and China is far less dangerous than all-out confrontation and can be moderated by diplomacy and responsive policies. Heightened tensions in all three regions do not imply an explosion into permanent warfare: Such tensions will be more difficult to manage than those of today, but they *will be* manageable. A Western Alliance with an uncertain capacity to act is far less worrisome than an alliance that fractures altogether, leaving its members on their own.

Even so, were this scenario to be realized, it would confront the United States with greater international troubles than today. Currently, the United States faces serious tensions in only two regions: the Middle East/Persian Gulf and Northeast Asia (Korea). Bosnia notwithstanding, Europe is stable. Minor frictions aside, Western relations with Russia and China are harmonious. If a dangerous world appears in the form of this scenario, the U.S. security agenda will expand greatly. It will be like a juggler who will have to juggle five weighty, unwieldy "balls" instead of a manageable two.

The United States' regional efforts will be pulled in wider directions, dealing not just with two zones of turmoil but with a third: East Central Europe and the Balkans. As the United States grapples with these regional instabilities, it will have to manage troubles with Russia and China, because they assert nationalist agendas in Europe and Asia partly at the expense of U.S. interests and those of its closest allies. To further complicate matters, troubled relations with Russia and China may impede U.S. regional policies, and regional tensions may intensify the United States' problems with both countries. The act of juggling these five "balls" thus will be made harder because the "balls" themselves will collide and bounce off each other.

The task will be made easier if U.S. alliances help, but far harder if they do not. Indeed, can the United States hope to manage a security agenda this complex if its allies do not lend strong support? Will alliances that defend only traditional borders be useful if the main problems lie outside those borders? The answers to these questions will identify U.S. priorities in a dangerous world.

THE NEED FOR STRATEGIC THINKING

This scenario is merely one illustration of what may lie ahead, and even it has many subvariations. If a dangerous world appears, therefore, the task will be more fundamental than preparing an action agenda and then implementing it with customary vigor. Because the Cold War and other twentieth-century conflicts produced great clarity (i.e., the "enemy" was easy to identify), the United States had the luxury of acting boldly, often without scrutinizing the exact problems being faced, the goals to be achieved, and the relationship between actions and objectives. This was especially the case for the Cold War, whose bipolar structure took shape quite early and remained in stasis for over 40 years.

Scrutiny or reflection was far from completely lacking, but it was most needed at the onset of new endeavors. Even then, the problems posed by the international system were straightforward, although the solutions often were not. The United States regularly was able to focus on means rather than on ends and first principles: on actions to be taken rather than on *why* they were being taken. Because the world was so static, this nation had the luxury of planning on the basis of extrapolation into the future: A single plan could be adopted, and with only modest variations, all U.S. programs could be tailored to support it. As a result, the United States learned to think at the margins: It became skilled at policy engineering and program management, but less adept at shaping new visions and strategic concepts.

What is meant by *reflection* is demonstrated by nineteenth-century Prime Minister Robert Cecil, Lord Salisbury. He found that the need to think carefully beforehand was more difficult than making fateful decisions and taking drastic steps. Such careful thinking involved forging conceptual order out of chaos, deciphering complex problems, weighing the issues and alternatives deliberately, then making reasoned choices that balanced competing concerns. A dangerous world will put a far greater premium on reflection, because its contours may be unclear and very complex: a unique blend of traditionalism and modernity that defies simple characterization. This world will deny the United States not only intellectual clarity but also moral simplicity, for realism will have to be joined with idealism in ways that produce a more complex policy calculation than before. The task will not be to subjugate a hegemonic enemy in a bipolar setting, to lead a galvanized alliance on behalf of a compelling moral vision in the face of an ideological threat. Instead, the task will be to deal with a fluid, multipolar setting, with countries that are neither permanent foes nor friends; to balance interests rather than promote absolutist values; and to coax reluctant allies to join ambiguous causes. Owing to all these complex dimensions, subtlety will be required, and it can be gained only through mature thought that prefers erudition and wisdom to sophistry and shibboleths.

Reflection may become a near-permanent state of affairs because the international system might not settle into a new stasis. Instead, it might undergo continuous, rapid change, veering sharply from one structural mode to the next, compelling the United States to think and rethink. Even if a new stasis comes about, the United States will need to forge a comprehensive vision, a design of the state of affairs it is trying to achieve.

As a result, the first-order task will be to set aside the impulse to act, and to ponder thoroughly the purpose of U.S. policy and strategy. Some argue that today's world allows the United States to muddle through: to address an issue on its individual merits, in the absence of an overarching strategic concept that provides visionary direction and guidance for coordinating multiple separate actions. Whether this approach is wise even in a stable world may be debated. Such an approach will not be feasible in a dangerous world, because events will be too interconnected and the consequences of error too great to permit anything other than an integrated policy and strategy.

TOWARD A NEW NATIONAL SECURITY POLICY FOR A DANGEROUS WORLD

Need for Coherent Policy and Strategy

A central conclusion of this study is that the quest for coherent policy and strategy should be guided by the premise that, if disengagement and isolationism are infeasible in today's world, they will be doubly so in a dangerous world. Nor will the United States and its allies be able to insulate themselves from the zones of turmoil that lie outside the Western Alliance. For many reasons discussed in the text, the West's own interests are steadily expanding beyond current borders, and outside turbulence easily could expand to the point of directly damaging the Western countries, including the United States. The United States will not be able to rely heavily on the United Nations and other multilateral organizations, because such organizations will lose effectiveness in a dangerous world that weakens global consensus. Nor will the United States be able to devolve full responsibility for security management onto the shoulders of its allies: If the allies are to be effective, they will need superpower leadership that only the United States can provide. For these reasons, a dangerous world will mandate a U.S. policy postulated on engagement, activist involvement in the zones of turmoil, and U.S. leadership of alliances.

An appropriate U.S. national security policy for a dangerous world— the kind of world reflected in the preceding scenario—would be very different from the policy of today. The current strategic policy is *enlargement*, a policy that assumes the international situation is inherently stable. It therefore judges that the spread of market democracy will be easily accomplished and that international economics can replace security as the principal focus of policy. Enlargement further emphasizes the building of a partnership relationship with Russia. Critics have charged that this is a "Russia-first" policy. Regardless of whether this accusation is fair, the current policy places high priority on establishing a strategic partnership with Russia. All these components must be modified if a dangerous world appears, because their premises will be invalidated.

Alliance First

To help promote dialogue, this study puts forth a revised approach, in Chapter Five—an "alliance-first" policy aimed at *systemic containment*: containment of multiple tensions for the purpose of preserving global stability. Under this policy, security management would be restored to a preeminent position at least equal to economics, and perhaps superior to it. The dominant goals would be to protect the vital interests of the United States and its closest allies, and to manage the turbulence of a dangerous world so that the occurrence of full-scale deterioration and catastrophic explosion is prevented. Containment would focus not on preventing expansion and aggression by a single hegemonic adversary but on preventing the violent forces of upheaval from consuming a dangerous world. The outward expansion of market democracy would still be pursued in regions where this goal is feasible and important to the West. But a first-things-first philosophy would be adopted: stability first, and, as a consequence, progress second.

Under this policy, the United States' first priority would be to preserve and upgrade the Western Alliance because healthy alliances capable of projecting security outward will be critical to maintaining stability. To that end, this policy would seek a new transatlantic bargain for NATO and a new trans-Pacific bargain in Asia. Both new bargains would seek to reorganize key U.S. alliances on the basis of U.S. leadership, but a leadership that would promote coequal distribution of influence and responsibility based on fair burden-sharing. The product of this reorganization would be new alliance partnerships for projecting involvement and security outward. By laying a foundation of security beyond current Alliance borders, the conditions can be created for encouraging the growth of market democracy in neighboring countries and gradually incorporating them into the Western community and Alliance. Enlargement thus would still take place, but it would proceed gradually, and it would move geographically outward from current Alliance borders.

Geopolitical Rivalry with Russia and China

This policy would endeavor to manage the reality of traditional Western geopolitical rivalry with Russia and China by means other than a futile quest for close friendship and partnership. Its goal would be to achieve a political equilibrium anchored on principles of legitimacy, mutual respect for vital interests, and agreed-upon rules of behavior that honor the sovereignty of countries on the periphery of Russia and China. These two countries thus would be accorded the respectful status of major powers pursuing their legitimate interests in a traditional era; however, they would not be allowed to pursue neo-imperial policies beyond their borders, especially if the outcome might be renewed military threats to the West.

To help achieve this goal, the United States and its allies would endeavor to maintain a stable military balance of power vis-à-vis Russia and China. The West's military approach would comprise defensive strategies and forces and would avoid offensive threats that could be considered provocative behavior by these two nations. The goal would be to maintain an atmosphere of peaceful dissuasion in ways that underscore political equilibrium and the security interests of nations on the borders of Russia and China.

Tensions in Europe, Asia, and the Middle East/Persian Gulf

The combination of revitalized alliances and equilibrium with Russia and China provides the framework for a U.S.-led effort to manage the regional tensions of a dangerous world. To manage Europe's growing tensions while not downgrading the Middle East/Persian Gulf and Asia, U.S. policy would broaden and U.S efforts would shift back and forth in response to the ebb and flow of tensions in these regions. The dominant goal will not be to resolve the tensions in some final sense, for they will be too deep-seated for that. Instead, the goal will be to contain the tensions: to prevent them from spreading in size and geographic scope, and especially to prevent them from escalating in ways that involve the major powers (i.e., the United States, Russia, China, Japan, Germany, and the European Union) and provoke confrontation among them. Intervention thus would not be indiscriminate or pursued for its own sake. It would be carried out selectively when warranted by vital U.S. interests, and for the limited purpose of crisis management and resolution. Moreover, it would be implemented only after a sound policy has first been fashioned to provide a coherent relationship between means and ends and to offer a feasible and affordable path to stability.

Requirements and Advantages of Policy

This policy thus is animated by a sense of *realpolitik*, yet it also offers a vehicle for promoting democratic values and cooperative community. It endeavors to strike a workable balance between realism and idealism. It also accords with the realities of a dangerous world that will allow for neither U.S. disengagement nor a moral crusade. The policy will require a traditional form of statesmanship by the United States—a patient and continuing superpower leadership that employs power on behalf of purpose and coherent strategy—and should provide an instrument for that kind of statesmanship.

To be sure, such a policy may run counter to the United States' domestic predilections, requiring sustained commitment of resources at a time when domestic priorities are being pursued. It also will require the United States to play the role of geopolitical manager, a role the country has normally shunned during ambiguous times when a clear moral cause was lacking. For both reasons, domestic support for this policy may be hard to maintain. Mature leadership by the Executive Branch and Congress will be required. To avoid the dangers of domestic overload, this policy must also be guided by a sense of proportion and restraint: Priorities will have to be set and peripheral involvements avoided. If these requirements are met, this policy can be implemented both in the near term and for 10 to 20 years or more.

For all its burdensome features, this policy offers important advantages for the coming decades if a dangerous world appears:

- It will permit the United States to continue pursuing domestic renewal even as it acts to contain global instabilities that threaten the nation's vital interests.
- It will reduce the risk of an international explosion that could compel abandonment of essential domestic programs.

- It is an affordable and feasible policy that focuses on vital U.S. interests.

- It downplays immediate hope for a peaceful democratic world in favor of an approach aimed at managing turbulence.

- Within the limits of what will be possible, it offers progress in slow but achievable ways.

- It will not allow the United States to escape history, but it will help enable the United States to make history its servant, not its master.

ANALYSIS OF FUTURE MILITARY CONFLICTS

Accompanying a sound national security policy will need to be a coherent U.S. military strategy that supports the policy and that is aligned with the requirements of the future. It will be especially important, therefore, that the Department of Defense conduct probing analyses of future military conflicts. In today's world, the Persian Gulf and Korea seem the most likely regions of war. But will they be in the years ahead? The answer will depend heavily on the root causes of future conflicts. Whereas, during the Cold War, the threat of global warfare stemmed from the ideological rivalry between democracy and communism, in today's world, geopolitical ambitions are the principal reasons for the threat of war in the Persian Gulf and Korea. In tomorrow's world, conflict might be triggered by ethnic hatreds, border disputes, minority troubles, conflicting economic agendas, nationalist ideologies, cultural antagonisms, historical rivalries, and competitive arms races (see Chapter Six). The myriad possibilities mean that wars might break out in different places and be fought in different ways. The United States will become involved only when its interests so dictate; in these potential situations, however, it might find itself fighting different enemies and supported by different allies than those who occupy its defense plans at present. To the extent feasible, strong efforts should be exerted to anticipate these conflicts as far in advance as possible.

MILITARY STRATEGY FOR A DANGEROUS WORLD

The United States will need to remain a superpower second to none, because a dangerous world implies that military power will be even more important than it is today. Current U.S. military strategy provides a frame of reference for gauging the future, but in all likelihood the strategy for the future will need to be quite different—a strategy of broader horizons (described in Chapter Seven).

The precise military strategy to be adopted will be a variable, not a constant. It will be influenced by the shape taken by a dangerous world. Indeed, if a dangerous world constantly changes shape, the future might witness the United States' regularly altering its military strategy: casting off one in favor of another much as a person changes clothes as the season changes.

If a dangerous world appears in the form of this study's main scenario, a new military strategy will be more than narrowly regional. It will not have to embrace a global conflict as during the Cold War; however, as with the U.S. national security policy, it will have to juggle many "balls" at once, owing to worldwide security troubles. More than today's strategy, it will pursue an expanded set of goals and priorities, deal with weightier responsibilities, and respond to a wider spectrum of situations. This strategy will still pursue deterrence and defense, but many standard precepts, e.g., forward defense and flexible response, will have to be modified or cast aside. Indeed, the meaning of *deterrence* itself might change.

Peacetime Shaping Function

In a new strategy, the peacetime *shaping function*—the act of guiding key regions toward stability—will acquire an even more important role than it has today. U.S. military power will be called upon to help perform five important functions that will be even harder to carry out than they are now:

- Projecting U.S. influence and resolve onto the world scene, especially into areas of vital geostrategic importance

- Maintaining control of vital sea-lanes for commercial, military, and strategic reasons

- Reassuring Allies and close friends, carrying out Alliance commitments, preserving Alliance cohesion, and promoting Alliance renewal.

- Maintaining a stable and dissuading military balance of power vis-à-vis Russia, China, and any other major power that might emerge as a Western rival

- Providing a military foundation for supporting U.S. policies aimed at dispelling turbulent regional tensions and managing crises that might occur.

Nuclear forces will still be needed, albeit at lower levels than today's. If proliferation occurs, the role of nuclear forces in U.S. military strategy may increase. Yet a dangerous world implies that conventional forces will play the lead role in U.S. strategy because military missions will be more diverse. In the years ahead, Europe seems destined to again become an important theater for defense planning, and in all three critical regions, the outer strategic perimeter seems likely to expand even as a dangerous world unfolds. In all three regions and at sea, moreover, the United States may confront both traditional adversaries and new and better-armed opponents, not only in peace but also in crisis and war (see Chapter Six).

Overseas Presence and Power Projection

U.S. strategy will continue to require a combination of overseas presence and power projection from North America. However, because a larger-than-current overseas presence may be needed, faster power projection may be required, not only into currently planned regions but also into new places, where U.S. forces may be called upon to participate in new conflicts. Most conflicts will take the form of limited wars in which political goals will determine military operations, and a host of nontraditional situations may be encountered: e.g., peacekeeping, peace enforcement, and crisis management. The Decisive Force Doctrine—a doctrine calling for use of overpowering force to achieve clear goals—will remain the model of choice, yet there will be a need for great flexibility to ensure that combat operations make both military and political sense.

FORCE PLANNING FOR A DANGEROUS WORLD

Conventional-Force Posture

A dangerous world implies a requirement for a conventional-force posture as large as today's posture, or even larger. The premium on readiness, agility, mobility, high technology, and modern nonlinear doctrines attuned to both offensive and defensive campaign plans will be even greater than today's. Likewise, joint operations and combined operations with allies—including new allies—will gain even greater importance. This outlook implies a compelling need to retain a force posture that is flexible and diverse: one composed of a balanced combination of ground, naval, and air forces that can work together to achieve military synergy (see Chapter Eight).

Posture-Then-Strategy Approach

Indeed, the capability to support not just one military strategy but several is a powerful additional factor that reinforces the need for flexible diversity and adaptiveness. Whereas the future may compel the United States to change strategies periodically, the nation will have only one posture because military forces cannot be changed with comparable speed. For this reason, the United States may be well advised to adopt an approach that is fundamentally different from conventional-force planning, whereby military strategy is forged first, after which defense posture is carefully tailored to support that strategy.

The great political fluidity of the years ahead may require the United States to shift paradigms by creating its posture first and its strategy (or strategies) later. If so, it will need a posture that permits it to rapidly change strategy directions, and perhaps more than once.

In the coming years, the nation will need to adjust its force posture, to discard unneeded assets, to optimize its assets, and to innovate. Strategic flexibility enables quick adjustment if the world turns upside down overnight, as happened in 1989 and may again. The United States possesses this flexibility today, but to continue possessing it will require adequate resources and intelligent planning that avoids the perils of distorted vision about military superiority.

Qualitative Superiority

Conventional-force planning will confront other changes and dilemmas in a dangerous world. Desert Storm showed that U.S. military forces today are qualitatively superior to those of their opponents. If this superiority can be preserved, the consequence will be greater security and a better capacity to win those wars that might occur. Yet the act of preserving this superiority should not be accompanied by false confidence that the goal will be easily attained, for future opponents will learn the lessons of Desert Storm and improve as well. The United States must guard against the kind of blind overconfidence that leads not only to slackened vigilance but also to a stripping away of the very assets that provide this superiority. High technology is not the sole factor that accounts for the current U.S. edge in quality. Equally important contributors are adequate overall size, multiple diverse assets, joint operations, training and readiness, staying power, modern doctrine, and others. If superiority is to be preserved, a balanced combination of all these assets must be maintained.

Canonical and Nonstandard Scenarios

Conventional-force planning should also avoid the temptation of becoming too locked into *canonical scenarios,* i.e., a few hypothetical conflicts that are deemed so representative of all future wars that U.S. forces can be designed mainly to fight them alone. Canonical scenarios can empower planning by providing specificity, but they can also imprison it by producing tunnel vision. Although their purpose is to allow U.S. forces to do some things quite well, it is not to do so at the cost of becoming unable to handle other problems effectively.

Today's two canonical scenarios are concurrent major regional conflicts (MRCs) in the Persian Gulf and Korea, which represent key present-day dangers and requirements, but which alone may not be a sound guide to preparing for the wars of the future. A dangerous world may serve up many different kinds of wars: U.S. forces may be called upon to fight enemies other than Iraq and North Korea, and to operate in theaters and oceans far removed from the Persian Gulf and Northeast Asia. They may be required to fight smaller conflicts for which the political agendas are more complicated than those for the two MRCs. They may also be asked to wage larger wars, against more powerful, better-armed opponents. And they may face enemies armed with nuclear weapons and willing to use them.

This prospect suggests that force planners may be well advised to broaden the set of scenarios and to examine nonstandard events that pose uniquely different requirements that might otherwise be overlooked. Indeed, U.S. planners might be best served by downgrading the primacy attached to scenario-based planning anchored on single events and threats.

Mission-Based Planning

An attractive alternative is generic planning on the basis of strategic missions, whereby forces are planned not only to fight two canonical MRCs but also to carry out a wide range of different missions in peace, crisis, and war. Employing generic standards to gauge requirements would enable force posture design that ensures that sufficient assets will be available for each mission category, then uses specific scenarios only to fine-tune the posture. This approach to planning admittedly would be more complex than that of today; however, the goal of planning is comprehensiveness, not simplicity. A dangerous world seems destined to be more complex than anything experienced in the past, and U.S. force planning may have to be broadened to capture its diversity.

CONCLUSION: THE INTELLECTUAL GYMNASTICS OF A DANGEROUS WORLD

Irrespective of whether this study's specific recommendations will prove worthy, a dangerous world means that the United States will need to think deeply not only about what must be done but also about why. History has judged Lord Salisbury and other nineteenth-century British leaders a success precisely because they proved adept at the deep-thinking, intellectual side of national security policy and military strategy in a complex age. Their legacy provides the United States a model to ponder as it faces a dangerous world.

ACKNOWLEDGMENTS

Important contributions were provided by James Winnefeld, Dean Millot, Paul Bracken, Paul Davis, Jonathan Pollack, Ron Asmus, Stephen Larrabee, Zalmay Khalilzad, Abe Shulsky, Charlie Kelley, David Gompert, and others at RAND and in the Department of Defense. The author alone is responsible for the material contained herein.

Chapter One

INTRODUCTION

This study addresses the following issue: What will be the consequences for U.S. national security policy if international conditions worsen in the years ahead? The troubling events transpiring abroad are rapidly making the prospect of worsening conditions—of a dangerous world—real enough to be taken seriously. This issue may soon become the most important on the national agenda, for if a dangerous world explodes around the United States with menacing force, the country will be compelled to make a major change not only in how it responds but in how it *thinks* about responding. The United States will need to shift its paradigm for its foreign policy, as well as that for its military strategy and defense planning. Indeed, its domestic agenda may also have to change, but planners would not have the luxury of addressing internal problems in a setting of relaxed optimism about the external environment.

THE ESSENCE OF A DANGEROUS WORLD

The phrase "a dangerous world" has a specific meaning in this study. All international systems contain dangers, and the system existing today is no exception. Yet there will be a critical difference between today and tomorrow if emerging negative trends bring about a major downturn. Today's world presents specific dangers that, for all their seriousness, are isolated from each other in geographic space, operating in separate spheres and thus not acting on each other. Above all, the dangers are the exception, not the rule: They do not dominate world affairs because they arise in an international system whose structural characteristics (as defined in Chapter Three) are stable. As a result, today's dangers may cause the international system to shudder and shake, but they do not threaten to plunge the entire globe into chaotic upheaval and chronic stress.

The difference between today's system and a dangerous world may be registered in a greater frequency of war or by the presence of an imperial superpower that pursues worldwide military dominance. But these are manifestations. What characterizes a dangerous world is its inherently great turbulence, which may wax and wane over time but is always severe and is greater by an order of magnitude than that of a nondangerous world. This turbulence, moreover, is manifested not only in specific instances but also in fundamental ways, in the underlying structural characteristics of world affairs. As a result, a dangerous world poses *more* threats to stability than a nondangerous world, and many of the threats are qualitatively far more serious.

Danger thus is the dominating rule, not the exception. Stressful conflict is endemic, and periods of tranquility are but welcome breathing spaces. Troubles are not isolated but overlap in ways that cause them to "feed" off each other, thereby worsening the situation. Most important, the very foundations of the international order are shaky, like eroding concrete pillars standing upon quicksand. And although a dangerous world can come in many different sizes and shapes— some versions are more unstable than others—what unites all versions is that they are constantly vulnerable to sliding into global chaos and turmoil, if they are not there already.[1]

A dangerous world thus is conceptually unique—a category only the events of a rare international era fall into. Today's world offers plentiful dangers, but it is not inherently *dangerous*. Indeed, by history's standard, today's world is remarkably undangerous. For today's world to become dangerous, it would have to experience more than a modest rise in tension; it would have to cross over into a new sphere of existence. Whether it will do so remains to be seen. But if it does, it will confront the United States with international troubles fundamentally worse than those of today. The exact nature of these troubles will matter greatly in determining the implications for global instability and U.S. policy.

---

[1] For a study of international relations theory, see Raymond Aron, *Peace and War: A Theory of International Relations*, Garden City, N.Y.: Doubleday, 1966.

Analysts naturally will want to be presented with compelling evidence of exactly where, when, and how conflicts will appear. Unfortunately, specificity of this sort is hard to produce; indeed, ambiguity may be at the heart of the difficulty confronting U.S. policy. Something more than vague generalities can be offered, however. In Chapter Four, several alternative futures with greater or lesser instability are postulated, and three interacting trends that will shape a dangerous world are identified: mounting regional tensions in Europe, Asia, and the Middle East; the emergence of traditional geopolitical rivalry of the West with Russia and China; and the potential weakening of the Western Alliance security system. Because this scenario does not involve global war or an irreversible slide into some other chaos of equivalent magnitude, its tensions are less severe than those of World War II and the Cold War. But this scenario embodies dangers considerably greater than those that exist in the relatively tranquil setting of today. The developments in this scenario will create the strategic framework within which specific conflicts and wars will unfold. They will also establish the framework for designing a coherent U.S. response aimed at moderating their effects.

A dangerous world of this type will confront U.S. policy with weighty strategic dilemmas. The problems posed will be manifold, and they will create pressures for assertive U.S. involvement in many geographic areas. Moreover, the need to anticipate, to pursue solutions before troubles have reached crisis proportions, will require clear thought and decisive action in the face of ambiguity. The United States needs to act with vision and purpose because international trends are already sliding downhill and the slide is accelerating. Such action will represent a shift, given the United States' long track record of waiting to react until impending catastrophe is unambiguously real. Such action must embrace the essence of statecraft, which is anticipating the future, acting in advance to prevent troubles, and being prepared for troubles if they arrive. A farsighted statesmanship of anticipation is called for, of long-range thinking and assertive action. The situation mandates adoption of prudent new policies that can help dampen the impending danger by preventing or controlling the negative international global trends now emerging. It also calls for the launching of new plans and programs that will prepare the United States if preventive efforts are not successful.

Current U.S. policy is focused on encouraging democratic progress while preventing a global downturn, and many will argue that this policy still stands a reasonable chance of success. Yet disturbing global trends undeniably are at work, as is amply demonstrated by the war in the Balkans, the threat of nuclear proliferation, faltering democratic reforms in Russia, ethnic strife, economic stagnation, and weakening international collaboration. The prospect exists that the entire international system—not just parts of it—will move toward chronic instability in the very plausible event that heightened regional tensions in many places are accompanied by renewed trouble with Russia and China.

The sheer complexity of the situation will require that a responsive U.S. policy and strategy for managing a dangerous world be forged. This study puts forth one alternative, in Chapter Five: an activist policy aimed at reinvigorating U.S. security alliances, maintaining equilibrium with Russia and China, and keeping regional tensions under control so that they do not spread outward. Regardless of whether other alternatives can be fashioned, the need for activism must be balanced by a sense of proportion and restraint. The United States cannot afford to carry all the world's burdens or hope to solve all its problems. U.S. policy, therefore, will need to focus on interests that are truly fundamental and problems that are truly threatening to global order. Inherent in such a policy will need to be respect for the costs and risks to be faced at the same time that the costs of activism are weighed against the costs of detachment. As the decades before World Wars I and II showed, a failure to engage carries risks of its own: The negative consequences often do not manifest themselves immediately, but when they take shape, they can be catastrophic and costly. Sometimes the cheapest solution is to become involved early, not to defer involvement until later, when the situation is more difficult. This may prove to be the case if a dangerous world manifests itself.

This study raises a warning flag. The dangerous world it hypothesizes is more than an abstraction whose sole purpose is to stimulate intellectual curiosity. It already is probable enough for notice to be taken, and it is becoming more real by the day.[2] Troubled times do lie ahead, and they may involve the United States sooner rather than later. Regardless of how a dangerous world is manifested, the consequences need to be understood to help prevent the United States from being caught off guard, as too often has happened in the past when unwarranted optimism was betrayed by real-world events. Optimism about the future also soared in the years immediately following the end of the Cold War. This development reflected prevailing emotions in many Western countries tired from Cold War exertions, but it also was buttressed by an emerging academic literature that underscored the intellectual credibility of an optimistic future. A great deal has been written about how U.S. national security policy should be recast to deal with the tranquil international era that allegedly lay ahead. This literature is reviewed in Chapter Two.

Warning cries have begun rising from several quarters, but there is not yet an organized literature on what the negative trends mean and how the United States should respond. Several scholarly books, discussed in Chapter Three, have signaled that the international future may be turbulent; as yet none has systematically portrayed the implications of such turbulence for U.S. policy. Likewise, official publications and speeches have noted the emergence of negative global trends, but they have focused primarily on explaining current U.S. policy, not on speculating in any depth about how this policy might have to be altered if such trends gain momentum.[3]

An analytic gap thus exists on this topic, and this study endeavors to help close it. Focusing on the coming two decades, this study looks into the future, to a time—perhaps in a few years, but maybe longer—when negative trends and undercurrents in world politics might manifest themselves. The events of the next 20 years are

---

[2]For an appraisal of the effect of a more tranquil world than today's on U.S. national security policy and defense strategy, see Richard L. Kugler, *U.S. Military Strategy and Force Posture for the 21st Century: Capabilities and Requirements*, Santa Monica, Calif.: RAND, MR-328-JS, 1994.

[3]An exception has been the formulations of former Defense Secretary Richard (Dick) Cheney and former Joint Chiefs of Staff (JCS) Chairman Colin Powell. While in office, both speculated about the effects of international trouble ahead, but they did not develop their analyses in detail.

within the frame of reference for U.S. planning, and they are near enough so that an effort to gauge them is more than an exercise in crystal-ball-gazing. Assuming that a dangerous world will emerge, this study seeks to assess the form that international politics might take and employs the resulting assessment to offer insights on the implications for U.S. national security policy, including military strategy and defense planning. The goal of this study is to offer a flexible model or approach rather than a fixed blueprint for managing the dangerous world that may be evolving. It presents a breadth of issues and alternatives that might lie ahead.

THE UNCERTAINTY AHEAD

The need to think seriously about a dangerous world is one part of a larger challenge confronting U.S. national security policy. What separates today's world from the Cold War world is not only a less threatening situation but also the need to manage great uncertainty about the future. The Cold War posed a dangerous bipolar confrontation across the entire globe, creating the ever-present specter of worldwide military conflict and nuclear war. The passage of the Cold War has pulled the world back from this deadly precipice; yet bipolar confrontation, for all its negative features, had the advantage of being remarkably static and predictable. The fundamentals of what existed at any one time could be counted on to prevail for as far into the future as anyone dared to forecast. This state of affairs is no longer, and what exists today may not exist tomorrow. Indeed, tomorrow may be vastly different and in ways that are difficult to foresee.

The primary reason for this uncertainty is that the collapse of bipolarity is interacting with other trends to bring about what can best be characterized as "tectonic changes" in world politics—the "plates" underlying the global security system are shifting in profound ways and are interacting with great force, thus bringing about the equivalent of a geologic upheaval in international affairs.

As with most geologic upheavals, the causal dynamics are poorly understood and the outcome is anybody's guess, ranging from a tranquil world to a quite turbulent security system and covering many permutations in between. Indeed, the future international system might not settle into a new stasis; rather, it might rapidly evolve from one structure to the next, thus failing to acquire the cast-in-concrete character of the Cold War. The outcome is unknowable, but what can be said is that we are no longer granted the comfortable assumption that the current international system will be the model for the future.

The challenge facing the United States will not be one from a utopian communist ideology wholly alien to the principles of market democracy,[4] nor one of dealing with a single hegemonic rival by leading a highly unified Western Alliance on behalf of a compelling moral vision of managing a bipolar structure and the risk of global war. And it may not be one of achieving deterrence in the regions that today seem most threatened, and against the specific military threats that today seem most menacing. The stresses of the future may embody less clarity, new challenges to Western values, several potential adversaries, less cohesive alliances, greater multipolarity, and different military threats and conflicts. If so, this dangerous world will be rendered all the more troublesome owing to the United States' own lack of recent experience in dealing with anything like it.

Consequences for National Security Planning

The combination of great uncertainty and the risk of a dangerous world has immense consequences for U.S. national security planning. During the Cold War, plans for the mid- to long term (e.g., 5 to 20 years) could be shaped with confidence in what the future would hold. Because the bipolar structure was so static, planning could be performed by what amounted to extrapolating the present into the distant future. The prospect of changes always had to be taken into account, but the changes were mostly technological and predictable, and did not threaten to overturn the underlying political status quo. Thus, planning was a relatively simple and confident exercise. Indeed, a single dominant plan could be prepared for a static future, and only a modest range of variation needed to be considered.

This state of affairs has now passed into history, and today the underlying political status quo itself is undergoing change. The

---

[4]A *market democracy* is a country that has a democratic political system and a capitalist, free-enterprise economic system.

transformation being experienced is huge. Changes of great magnitude are coming from many different directions. Although such changes can be influenced by concerted policy action, to control them ultimately lies beyond the capacity of any single nation. Such changes defy an ability to predict their consequences: They are too complex and are driven by too many interacting variables to permit confident forecasts about where they are headed. Moreover, they seem to be occurring at an ever-accelerating pace.

The United States cannot afford to wait passively for the future to unfold for good or ill. Passivity would enhance the chances of a more dangerous world's evolving and perhaps leaving the United States unprepared to deal with it. The United States will need to pursue vigorous policies that not only manage today's situation but also prevent new dangers from emerging. Current policy must also endeavor to shape the future, to propel it—against opposing forces— toward destinations conducive to U.S. national interests and moral values. The United States requires a policy and a strategy that not only are preventive but also are anticipatory and curative.

In the event a dangerous world takes shape, the United States will not face an immediate mortal threat to its survival, yet its enlarging overseas interests will be at greater risk than they are today. Increased dangers will have to be controlled before still-existing opportunities can be capitalized upon. Therefore, realism will need to be embraced by U.S. policy, for it will provide the only viable avenue along which idealist visions can be pursued, as during the Cold War, when the United States was able to master the difficult art of synthesizing realism and idealism. In different ways, it will need to do so again.

The central implication is that, if stability is to be preserved and the goal of peaceful market democracy is to be advanced, U.S. power and leadership must be asserted even more than they are today. The chief task will become one of global security management, guided by U.S. interests as well as by democratic values and a broad conception of stability that is anchored not only on diplomacy but also on a balance of power (see Chapter Five). For this purpose, American military power—backed by contributions from still-energetic but transformed security alliances—will need to play a central role in peace, crisis, and war (see Chapter Seven).

Unlike during the Cold War, the main task will be *systemic containment*: containing multiple sources of instability in a more traditional era of conflicting national agendas devoid of utopian ideological content but animated by new forms of conflict. In the near term, the chief concern may continue to be control of regional strife, especially in the Persian Gulf and Korea. Over the longer term, new dangers are likely to arise. Europe may reappear as an unstable region, and the emergence of the West's traditional geopolitical rivalry with Russia and China may add management of stressful relations among the major powers to the international security calculus. If so, the U.S. security agenda will be far different and broader in scope than it is today.

The United States will need to become skilled at dealing with the phenomenon of major changes in the international environment, which means that, at a minimum, the United States will need to develop the agility to deal with new and very different problems, many of which are only dimly foreseeable today, but could appear suddenly tomorrow. Because many plans and programs set in motion today will have their greatest effect in the distant future, such efforts will need to be evaluated on their ability to perform the specific tasks for which they were originally designed and on the flexibility they provide. In grappling with the future, the United States may find that the capacity to quickly adapt and to do several things reasonably well may prove to be more valuable than the ability to do only one thing perfectly.

Beyond this, the prospect of an ever-changing dangerous world means that the United States may well have to develop the capacity to radically alter basic policy and strategy with greater frequency than in the past. The scope of policy change may go well beyond concrete programs and actions abroad. Intellectual precepts underlying U.S. programs and actions might themselves have to undergo major uprooting, and new perceptions of the international situation might have to be adopted.

Indeed, a new security vocabulary might have to be created, altering especially the manner in which national interests are defined. Whereas, during the Cold War, the United States defined its interests as either *vital* or *peripheral* according to its willingness to use military force to defend them, in the years ahead U.S. interests appear likely to expand in both geographic and functional scope, mandating that a new category be adopted. The new category, e.g., *major interests*, may be suspended halfway between vital and peripheral, neither automatically qualified nor unqualified for protection by force. The United States might also be compelled to extend security assurances to countries that lie well outside its Cold War Alliance networks, and even outside traditional interpretations of its outer geostrategic perimeter. New approaches might also be needed for dealing with important countries that are neither friends nor enemies, but in a gray, in-between area. And such concepts as deterrence, flexible response, and forward defense might have to be replaced with new concepts that accord with new realities.

Difficulties Posed by Changes in Policy and Strategy

The prospect of policy and strategy change confronts the United States with immense difficulties. Because most countries are primarily regional powers, their policy and strategy have a limited scope. For them, change may be troublesome, but it does not pose overpowering dilemmas or massive consequences. For the United States, the situation is different because it is a superpower with global involvements, multiple objectives, and many problems to be handled. As a result, the United States is faced with a far more complex calculus than most other nations, a calculus that will require intellectual dexterity.

Intellectual dexterity will necessitate deep thinking of the type practiced by other nations, especially countries in Europe, which have long experience in regularly switching policy to accommodate new troubles and ever-changing geopolitical situations. Britain, for example, regularly changed alliance partners and its own military strategy in its quest for a European balance of power, as did both France and Germany.

The United States lacks such experience. It emerged as a powerful actor on the world scene only in the last half of the twentieth century, an era dominated by the continuing clash between democracy and totalitarianism. Early in the Cold War, the United States altered its military strategy several times within an established policy framework of containment and deterrence. By the early 1970s, U.S. policy and strategy had been firmly shaped and remained that way for the duration of the conflict. The Cold War was won not because the United States showed agility at switching strategies but because it displayed the willpower to relentlessly carry out one dominant strategy.[5]

Need for Change in Intellectual Style

Some observers have accused the United States of an engineering mentality that favors the mechanics of implementing policy at the expense of conceptual thinking about first principles. This criticism identifies a predilection for simplicity and clarity in the American intellectual style that might not be suited for the era ahead. Since the Cold War's end, the crafting of a new strategy, a single strategy that will endure for the coming years, has received emphasis. Yet, because any strategy reflects a specific external environment, no one strategy can meet the requirements of all international systems. If the security system of today gives way to something radically different tomorrow, then, in all likelihood, U.S. strategy will have to change as well. The capacity to adopt new strategy departures rather than to single-mindedly execute one strategy may be the hallmark of a successful foreign policy in the coming era. If so, the United States will have to learn this art in which it is not an experienced practitioner.

The ability to make strategy innovations requires that thinking be done in advance. In theory, policy and strategy can be altered quickly, for they are composed primarily of ideas—goals and action plans—that can be discarded readily in favor of something better suited to different times. In reality, however, policy and strategy renewal does not take place overnight: Although outmoded ideas can be instantly discarded, the act of creating suitable replacements can be time-consuming, taking months or longer when a major intellectual refinement is needed. The United States is best advised to perform as much of its thinking in advance as possible.

---

[5]For more detail, see Richard L. Kugler, *Commitment to Purpose: How Alliance Partnership Won the Cold War*, Santa Monica, Calif.: RAND, MR-190-FF/RC, 1993.

Need to Develop Strategy Resources

Ideally, the United States would develop a set of strategies that can be kept on the shelf, for use as the situation demands. Perhaps uncertainty about the future will prohibit this degree of sophistication, but, at a minimum, it should be possible to develop alternative scenarios of future global affairs, as well as the core precepts of strategies for dealing with such scenarios. Conceptual efforts of this type could help alert U.S. planners to what might lie ahead and reduce the upheaval if major strategy departures become necessary.

Need to Develop Assets

Equally important, national security planning will need to apply a broader calculus to the development of the physical means that will be required to carry out policy and strategy. Whereas the intellectual components of new approaches can be created in a few months, the physical components can take years to build if the effort must be started from scratch, which is seldom necessary. Nevertheless, the assets needed to carry out a new strategy often differ from those mandated by its predecessor. To the extent that the necessary components are lacking when a new strategy is formulated, the United States may be left unable to implement that strategy, even if the act of intellectual refinement has been fully accomplished. Policy and strategy are meaningless if the physical means to bring them to life are lacking.

The need for being physically prepared applies especially to new military forces, which can require anywhere from three years to two decades to assemble. For example, the forces, weapon systems, and support structures being built today will be those at the United States' disposal tomorrow. Consequently, defense planning will need to do more than simply identify the requirements that must be met for today's strategy; it also will need to devise a force posture that has inherent flexibility to meet tomorrow's demands while meeting contemporary needs. During the Cold War, the United States required a defense posture closely tailored to a single, enduring strategy. For the coming era, it may require a posture that can rapidly be adapted to fit several different strategies of very dissimilar composition.

TOWARD A DANGEROUS WORLD?

The Global Security System

The act of preparing for a fluid future will be facilitated if the global security system evolves toward ever-greater stability, tranquility, and community. The primary task facing the United States, then, would be to recast its national security policy downward: diminishing requirements, halting old endeavors, and retiring existing capabilities. A far more difficult situation will arise, however, if the global system evolves toward greater instability and strife. The task will not be to downsize but to adapt, refocusing policy and strategy toward new horizons and meeting new dangers. It might involve the reconstitution of old assets or even the building of entirely new capabilities. For this reason, the demands posed by a more dangerous global system merit careful appraisal.

The risk of a more dangerous world was acknowledged by former Secretary of Defense Les Aspin, who in mid-1993 said that the failure of democratic reforms in Russia might necessitate major alterations in U.S. defense strategy. The dangers of the future include the reappearance of an adversarial Russia, but they are not limited to this development alone. During 1993, a new academic literature appeared in the United States, forecasting a whole set of troubles ahead, not only in Europe but in other regions as well. The picture sketched by this literature is of a turbulent global system, one marked by chaotic change, conflicting values, frustrated ambitions, great stress, competitive rivalry, and growing violence (see Chapter Three). If the worst transpires, the United States could face a world of nineteenth-century politics, twentieth-century passions, and twenty-first-century technology: a lethal combination of unstable multipolar rivalries; intense conflicts over core values, with resurgent nationalism as the common denominator; and widespread access to weapons of immense destructive capacity.   Even if the worst does not transpire, something short of it might prove trouble enough.

This dismal forecast is not necessarily accurate, but it serves as a useful counterweight to the heady optimism that prevailed only a short time ago (see Chapter Two). Above all, it calls attention to the need to remain alert and to think in systemic terms. As Secretary

Aspin's *Report on the Bottom-Up Review* asserted, we face today a world of multiple dangers: nuclear proliferation, regional conflicts, failed democratic reforms, and economic dangers. Yet even Aspin's worried formulation may be inadequate for the more distant future. If the pessimists are correct, the world might offer dangers that are more fundamental and widespread than those contemplated by the Bottom-Up Review. Therefore, a compelling need is to identify the potential dangers and the implications posed for future U.S. policy and strategy.[6]

The kind of U.S. policy and strategy to be adopted will depend heavily on the specifics of the situation to be encountered. For example, an increase of regional tensions might require one form of strategy response and the reappearance of rivalry with Russia and China, a quite different response. If the Western Alliance holds together, the United States will be able to continue pursuing a coalition strategy; if not, a strategy embodying greater reliance on unilateral action will become necessary. A troublesome combination of heightened regional tensions, renewed major-power rivalry, and weakened alliances would require yet a different kind of response.

Analysis of Future Military Conflicts

For the Department of Defense, probing analyses of future military conflicts will be especially important. In today's world, the Persian Gulf and Korea seem the most likely regions of war. But will they be in the years ahead? The answer will depend heavily on the root causes of future conflicts. Whereas, during the Cold War, the threat of global warfare stemmed from the ideological rivalry between democracy and communism, in today's world, geopolitical ambitions are the principal reasons for the threat of war in the Persian Gulf and Korea. In tomorrow's world, conflict might be triggered by ethnic hatreds, border disputes, minority troubles, conflicting economic agendas, nationalist ideologies, cultural antagonisms, historical rivalries, and competitive arms races (see Chapter Six). The myr-

---

[6]See Les Aspin, *Report on the Bottom-Up Review*, Washington, D.C.: Department of Defense, 1993.

iad possibilities mean that wars might break out in different places and be fought in different ways. The United States will become involved only when its interests so dictate; in these potential situations, however, it might find itself fighting different enemies and supported by different allies than those who occupy its defense plans at present. To the extent feasible, strong efforts should be exerted to anticipate these conflicts as far in advance as possible.

THE EMERGING DEFENSE AGENDA

The prospect of a more dangerous world, one very different from that of today and prone to fast-paced change, imposes a new agenda on U.S. defense policy. Although specific requirements are unclear, the U.S. defense posture will need to remain strong, flexible, and diverse. Nuclear requirements may loom larger than they do today if proliferation occurs and major-power rivalry reappears; yet, even more than during the Cold War, conventional strength will be central to a viable U.S. military strategy.   U.S. military power will need to be viewed as more than a last resort, an instrument to be employed only when diplomacy and other efforts fail. Along with other instruments, it will need to be regarded as a key vehicle by which peacetime foreign policy is carried out and national security is preserved in a dangerous world (see Chapters Seven and Eight).

Away from Canonical Scenarios

Insofar as uniquely new conflicts lie ahead, the United States should avoid the temptation to base its defense plans on stylized thinking as represented by canonical scenarios. The Cold War allowed for the use of canonical scenarios, and, today, hypothetical regional conflicts in the Persian Gulf and Korea are acquiring a canonical status of their own. These scenarios undeniably reflect current realities, but do they represent the conflicts of tomorrow's world to the point of warranting confidence that U.S. forces designed to fight them will be able to handle all other challenges? Other questions arise: Can the favorable political-military conditions encountered in Desert Storm be relied upon to repeat themselves anytime soon? Is the key defense requirement to be prepared to wage two major regional conflicts, or is it also to be capable of performing a wider spectrum of missions, in different regions and against different adversaries? If emphasis is to shift away from an overseas presence toward power projection from the United States, what is the proper mix? How can timely power projection be accomplished to enable the United States not only to conduct decisive military operations but also to deter wars from occurring in the first place?

The prospect of a more dangerous world suggests that the answers to these troubling questions may be very different tomorrow from those of today. Regardless of the answers, these questions must be addressed. Successful planning can be accomplished only by taking off intellectual blinders. U.S. forces must be rendered capable of fighting the wars of the future, not those of the past. And the U.S. defense planning framework must be attuned to the challenges of tomorrow, not just those of today. The challenge will be not only to identify compelling defense requirements but also to maintain public support for a strong defense posture in an ambiguous era that offers great danger but few clear enemies. The techniques of force planning that were developed during the Cold War, and that continue to be applied in altered form today, may have to undergo far-reaching change. Imagination and innovation of a kind not commonly practiced for many years may become the order of the day.

Contribution Needed from Overseas Security Alliances

Adequate and flexible U.S. military forces will be needed, especially if a more dangerous world evolves. Yet U.S. force levels, military budgets, and overseas presence are scheduled to become lower than those during the Cold War. For this reason and many others, an assertive U.S. policy agenda will require powerful contributions by overseas security alliances. A great danger is that existing U.S. alliances will erode from the lack of a clear threat. A more subtle but equally grave risk is that such alliances might elect to rely on their old missions and successes, and thus fail to meet tomorrow's challenges, which will lie beyond current Alliance borders.

This risk applies to NATO, which can ill afford to ignore the dangers posed by great instability in the troubled zone to its east. This risk also applies to U.S. alliances with Japan and Korea, countries that cannot afford to live in isolation if the entire Asian region slides toward turbulent instability. It also applies to the Middle East and Persian Gulf, where the lack of strong security alliances has been a chronic source of troubles in the past and could become even more so in the future. In all these regions, the beckoning agenda is that of Alliance transformation to develop the capacity—anchored on Coalition defense, fair burden-sharing, and responsive roles and missions—to meet new dangers and capitalize on emerging opportunities.

METHODOLOGY AND ORGANIZATION

This study employs an interdisciplinary methodology to fashion a conceptual framework of policy-related issues. It focuses on what may be the most important implications of a worsening global situation over the coming decade and beyond and aspires to show the interrelationship of several dangerous trends. It surveys the many components of strategic planning—from portrayals of the global future, to scenario-writing, to analysis of U.S. national security policy, to military strategy, to conventional-force planning—to demonstrate how they interrelate. Trend analysis and forecasting techniques are used to assess international futures and develop alternative scenarios. Policy analysis is employed to examine future U.S. policy and strategy options. Defense analysis is used to examine the implications for U.S. military strategy and force planning.

These methods telescope downward from the general to the specific and from trend analysis to policy appraisal. Chapter Two initiates the analysis by examining the reasons why the postulates of international optimism may no longer provide a basis for projecting the future. Chapter Three examines the reasons why a more dangerous world may lie ahead; it includes a survey of the recent pessimistic literature, which offers concrete projections of the unfoldings of a dangerous world. Chapter Four develops strategic scenarios for a dangerous world, each with different characteristics and unique challenges for U.S. policy. Chapter Five analyzes the implications of a dangerous world for U.S. national security policy. Chapter Six assesses the military dynamics of a dangerous world, including nuclear and conventional-force balances in key regions. Chapter Seven analyzes the implications for U.S. military strategy, and Chapter Eight analyzes those for U.S. conventional-force planning. Chapter Nine offers conclusions.

Chapter Two

THE LIMITATIONS OF INTERNATIONAL OPTIMISM

STABILITY AND UNCLEAR TRENDS

If a dangerous world lies ahead, it will be for reasons that transcend the current international security system, which is stable compared with the worldwide frictions of the Cold War or the 1930s or the late 1800s. This stability, which may be only temporary and to some seems uneasy and tentative, exists undeniably and owes heavily to the low-to-medium-grade severity of regional tensions today. Although regional political strife abounds, the numerous military conflicts of the post–Cold War era have thus far been mostly local, small, and containable. They might escalate outward by drawing in other powers, but for now they do not yet pose a threat to the system as a whole. The only exception has been the Persian Gulf War, but this conflict ended on terms that seemingly quashed prospects for a further flare-up of major Gulf conflict anytime soon. For all its murderous violence, the Balkans conflict confirms the rule because it thus far has been confined primarily to Bosnia.

Another important contributor to stability is the recent tranquility of relations among the major powers—unusual for countries that have long track records of opposing each other. The United States finds itself allied with Germany and Japan and pursuing cooperative relations with Russia and China. In Europe, Germany and Russia are in harmony; in Asia, the complex triangular relationship among China, Russia, and Japan is free of deep frictions. Whether this state of affairs will continue once these nations rebound from their current inward-looking stances and again begin pursuing activist foreign policies is uncertain. At the moment, however, tranquil relations among these powers are a powerful contributor to a generally peaceful world scene.

As for the future, available data suggest unclear trends. Whereas pessimists can point to several worrisome developments that have emerged recently, optimists can point to offsetting developments that, in their view, augur a tranquil future. For example, although Vladimir Zhirinovsky's success in Russia's elections of late 1993 can be seen as a harbinger of fascistic nationalism, the simultaneous approval of a new constitution can be interpreted as laying the foundation for democracy. The future may offer neither optimism nor pessimism but only profound uncertainty and ample room for debate.

An effort to address how a more dangerous world might evolve, therefore, must look beyond contemporary events and peer into the future through conceptualization and theory-building. From such scrutiny, a set of plausible and internally consistent propositions must be assembled, examined for their internal characteristics, and judged according to formal criteria of evaluation. A review of the scholarly literature that has appeared over the past two to three years is the best starting point for such scrutiny.

During the Cold War's waning years, the academic literature on global security affairs did not figure heavily in U.S. national security planning. For the most part, the international system was so stable, monolithic, and well understood that academic appraisals offered little that was new or useful. Because the post–Cold War era is proving so fluid and complex, this situation is changing. Confronted by enormous uncertainty, the U.S. government now has a need for insightful estimates of the future, and the emerging literature offers such estimates. This literature puts forth only propositions, hypotheses, and conjecture—not ironclad predictions. But it does present a set of alternative visions, offering an opportunity to gauge how some of the best observers of global politics are assessing the future.

POST–COLD WAR OPTIMISM, THEN PESSIMISM

During 1991–1992, an optimistic academic literature emerged that portrayed a tranquil future, owing primarily to the political collapse of European communism and the military defeat of Iraq. This literature acknowledged that dangers remain on a regional basis, and it called upon the United States to stay engaged abroad, especially in pursuit of its economic interests. Its underlying theme, nonetheless, was one of relaxed optimism about the future. It assessed still-existing dangers as having limited scope and as dwindling because of the expected adoption of liberal democracy and cooperative foreign policies in many new places. The implication was that the United States, now facing a stable external environment, could safely concentrate on domestic problems while adopting a downsized and refocused security policy, a policy less concerned with military threats to vital U.S. interests and less indebted to Cold War security alliances.

As 1993 unfolded, several books and provocative scholarly articles in key journals appeared as a beginning of a more pessimistic literature. The result is an emerging debate within the scholarly community whose outcome is not yet in sight. The new literature responds to disturbing events in the international arena since 1992.

This pessimistic literature suggests that the future international system might be more turbulent than that postulated only a few months before. Whether this worried literature accurately assesses the future is an imponderable. The authors themselves acknowledge uncertainty and the tentative nature of their judgments. Their assessments by no means are identical; they point to different types of tension and conflict, not all of which will directly influence U.S. security planning. Nonetheless, they suggest that in the years ahead, the world will become a far more dangerous place than it is today. Moreover, they imply that this more dangerous world may impose demands on U.S. policy, strategy, and force posture that are different from those being contemplated today. For these reasons, this literature must be pondered by American planners. This chapter sets the stage for analyzing the pessimistic literature by appraising the optimistic school.

THE POSTULATES OF OPTIMISM

The origin of today's debates between optimists and pessimists goes back decades. Intellectual historians might cite the nineteenth-century British debates between Benjamin Disraeli and William Gladstone, or even earlier debates between eighteenth-century conservatives and liberals. The American debate "broke out" after World

War I, taking the form of a prolonged and still-unresolved fight between idealists and realists. The conflicts between these schools are detailed in Chapter Three.

Background

As a brief background here, the idealists took their inspiration from Woodrow Wilson, who aspired to create a new moral order aimed at preventing the competitive interstate (*state* in the international sense) rivalries that led to the Great War. Wilson postulated that interstate conflict and war were abnormal, a product of flawed ethical principles and improper diplomatic conduct. He therefore proposed a cure of democracy, open diplomacy, collective security, and self-determination. Realism emerged in the 1930s, in reaction to the failure of Wilsonian idealism to prevent the European downturn that gave rise to Hitler and Stalin. Judging that conflict and war were not solvable through moral posturing, realism proposed a policy agenda of military strength, formal alliances, and a firm stance against aggressors.

In important ways, today's optimists are modern Wilsonian idealists, although the appearance of their literature was a direct by-product of undeniably favorable events, especially in Europe and the Persian Gulf, that took place in 1989–1991. The result was a stream of books that projected these events into the future and generalized their implications. Good examples of this literature are the following:

- Francis Fukuyama, *The End of History and the Last Man*, New York: Free Press, 1992.

- Samuel P. Huntington, *The Third Wave: Democratization in the Late Twentieth Century*, Norman, Okla.: University of Oklahoma Press, 1991.

- Graham Allison and Gregory F. Treverton, eds., *Rethinking America's Security: Beyond Cold War to New World Order*, New York: W. W. Norton and Co., 1992.

- James Chace, *The Consequences of the Peace: The New Internationalism and American Foreign Policy*, New York: Oxford University Press, 1992.

- Richard H. Ullman, *Securing Europe,* Princeton, N.J.: Princeton University Press, 1991.

- Bruce Russett, *Grasping the Democratic Peace: Principles for a Post–Cold War World,* Princeton, N.J.: Princeton University Press, 1993.

Whereas Huntington's book offers an empirical analysis that records the adoption of democratic governments by many countries in recent years, Fukuyama boldly projects positive global implications for the future. The books by Allison and Treverton, Chace, and Ullman all offer upbeat appraisals, but they are more guarded in their proclamations and less penetrating in their analyses. The Russett book is noteworthy for its empirical assertion of the idea that democratic nations do not wage war against each other; however, it expresses concern that this rule may be violated by newly emerging democracies in countries embracing ethno-nationalist values. Of these works, Fukuyama's has attracted the most attention.

Heavily focused on the evolution of Western political philosophy during the eighteenth and nineteenth centuries rather than on international relations theory or empirical sociology, Fukuyama examines the role of ideas in shaping social action, and pays special attention to the overlooked roles of philosophers Georg Hegel and Friedrich Nietschze. Asserting that people of all historical eras pursue not only material satisfaction but also prestige (*thymos*), often by trying to dominate each other, Fukuyama is far from blind to humanity's foibles. Nor is he indifferent to the energizing effects of social conflict or to the risks of continued turbulence in the decades ahead. Nonetheless, he asserts that the great ideological struggle between the two modern forms of government—democracy and totalitarianism—has at last been settled permanently. In this sense, he asserts, history has come to an end: Because democracy has won out over competitors, we are witnessing the end of an age-old debate over the best form of government. This development, he reasons, gives cause for resurrecting nineteenth-century optimism, which was dealt cruel blows by the warlike twentieth century. Fukuyama does not predict utopia anytime soon, but he does conclude that in the political realm, the final stage of Hegel's dialectical idealism has been reached, and the synthesis is liberal democracy.

In his book he argues that the outward spread of liberal democracy will especially benefit populations in countries that are newly adopting this system. The reason is partly that market capitalism generates greater prosperity than command economies, but more important, that liberal democracy provides for personal freedom and a civic culture. Beyond this, he asserts, such development augurs international peace because democracies typically do not wage war against each other. To the extent this statement is true, he says, interstate military rivalry and war are becoming conditions of the past, to be replaced by growing community. With liberal democracy prevailing in ever-larger parts of the globe, peaceful cooperation will become the rule, not the exception, and the desire for both material rewards and prestige will be channeled in directions other than interstate aggression. The principal challenge, he says, will be for human beings to learn to find self-fulfillment in peace.

The other books refrain from visions this bold, but they celebrate the prospect of more-tranquil days ahead. They agree with Fukuyama that the triumph of democratic ideals is a principal cause, but they also cite other influential factors. One factor is economics—which allegedly has now replaced security affairs as the axis of world politics—because, the books assert, the modern world economy removes any need to pursue war by giving all states access to necessary resources through normal trade and competitive capitalist dynamics. A related assertion is that fear of losing membership in the world economy will create barriers to rogue conduct because states would be fatally undercutting their own prosperity. Another factor is modern communications, which presumably enables societies to see through false propaganda and comprehend that peaceful prosperity will be the reward for democratic practices and benign foreign policies by their governments. Yet another factor is the modern state's becoming too embedded in multiple internal and external constraints to pursue war. A final factor is growing international recognition that resort to coercive military power simply does not pay off and that the best path to a successful foreign policy is cooperation with other countries.

Conclusions of the Literature

The conclusions of this literature, while not utopian, are decidedly upbeat. Now that the danger of a hegemonic rival has vanished, they reason, global war is no longer a threat, and the principal dangers will be regional and small. In particular, this literature implies, Europe is now rendered stable, but the other key regions are not far behind. Moreover, the prospect of partnership with Russia enhances the United States' latitude for employing multilateral cooperation to handle remaining troubles. The United States will need to remain alert to the still-existing dangers, this literature says, but attention can shift to capitalizing on the great opportunities ahead. Worried pessimism can give way to a sunny disposition, for as the number of enemies rapidly fades, the United States' circle of friends can be greatly expanded. Preoccupation with military preparedness can now give way to a predominant emphasis on economic recovery and building a viable world economy guided by cooperative democratic partners. U.S. national security policy for the coming era thus can be very different from that of the Cold War. In essence, the earlier approach, which would have pleased militaristic Sparta, can be replaced by a more hopeful and enlightened policy that would find favor in peace-loving Athens.

The strength of the books lies not only in identifying opportunities for community-building but also in pointing to the powerful role played by ideas in international affairs. The authors present their arguments in subtle terms that acknowledge the complexities ahead and the difficulty of making firm forecasts. Many of them have since altered their own opinions in response to unsettling international developments that have called their original conclusions into question. Nevertheless, this literature offers a basically optimistic appraisal that, understandably, was shared at the time of its publication in many quarters of the American intellectual community. This appraisal was embraced in scholarly journals, newspapers, and by many political leaders across the spectrum. For a time, it came to reflect a consensus.

This consensus responded to the change in the direction the international wind was blowing. The United States stood tall as the globe's only superpower, and the Western Alliance remained strong. In Europe, the menacing Warsaw Pact had vanished, and Russia and all of Eastern Europe were voicing intent to embrace market democracy. In Asia, China was subdued, with its economy pointed toward capitalism, its totalitarian government besieged by internal opposition, and its military too weak to project power abroad. In the Middle East, the Persian Gulf oil fields seemed permanently secure, Iraq and Iran were on the defensive, and hope was raised for settlement of the Arab-Israeli dispute. In the United States, consequently, talk was rife of a future in which the opportunities far exceed the dangers. In the eyes of many, a century of peace seemingly lay ahead, and the principal task would be to carry forth democracy's final worldwide victory—a task that could be accomplished with a modicum of effort. Cautionary words came from some quarters, but for the most part they were either not heard or were casually dismissed.

Although this intellectual construct continues to be embraced in several quarters, following this construct's appearance have come multiple unfavorable developments in and around Europe: the outbreak of savage ethnic war in the Balkans, rampant conflict in the Caucasus and Central Asia, great political-economic upheavals in East Central Europe and Russia that are calling market democracy into question, and a worrisome decline in the cohesion of both the European Union (EU) and NATO. What was to have been the globe's most stable region is now becoming a hotbed of violence, nascent extremism, renationalized policies, proliferation, other unhealthy security dynamics, and growing worry among virtually all governments there. The outcome is uncertain, and these negative trends might yet be reversed. Unless the downslide can be halted, many Europeans are coming to conclude that the future is likely to be more like the dark past than the rosy portrayal offered by American academics.

If this is so for Europe, it also applies to other regions that are regarded warily even by the optimists and that have themselves shown signs of renewed turmoil in recent months. Will Asia emerge as permanently stable now that the rigid bipolarity of the Cold War is giving way to a more fluid multipolarity driven by new and untested economic-security dynamics among nations that have long been rivals? What of South Asia, where India and Pakistan remain bitter ethnic-religious enemies although both are becoming democracies? And what of the Middle East and the Persian Gulf, where progress is being made toward resolving the Arab-Israeli dispute, but where the future is threatened by mounting Islamic fundamentalism, poverty, and growing national ambitions of Iraq, Iran, and others? In all these regions, governments are aware of the enticing prospects of a cooperative future; however, they are also worried about resurgent historical animosities and the new threat of nuclear proliferation. Perhaps enduring stability will be the outcome everywhere, but exactly how is a mystery not resolved by the optimistic literature.

CONCEPTUAL FLAWS OF OPTIMISM

Recent troubling events have not dispelled all hopes for a tranquil future, but they suggest that the literature of optimism may be guilty of a premature judgment that stems from a lack of historical perspective and analytical depth. The result is a framework that offers high normative appeal and engages in self-congratulation of the West's alleged moral superiority while oversimplifying a complex reality. The wish appears to have fostered the thought in ways that misinterpret the manifold sources of human conflict and therefore overlook the enduring nature of such conflict. This section identifies seven flaws of optimism.

Collapse of Unstable Old Order Begets a Stable New Order

A first, core flaw of this literature is its implicit assumption that the collapse of an unstable old order automatically begets a stable new order. As history has shown many times over, tranquility need not be the consequence when one form of turbulence passes from the scene. The outcome can be a new form of turbulence as bad or even worse than what came before. Although the future is not governed by irreversible laws inherited from history, the past can be prologue if underlying causal dynamics remain unchanged: The collapse of communist ideology does not itself mean that Western values will fill the void, for these values may have less-than-universal appeal and relevance, most noticeably in regions that are influenced by histories and belief systems radically different from those of the West.

Democracy and Capitalism Operate Together Under Market Democracy

A second, related flaw is this literature's implied logic that democracy and capitalism go hand in hand under the mantle of "market democracy," and that the two philosophies work together to breed nonthreatening and cooperative ("innocent") foreign policy.   In truth, they do not go hand in hand, for there can be democracy without capitalism and capitalism without democracy. In today's world, some West European countries approximate the former model, and both Pinochet's Chile and China have aspired to the latter. The question thus arises: Is it the combination of the two that produces a peaceful foreign policy? If so, hybrid systems embracing one but not the other (e.g., market socialism) presumably are condemned to less pristine external conduct. If not, then which one is the true source of innocence? The answer is unclear, for both institutions were born in blood in ways that belie any claims to innocence for either. Before they could be adopted, capitalism had to crush feudalism and democracy had to repress monarchy—tasks that were accomplished with brutality and ruthlessness. With origins like this, can either lay claim to unique virtue?

Lenin and like-minded nineteenth-century theorists would blanch at the idea that capitalism promotes benign foreign policy. To them, capitalism *is* the root cause of imperialism, the ultimate form of foreign policy malevolence. Perhaps they exaggerated, but the core reality is that capitalism celebrates individual profit-seeking. It does endorse cooperative values when the outcome is mutual profit, but when economic dynamics produce winners and losers, it has no hesitations about who comes first. Lenin and his colleagues grossly miscalculated the comparative economic dynamism of the two systems, but they did touch capitalism's ethical fault lines by showing that its moral premises are one step removed from a foreign policy of exploitation and coercion. After all, the early capitalists were mercantilists, and some of their descendants were, in fact, imperialists. The twentieth century has shown that capitalist powers can cooperate on behalf of common growth. Yet the fact remains that although capitalism can promote collectivist values, it does not do so automatically.[1]

The real source of benign foreign policy must, therefore, be democracy. Surface appearances suggest that it is, but underlying realities give rise to a more complex interpretation. Democracy's embrace of collectivist values is less than total: Whereas democracy protects individual rights and establishes rules for peacefully resolving conflict, its main purpose, even in domestic affairs, is to promote freedom, *not* equality. It offers all citizens the equal opportunity to compete in the marketplace, but it does not guarantee success for all or even an equal distribution of rewards. Although modern-day policies have established antimonopoly laws and welfare safety nets for the unfortunate, many democracies preside over capitalist economies that breed high social stratification and that also tolerate varying degrees of economic exploitation. If democracies are willing to tolerate hierarchy and exploitation within their own borders, why would they be unwilling to practice them outside, in the anarchical international system that determines the standing of states?

Moreover, even domestic freedom has its limits, for democracy unavoidably places an equal premium on social control. Virtually all democracies are willing to use force to quash those who violently dissent from majority rule, even if majority rule yields policies that are patently unfair. Democracies also react poorly to secessionist movements: Witness the U.S. Civil War. And knowing that their internal health is best ensured if the external environment is brought under control, they are capable of pursuing their own strategic good and greater glory. They thus have a sense of *realpolitik* of their own, for they use coercion at home and abroad to accomplish their purposes, idealistic or otherwise. None of these compromises with collectivist values compels democracy to embrace malevolent diplomacy as a matter of principle; however, such compromises do imbue democracy with a keen sense of economic competition and power politics. They thus provide ample latitude for democracy to pursue foreign policies that depart from the norms of innocence.

---

[1] See F. Parkinson, *The Philosophy of International Relations: A Study in the History of Thought*, Beverly Hills, Calif.: Sage Publications, 1977. See also Louis Fischer, *The Life of Lenin*, New York: Harper and Row, 1964.

How then do democracy and capitalism interact, and what are the consequences of that interaction for foreign policy? If enduring innocence is the product of their mixture, then these systems must cancel out each other's moral blemishes: Democracy must tame capitalism's self-serving impulses, and capitalism must sand off democracy's rough edges. If this is the case, why, as a matter of logic, is it so? Is it not possible—in theory—that the two could bring out the worst in each other, or at least have no taming effect? Can capitalism lead a nation into wars that democracy would not normally approve of, or at least not foster? If democracy is driven by angry popular passions, can it produce wars that make little sense to capitalism? And if nationalist passions interact with capitalist imperatives, can the consequence be external aggression beyond that normally pursued by an authoritarian government with a noncapitalist economy?

Many nineteenth-century theorists might answer "yes" to these questions. Today's answers are more complex, for twentieth-century experience has shown that, even if market democracy often operates imperfectly, the alternatives regularly operate far worse. Even so, a sense of perspective is needed to assess the extent of market democracy's positive effects. Democracy can encourage international peace by promoting the same collectivist values externally that guide its structure internally. Capitalism can foster prosperity in both the domestic and international arenas, thereby enhancing material satisfaction and creating a sense of shared economic destiny. Together, the two can have a multiplicative effect.

But such an effect may not always occur, especially when all other barriers to international peace are swept aside. As a matter of deductive logic and empirical theory, the effects of market democracy on international conduct are best seen as variables, *not* constants. The effects depend on exactly how democracy and capitalism operate at home and abroad. The mere fact that many Western market democracies today tend to pursue cooperative foreign policies does not mean that the foreign policies of all market democracies, everywhere and for all time, are destined to be always innocent. For this reason, the recent spread of market democracy to new corners of the world may be a sign for the better, but it is no cause for concluding that a peaceful millennium has automatically arrived.

Incompatible Political Ideology Is the Source of Interstate Conflicts

A third flaw lies in this literature's tendency to present incompatible political ideology as the alleged primary source of interstate conflict, and the lack of ideological strife as the begetter of peace. Ideological warfare undeniably has dominated the twentieth century. However, in previous centuries, before contemporary ideologies appeared on the scene, interstate conflict was rampant and stemmed from more traditional causes.

In Europe, the modern era began about 1500. For the next 150 years, many wars were waged, primarily for religious reasons. The secular nation-state system emerged in 1648 with the signing of the Treaty of Westphalia. From that point, religion ceased to be a central cause of strife. And because monarchical rule was viewed as legitimate almost everywhere, political ideology was widely agreed on. Yet wars continued to be fought with equal or greater ferocity as the seventeenth century gave way to the eighteenth and nineteenth centuries. The causes were varied but most often stemmed from mercantilism, territorial disputes, military competition, mounting nationalism, and unabashed status rivalries. These traditional causes of interstate conflict were suppressed during the twentieth century. Now that ideological clashes are diminishing, the danger is that these traditional causes will return to life. If so, ideological friction may pass into history, but war will not accompany it.[2]

Economics Has Peace-Enhancing Effects

A fourth flaw is this literature's tendency to exaggerate the peace-enhancing effects of economics. Economists, historians, and political scientists have long recognized that economics can be a cause of war, not peace. Just as cooperation can build peace, exploitation can produce conflict. And in today's world, some states still exploit each other. That many states have access to resources does not mean that all states feel adequately endowed or have concluded that resorting

---

[2]See Russell F. Weigley, *The Age of Battles*, Bloomington, Ind.: Indiana University Press, 1991. See also Bernard Montgomery, *A History of Warfare*, New York: William Morrow and Company, 1983.

to coercion will gain them nothing. Although an interdependent world economy has existed for the past century and more, neither membership in it nor entangling trade relations have deterred neighbors from waging war against each other. Indeed, the region with the greatest economic entanglements—Europe—has been the one most prone to war.[3]

Modern communications similarly cuts both ways. A heightened flow of information can make societies more aware of the peaceful intent of other countries, but it can also alert them to malevolent intent and exaggerate the effects of such malevolence. It can convey messages quickly, but not always for the best. It can resolve misunderstandings, but it can also deepen them. It can promote sophisticated appraisals, but it can give rise to simplistic images and slogans. It can dampen passions, but it can also excite them. It can help societies influence their governments, but it can enable governments to control their populations. Indeed, modern communications provides the foundation for totalitarianism, and it is not a recent invention.

Technology has improved recently, but the core phenomenon has been present throughout the twentieth century—history's most violent era. People have television now. Before that they had radios and newspapers, and they were no less informed. Yet they regularly marched off to war. Again, Europe was the primary beneficiary, and it was the globe's most violent region.

Conflict Stems from the Nation-State System

A fifth flaw is this literature's tendency to see conflict as stemming from the nation-state system. Governments are the primary vehicle for organizing military forces and carrying out aggressive foreign agendas. But it is human beings that engage in conflict, not institutions. From Sigmund Freud and Carl Jung onward, modern psychology has asserted that human conflict has its origins in the pathological forces that often motivate individual behavior. Unfortunately,

---

[3]For an analysis of the relationship between international politics and economics, see Robert Gilpin, *The Political Economy of International Relations*, Princeton, N.J.: Princeton University Press, 1987.

modern times have not eradicated psychopathology; indeed, some observers claim that psychopathology is on the rise, owing to the pressures of modern life. Regardless of whether an increase is occurring, the human being has not yet reached perfection, even if, in the minds of some, clashes over political values have finally been settled.[4]

Building upon this observation, modern sociology and social psychology have concluded that when social groups are formed and confront each other, the outcome can be stressful group conflict. Social groups are capable of extending human rights to their own members but of denying those rights to outsiders. They also are capable of hating each other for reasons that transcend political ideology or even the outer boundaries of rationality. Reinhold Niebuhr observed that as the level of social organization increases, the propensity to exercise individual responsibility and moral restraint often declines. In essence, mass psychology takes hold, and it can result in unreasoned conduct of the type that individuals would not pursue if left to their own devices.[5]

Group psychology has important implications for international politics because it can influence the behavior of all countries, irrespective of the political ideology that is embraced within national borders. The modern *state* is often defined in terms of its governmental institutions, but the modern *nation* is defined in terms of the large social group that constitutes its population. Governmental bureaucracy can influence society, whereas, especially in the modern pluralist country, society can influence government. Interstate conflict can be caused by the decisions of governments to oppose one another absent any impulse from their societies. But interstate conflict can also be caused by societies that propel their governments

------

[4]Freud began his psychoanalytic career by arguing that sexual impulses are the cause of social conflict. In his later years, he altered his position to argue that human beings are inherently aggressive for many reasons. This conclusion is expressed in his last book, *Civilization and Its Discontents*. Jung seems to have felt that humans were made in the image and likeness of a God who was part good, part evil. See Peter Gay, *Sigmund Freud: A Life for Our Times*, New York: Anchor Books, 1988. See also Barbara Hannah, *Jung: His Life and Work*, Boston: Shambhala, 1991.

[5]See Reinhold Niebuhr, *Moral Man and Immoral Society*, New York: Scribner's, 1960. Also, see Seymour Martin Lipset, *The Politics of Unreason*, New York: Random House, 1972.

to war for reasons stemming from group animosities. Resurgent ethno-nationalism is one manifestation of this phenomenon, which has not vanished into history simply because debates over the proper form of governmental life have dissipated.

Military Power Has a Discounted Role in Preserving Global Peace

A sixth flaw of this literature is prematurely discounting the role that military power must still play in preserving global peace and promoting democratic values. Unlike left-wing treatises, this literature does not perceive military power as a uniform source of evil in world affairs. It is prepared to grant that in the hands of market democracy, military power can be used constructively. But it tends to perceive military power as an instrument to be used only at times of great danger and for the purpose of dealing with imminent threats. On other occasions, it implies, military power can be retired, to be reconstituted only when another threat appears. Its theory of military power thus is reactive, not proactive, and is focused on crisis management, not peace-building.

Underlying this reactive theory is the premise that, because the Cold War is now ended and twentieth-century ideological battles are over, the international system can be relied upon to remain stable on its own, without propping up by conscious security policies backed by military power. A related premise is that market democracy will spread for reasons of its own and does not require a supporting foundation of the same type needed to preserve stability. Are these premises correct? As discussed in the next section, there are reasons for concluding that global stability and market democracy are not ensured and that progress toward these goals will require a strong foundation of security management and military strength: a different calculus that applies proactive and peace-building standards to judgments about the use of military power in the coming era. Required here is deep thinking about cause and effect, not simple formulas. Relationships must be viewed as variables rather than as constants.

None of these first six flaws in the optimistic literature validates philosopher Thomas Hobbes' dire claim that life is nasty, brutish, and short. Nor do they imply that all hope for enduring tranquility is lost, nor that interstate warfare can never be tamed. But they do imply using a sense of caution toward sweeping claims that human conflict and the interstate rivalries that grow from it are passing into history. The clash between democracy and totalitarianism may have been settled, and capitalism is proving a better vehicle for economic management than a command economy. Yet these developments, for all their positiveness, do not settle everything or even most things, for the sources of human conflict run far deeper.

Democracy Has Tranquility-Inducing Effects

Especially because human conflict is deep-seated, this literature suffers from a seventh flaw: exaggerating the tranquility-inducing effects of democracy. It does so partly because it embraces a single-cause interpretation of international politics. It postulates that the character of a country's domestic political order shapes its foreign policy in ways overpowering all other influences. Because this postulate equates democracy with benign foreign conduct, it projects that global peace will flow from the expansion of democracy into many new nations.

Irrespective of its appeal in many quarters, this postulate violates the predominant body of social science theory, which concludes that foreign policy is a product of many variables, including not only domestic institutions but also social values and the class structure of society, a country's geostrategic setting, vital interests, economic situation, and external environment.

To the extent that other factors are granted influential roles, they dilute the all-encompassing power of democracy. The presence of these factors implies that, although democracy may create a predisposition in favor of benign conduct, it is no cure-all; other variables can intervene to produce a different outcome. Other things being equal, democracies may be less likely to commit aggression than autocratic or monarchical regimes; however, if the conditions are right, in theory they are capable of acting in nonbenign ways. The core reality here is that the international system remains composed of sovereign nation-states, and, to a still-important degree, the liberal values of even democratic states can stop at their borders. As a matter of deductive logic, there is nothing to stop democratic states from using force abroad even though their normative values call on them to resolve disputes peacefully within their own territory, because the laws of nearly all democratic states permit use of military force externally in defense of their sovereign and legitimate interests.

Even today, most democratic states retain military forces that are intended not only to protect sovereign borders but also to project power abroad. To be sure, the stated intent of these nations is to employ force only within the framework of international law, but all retain the legal right to act unilaterally, subject to their own judgments. Nearly all also retain the right to use force not only against nondemocratic countries but also against other democracies when those democracies violate the legitimate interests of the parent state. This state of affairs implies that irrespective of their hope for the future, most such states are far from concluding that a democratic peace has settled permanently over the globe or that all other democracies can be fully trusted.

This literature properly notes that although democracy contributes to the cause of peace, the limitations on that contribution need to be clearly understood. What democracy helps ensure is that choices regarding foreign policy and military strategy are made through pluralist means, e.g., consensus-building, thereby safeguarding against the arbitrary decisions that autocratic or authoritarian governments can be prone to make. Simply stated, autocracies can go to war on the whim of a dictator, and authoritarian systems can go on the wishes of a small ruling class. Democracies, however, can go to war only through a complex exercise in consensus-building that requires the support of several institutions and even the populace. Yet the degree of constraint placed on arbitrary decisions depends on the type of democracy, and democracy comes in different forms.

A democracy dominated by presidential leadership or a single party may impose relatively light constraints because decisions are made by centralized means. The constraints are greatest in Western-style democracies, in which there is a separation of powers between the Executive and Legislative Branches, a division of powers between the federal government and regional bodies, and a sharing of powers among multiple political parties. But even in Western democracies, decisionmaking on national security policy has tended to be concentrated in the Executive Branch, a contribution that diminishes the effectiveness of institutionalized constraints.

In any event, democracy is no barrier to war if there is a solid domestic consensus to pursue it. Indeed, democracy can increase the likelihood of war if public opinion favors resort to military force, because democracy can weaken the ability of governmental institutions to withstand popular pressure. This phenomenon contributed somewhat to the outbreak of World War I, for several governments were goaded into war, despite their reservations, by public pressure inspired by nationalist sentiment. Democracy, therefore can act as a two-edged sword: sometimes erecting powerful barriers to war, sometimes knocking such barriers down.

The political values of a democratic government and society, then, not institutions, have the strongest influence over foreign policy. Yet even in a democracy, values are a variable, not a constant. If a democracy embraces liberal values that are applied not only at home but also abroad, it will promote international peace. But if it fails to apply liberal values to external conduct, then it may act no more peacefully than a totalitarian country. To presume that, as a matter of definition, democracy embraces liberal values that mandate a benign foreign policy is to engage in a tautology that makes a postulate true by means of its internal logic alone. Although some democracies embrace liberal values, not all do. Doing so certainly is not dictated by some immutable political law.

In fact, democracies across the world vary considerably in their respect for democratic principles. Whereas some perform well in this regard, others suppress their own minorities by denying them constitutionally guaranteed rights. Still others fail to respect the rights of other states, which makes them a threat to peace, not a protector of it. Moreover, democracies do not emerge pristine from the moment of their creation, but instead tend to mature as they age, passing through a "turbulent adolescence" along the way.

An important hallmark of democracy is its emphasis on laws. However, a large range of discretion exists in policy choice, and especially so in foreign policy. Policies may be chosen on the basis of majority rule, but the majority is not necessarily on the side of liberal values simply because it is a majority.

THE COMPLEX RELATIONSHIP BETWEEN DEMOCRACY AND PEACE

A question for the future is whether ideology—in all forms of government, democratic and otherwise—is dead in international affairs. The optimists assert that the end of the titantic clash between democracy and communism means that an ideology of cooperative conduct will arise in its wake. But will this be the case? Will most countries now settle into an enduring era of bourgeois tranquility encouraged by common domestic values and participation in an interdependent world economy? Or will nationalism again rise to the fore, thus driving many countries into conflict with each other? Will ethnicity become a dominant ideology of its own? Will culture and religion emerge to propel states and communities toward conflict? To the extent that these rival ideologies muscle out cooperation in the battle for controlling human passions, the future may be less tranquil than forecasted by the optimists.

Historians of Europe during the nineteenth century would find puzzling the assertion that democracy brings peace, for democracy was born in Europe in that period. The nineteenth century there witnessed substantial imperial conduct by democracies, as well as a long-enduring adversarial relationship between the two great democratic powers of the day, Britain and France. These two rivals did not fall into many wars after Napoleon's downfall because of Britain's success at maintaining a balance of power to contain France. Democracy did little to temper their rivalry; in some ways, it enhanced this rivalry by fanning nationalist sentiment.[6]

Indeed, most observers at the time felt that democracy incited interstate tensions by exposing governmental policy to populist pressures. The prevailing theory then was that government by aristocratic monarchies brought peace because the ruling families shared the common bonds and commitment to civility that encouraged restrained conduct. By introducing the masses into government, democracy was thought to unleash explosive passions—including nationalism, ethnic hatreds, and demagoguery—that would bring about perpetual war. Seasoned diplomats feared that Europe's deli-

---

[6]See David Thomson, *Europe Since Napoleon,* New York: Alfred A. Knopf, 1964.

cate equilibrium, which required the give and take of compromise, could not be maintained in the presence of mass politics. Their fears were somewhat borne out by Europe's catastrophic move toward World War I, which was driven strongly by nationalist passions.

Europe's turbulent history suggests that the causal relationship between democracy and peace is not single-dimensional (i.e., it does not occur in isolation) but instead quite complex. Normally, democracy cannot be imposed from above but must be nurtured in favorable soil by a healthy climate. Especially important to the growth of democracy are a healthy capitalist economy, a stable society with a strong middle class, and a sense of being secure from outside threats. Once democracy takes hold, it does encourage peace by promoting liberal values. But it is not the equivalent of an antibiotic that can be injected into an unhealthy political situation and relied upon to produce peace through its healing effects alone.

Democracy can contribute to peace but is not a sufficient condition for it, primarily because the decision of countries to pursue benign and cooperative foreign policies toward other nations is influenced by many factors other than common political ideology: the strength of the social and economic bond existing among the societies of countries, especially neighboring countries; the maturity of nations being sufficient to realize the disastrous effects of aggressive conduct; and the extent to which neighboring countries have resolved their geostrategic conflicts and have come to see virtue in cooperating. It is this transformation, not the presence of democracy alone, that determines when enduring peace and community are established. Moreover, this transformation most often does not occur overnight but is, instead, an outgrowth of time, experience, periodic setbacks, and accumulated successes: an evolutionary product of many small steps, not an instantaneous "big bang" of political awakening.

The arrival of democracy in a turbulent region, therefore, is no guarantee of immediate peace. In fact, it may exacerbate problems by giving greater scope for the expression of nationalism and exclusive ethnicity. Over time, the liberal values of democracy can encourage cooperative diplomacy. The real engine of peace is cooperative diplomacy, which is best practiced by democracies but nonetheless can be pursued by other forms of government. Once diplomatic cooperation takes the place of coercion, an environment of security is established, and liberal democracy can then flourish, thereby reinforcing the tendency toward peace. The causal relationship between democracy and peaceful interstate relations thus is a two-way street.

The reality is not that liberal democracy brings peace but, rather, that peace brings liberal democracy. The complex interaction between peace and liberal democracy begins with an already-existing system of authoritarian states in deep conflict with each other. Authoritarian rule propels each country toward a militaristic foreign policy of hostile paranoia and brutal exploitation. Stressful interstate relations, in turn, reinforce the incentives for authoritarian rule to preserve a mobilized society. The process of breaking this damaging cycle can begin in response to democratizing trends within each state. Yet democratization normally starts taking firm hold only when diplomacy has begun to resolve interstate frictions in ways allowing for a more relaxed internal order.

In the complex cycle that then unfolds, a lengthy period must be passed through during which democratizing nations find themselves still in a conflict with each other that is animated by nationalist passions, which typically emerge during democracy's adolescent stage. The propensity to conflict is further increased if dissimilar development cycles leave paranoid authoritarian states confronting immaturely boisterous and intolerant democracies. Yet parallel development cycles do not translate into benign foreign policies, for immature democracies can find compelling reasons for mutual animosity. Military competition may govern interstate relations, and bitter wars may be fought over borders, economics, and other claims.

Over time, conflicts are resolved on the basis of diplomacy and satisfactory mutual adjustments, and distaste for war gives way to a desire for tranquility. At this juncture, interstate community begins to take shape and conflict gives way to growing cooperation in security affairs and economics. This development, in turn, provides the sense of safety that allows liberal democracy to flower within states and that encourages these states to apply liberal values toward each other. The ultimate outcome is liberal democracy and peace, but the causal process was not one in which the former produced the latter single-dimensionally, with no trouble along the way.[7]

REALITIES OUTSIDE DEMOCRACY'S ORBIT

Even if the term "stable democracy" is interpreted loosely, this form of government obtains in only about one-half of the world's nations. Owing to its rapid march into new regions over the past 20 years, it dominates in North America, Western Europe, Latin America, and the western Pacific region of Asia. But it does not hold sway in most of Eurasia and the Middle East, and these vast regions appear to be the most susceptible to widespread turbulence and upheaval in the years ahead. The role of nondemocratic China will figure largely in Asia's future; in the Middle East, prospects for peace will be influenced by the large number of authoritarian governments that still rule there. If the presence of democracy helps encourage peaceful interstate relations, then its absence seems likely to act as an impediment, and democracy will be absent from many places in tomorrow's world.

Former Soviet Bloc

Particularly important will be developments within the former Soviet bloc. Most of the new nations there have cast aside communist rule and command economies, and are conducting experiments in market democracy. Some form of capitalism seems likely to be adopted for reasons of economic survival alone. Whether democracy will be successfully implanted is less certain, principally because these countries lack not only a historical legacy of democracy before communism was established but also the social and economic conditions that played a critical role in democracy's survival in Western Europe. Indeed, most countries suffer from deep social cleavages, the absence of a merchant middle class, and varying degrees of poverty: elements conducive to authoritarian rule, not democracy.

---

[7]See Appendix A for an historical treatment of the unfolding of the relationship between democracy and peace in Europe and Asia.

As matters now stand, market democracy has taken root deeply only in Poland, Hungary, and the Czech Republic; the Baltic states and a few other small countries are also good candidates. Hope for its flourishing will be much higher if Russia completes its own revolutionary transformation to market democracy, so that huge country will radiate the resulting value system outward to its smaller neighbors.

The troubled events of late 1993 and afterward, however, have raised doubts about whether this transformation will occur in the ways envisioned by optimists. By early 1994, President Boris Yeltsin had emerged as a leader ostensibly in search of a strong Russian state, not full-fledged market democracy. He presided over a cabinet of anti-reformers, a nationally elected parliament led by ex-communists and neofascists, a once-liberal foreign minister now talking in terms of neo-imperial restoration, and a military clearly gaining political influence. Yeltsin continued to speak in terms of democracy and economic reform, but events belied this vision.

Although some observers express hope that this troubled situation will be overcome, the future at best seems pointed toward a Russia marked by a strong president whose support for parliamentary democracy is lukewarm, an erratic and incomplete march toward market capitalism, and a tough-minded and interest-based foreign policy. Even worse, an authoritarian government and an imperial foreign policy might be the outcome. If a catastrophe occurs, a descent into fascistic nationalism cannot be ruled out. Also plausible is the fracturing of the Russian state itself, owing to weakened central control in Moscow, which allows headstrong republics and regions to go their own ways, setting the stage for civil war among Russia's competing political factions. A country dominated by regional warlords might be the outcome. Yet because Russia has always managed to maintain its unity and has compelling reasons to do so, civil war seems likely to produce an eventual restoration of an authoritarian dictatorship, perhaps under a fascist flag.

In the very long term, perhaps irreversible trends will produce a stable market democracy in Russia. But the time required for these trends to overpower all barriers is measured in decades and maybe centuries, not months and years. Nor is it inevitable that the dynamics that shaped the West's evolution will play themselves out in the same way in Russia: Russia has been a non-Western country for over one thousand years. Its origins lie in the Kievan state that formed at the end of the first millennium. The modern Moscow-dominated Russian state began emerging in the fourteenth century, when feudalism still ruled Western Europe. Throughout these many centuries, Russia steadfastly resisted the pressures for conformity emanating from Western Europe. Perhaps it will do so again.[8]

In any event, what matters now is not far-distant centuries but the coming period of history: the next two decades. Any restoration of communism seems out of the question; yet some of the old traditions of czarism (e.g., an assertive foreign policy reflecting the national interest) may be revived. During the coming years and decades, Russia may well move toward an economy with important capitalist features, but it also is likely to preserve strong central-control mechanisms and public ownership of industry, and authoritarian rule. If this is the case, it will reflect Russia's age-old pattern of adopting only some of what the West offers: not mimicking the West, but instead blending Western modernization with Russian traditionalism. Present dynamics seem pointed toward a restored Russian state and a mixed system of authoritarian capitalism. Some Western analysts insist that this outcome is impossible, for authoritarianism allegedly cannot exist in the presence of capitalism. But Russia may show that this outcome is indeed possible.

Even short of any immediate descent into fascism, Russia's future does not bode well for the independence of states within the Commonwealth of Independent States (CIS), to say nothing of market democracy there. Indeed, Belarus is trying to regain union with Russia regardless of whether democracy takes hold. Ukraine is waging a tough battle to stay free, but Ukraine itself is far short of market democracy. The same judgment applies to many of the fledgling states in the Caucasus and Central Asia. What might emerge is a restored Commonwealth under Russia's leadership, but not one guided by the principles of market democracy or warm friendship toward the emerging democracies on its western flank.

---

[8]See Herbert J. Ellison, *History of Russia,* New York: Holt, Rinehart, and Winston, 1964.

By itself, democracy's taking hold in the former Soviet bloc does not guarantee an era of peaceful interstate relations. Throughout this region, troublesome conflicts bar the way to diplomatic cooperation, much less the emergence of healthy community life. Among the causes of conflicts are unsettled borders, large ethnic minorities, economic frictions, religious antagonisms, historical animosities, emerging military competition, a lack of security guarantees, and a legacy of imperial conduct. Similar troubles once existed in Western Europe, and they were eventually resolved through diplomacy and mutual accommodation. But this process took many decades to accomplish; indeed, it took centuries. Along the way, a large number of wars were fought. The former Soviet bloc is not necessarily doomed to repeat this painfully long quest for peaceful community; however, if it does, enduring tranquility may be many years off.

Also important to this region's future will be the attitude adopted toward military force and war. In the West, bitter experience has dispelled the once-influential belief that aggressive war can be a positive instrument of statecraft and even an uplifting moral adventure. As a result, war is viewed as something to be embarked upon only as a last resort and for legitimate defensive purposes. But even in the West, this development is a relatively recent phenomenon. Before the twentieth century, conservative philosophers felt otherwise, and even some liberals shared their view. The disasters of World Wars I and II and the threat of nuclear holocaust during the Cold War produced the contemporary Western view.

Whether war is viewed in similarly negative terms outside the West, and especially within the former Soviet bloc, is an open issue. (European countries have been inflicting savagery on each other for *centuries*, but that does not seem to have deterred them from fighting again.) What can be said is that most of these countries possess ample means to wage war against each other as well as against other nations. Whether they will employ these military assets remains to be seen. The mere existence of these assets creates options for aggressive conduct and thus is grounds for concern in itself.

China

What applies to Russia's political and economic future may also apply to China. A millennia-old country, China has a mammoth population, nearly twice that of Western Europe and the United States combined.   The winds of change clearly are blowing over China, but not necessarily in the directions favored by Western philosophies.   China is slowly moving toward a capitalist economy, and the result has been a remarkable upsurge in productivity, which, if it continues, will make China an economic powerhouse in the decades ahead.   But China is not simultaneously trying to embrace democracy. Indeed, fear of warlordism and explosive civil war seems to have produced a consensus among its ruling elite for continued authoritarianism.   Doubtless communism will mutate.   The alternative may not be Western parliamentary democracy but, instead, a strong state, an authoritarian government, and an economy of "corporatist capitalism."[9]   Can this model work?   Western analysts are doubtful.   As with Russia, China may show similar single-mindedness in its foreign policy, which might not be one of communal cooperation with the West but, instead, strong-minded assertions of Chinese interests, as determined by the Chinese themselves.[10]

Middle East

A similar future of not emulating the West evidently awaits the Middle East and the Persian Gulf, a vitally important region where, apart from Israel, Western market democracy shows little sign of embedding itself.   Indeed, the recent trend has been in favor of Islamic traditionalism, not Westernization.

Today, Iran is governed by a theocracy. Iraq and Syria are ruled by dictators showing strong staying power. All the Persian Gulf states are ruled by conservative sheikdoms. Egypt is still heavily authoritarian. Libya is ruled by a quixotic Muslim dictator, and Algeria may be moving in the direction of Islamic fundamentalism. For these countries, stasis may dominate the future. If major change occurs, Islamic fundamentalism may be the ideology of choice, not Western democracy.

---

[9] *Corporatist capitalism* means an economic system that is heavily managed by government, with many of the industrial assets concentrated in a few large corporations.

[10] See Barber B. Conable, Jr., and David M. Lampton, "China: The Coming Power," *Foreign Affairs,* Winter 1992–1993.

Communal cooperation with the West is not necessarily the wave of the future for this long-turbulent region. Indeed, these countries may well display growing xenophobic hostility to the West, coupled with continued inability to get along with each other. If a cooling of hostilities occurs because the Israeli-Arab conflict is finally resolved, the process of cooperation likely will be slow, and it may be far from complete.[11]

GUARDING AGAINST NAIVE OPTIMISM

This brief global overview suggests not only that a guarded stance must be taken toward optimism but also that a stock-taking is needed of the United States' ability to understand what is happening abroad and where the future may be headed. The United States possesses far greater analytical resources for gauging events overseas than do other nations. These resources include a sizable intelligence apparatus, an extensive overseas presence by the U.S. diplomatic corps and the military, a large academic community, a robust journalistic sector, and a massive global communications network. But resources do not automatically translate into estimative capability. Although the United States is capable of gathering more information than other countries, can it process the information and interpret it? Does the United States know how to think clearly and judge accurately?

If optimistic judgments have been embraced prematurely, the reason may lie in U.S. inexperience with a more traditional form of international politics about to reappear on the world scene. The United States became globally active only during the twentieth century, which has had a historically unique international politics. The United States pursued isolationism during the nineteenth century, so it acquired no seasoning in the traditional politics of nationalism and multipolarity that dominated then. To the extent that nineteenth-century politics is making a comeback under twenty-first–century conditions, the United States may lack the intellectual tools needed to perceive where the future lies. If so, the task ahead will be to as-

---

[11]See Bernard Lewis, "Rethinking the Middle East," *Foreign Affairs*, Fall 1992; and Robin Wright, "Islam and Democracy," *Foreign Affairs*, Summer 1992.

semble better analytical capital before firmly embracing sweeping theories of the future.

Something more fundamental is involved than merely gathering more data and recalibrating predictions of the future. Forecasts are based on more than perceptions of empirical events that are projected in time. Intellectual predispositions—not only conceptual frameworks but also normative values and expectations—play a major role in shaping forecasts, and these too need to be thought about carefully. The optimistic literature reflects an inherent American tendency to underestimate the inbred permanence of conflict in a global system that remains structurally anarchic regardless of periodic changes in its surface characteristics (see Chapter Three). It also may reflect a flawed tendency to embrace idealism at the expense of *realpolitik*, and an unhealthy cultural chauvinism that projects Western visions upon the rest of the world, including to regions where they are not shared. The fault may lie not only with the optimistic literature but also with many American citizens across the entire political spectrum.

Several times in the past, as many scholars have written, the United States has embraced naive overoptimism in the immediate aftermath of a global crusade that vanquished a powerful enemy. Today, no hegemonic rival threatens to replace the USSR or Nazi Germany, but the absence of a single militarily powerful opponent embracing a totalitarian ideology does not mean permanent peace. Serious dangers can arise from other quarters and for other reasons. Indeed, an uncertain political environment can itself be destabilizing by influencing nations to pursue policies of self-protection that are perceived as threatening by others. To a degree, these dynamics caused World War I: a product of nineteenth-century European politics driven not by ideological confrontation in a bipolar setting but by nationalist conflict in a multipolar setting. If negative dynamics unfold again, the United States will compound the problem if it repeats its past susceptibility to falling victim to excessive optimism and naïveté.

Today's global system is still in the early stages of a profound upheaval, the outcome of which lies beyond the U.S. capacity to predict or control. Forces of integration are at work, as are forces of disintegration, and their competing dynamics cannot be accurately gauged by the academic theories of today. The optimistic literature offers a still-useful hypothesis for helping organize thinking about the international future, but it falls short of providing unshakable premises for building U.S. national security policy. U.S. national security needs intellectual guideposts. In constructing these guideposts, however, *hubris* should be avoided. What is needed is the capacity to remain open-minded, to suspend judgment, and to think deeply. The United States may be best served by relying on competing theories of the future, all of which are appraised for their respective strengths and are embraced in ways that do not erode flexibility. The next chapter presents theories in competition with optimism.

Chapter Three

THE WORRIED VISIONS OF INTERNATIONAL PESSIMISM

Representing a reaction against the optimistic school, the pessimistic literature reflects more than the negative developments of the post–Cold War years experienced thus far. It also reflects expectations for the shaping of the future by powerful systemic factors operating below the surface, unobserved, at least by the public. This chapter begins by discussing the theory of realism, which undergirds much of today's pessimistic literature. It then turns to a detailed description of that literature, including several subschools. The chapter concludes with a critique of the pessimistic literature.

THE POSTULATES OF REALISM

The stage for discussing the pessimistic literature can best be set by first reviewing the realist theory of international relations (or "neorealism," as it often is called today). In its premises and postulates, realism is the polar opposite of idealism, the theory that provides the intellectual underpinnings for the optimistic literature. Hans Morgenthau is the best-known proponent of realism,[1] but a more recent account has been written by Kenneth Waltz in his 1979 *Theory of International Politics* (Reading, Mass.: Addison-Wesley). A good scholarly appraisal of this school is presented in Robert O. Keohane's *Neorealism and Its Critics* (New York: Columbia University Press, 1986).

---

[1]See Hans J. Morgenthau and Kenneth Thompson, *Politics Among Nations: The Struggle for Power and Peace*, New York: McGraw-Hill, 1985.

What the realist school offers is the core postulate that conflict is a normal state of affairs for international politics and that instability typically grows as multipolarity increases. Because today's international system is moving away from Cold War bipolarity toward greater multipolarity, the negative trends identified by the pessimistic literature are rendered all the more valid—and serious. In essence, these trends apply great stress to an emerging international system that already may be prone to fracturing because of fragility in its underlying structural characteristics (see the "Alternative Security Systems" section of this chapter).

Whereas idealism stresses the ability of nations to cooperate on behalf of community-building and peaceful resolution of disputes, realism postulates a world in which nations pursue their own interests amid largely anarchical conditions. Realism does not forecast endless war: It expects peace when nations harbor no opposing interests. But it does forecast political conflict when interests are not in harmony. Realism holds that conflict regularly emerges because nations in collision endeavor to coerce each other, often through the use of military power when diplomacy fails. Equally important, realism argues that conflict can emerge inadvertently—even when nations do not pursue overtly incompatible agendas—because most nations amass military and economic power to safeguard themselves from an uncertain future. The result is a competitive dynamic borne of mistrust from which can spring wars spawned by nothing more deep-seated than a fearful desire to prevent a neighboring country from becoming dominant during peacetime and using that advantage sometime in the future.

Conflict

Realism is anchored on the assumption of the imperfectability of human nature and the enduring reality of group conflict. This assumption contrasts sharply with the judgments of idealist theories, but it squares with the views of many eminent observers, including political philosophers John Locke and Edmund Burke, who played key roles in establishing modern democratic theory. Reflecting the conclusion that at least some men everywhere remain perpetually aggressive, especially when they are angry and dissatisfied, realism regards human avarice as a permanent state of affairs, not a primitive failing that will be overcome as the human race gains moral maturity.[2]

In realism, interstate conflict is but one form of social strife, yet it is key to shaping the conduct of international affairs past, present, and future. Realism asserts that the causes of interstate conflict are manifold but are dominated by geopolitical rivalry, territorial disputes, antagonistic security agendas, and military competition. Realism also judges that interstate conflict can grow out of economic friction, including struggle over control of resources and markets. It rejects the postulate, advanced by liberal economic theory, that the international marketplace and growing wealth can be relied upon to bring prosperity to all, thereby alleviating interstate tension and producing global tranquility.

Economics

Realism acknowledges the pacifying effects of modern prosperity and cooperative trade relations, but, aware of history, it asserts that international economics often is marked by policies of statism, mercantilism, imperialism, and coercive exploitation—all of which exacerbate tensions. It notes that wars often have been directly caused by economic conflicts, with especially important roles played by control of resources and access to markets. Perhaps poor countries lacked the means to pursue aggression and rich nations lacked the incentive, but actors in between had both the means and motives and often were propelled outward by their own rising expectations.

Realism notes that, even today, economic conditions vary a great deal—differences, realism notes, that are still an important cause of interstate strife, for the less wealthy often feel exploited by the rich. Realism asserts that global economic trends are cyclical, with periods of sustained growth followed by cycles of recession and depression in which discontent breeds. Even in the best of times, realism points out that growth rates are distributed unevenly. Different levels of competitiveness make some countries "winners" and others "losers." For all these reasons, realism regards economics as an important

---

[2]See Leo Strauss and Joseph Cropsey, *History of Political Philosophy*, Chicago, Ill.: University of Chicago Press, 1988.

variable in the stability calculus: When economic conditions are healthy, stability is enhanced; when conditions are unhealthy, the opposite is the result. Indeed, in realism, economic frictions can themselves become a cause of security rivalry and war.

History

Owing to its assessment that the causes of interstate friction are manifold and perpetual, realism embraces an interpretation of history that contrasts sharply with that of idealism, in which history is a story of progress, a record of mankind's steady march toward peace, prosperity, and community. Realism, by contrast, offers a less up-beat appraisal. It acknowledges progress in the form of technological achievements, economic growth, institution-building, and increasingly complex social structures. But realism does not expect a peaceful international millennium anytime soon. Instead, it views interstate conflict as permanent, with only the forms of conflict changing from era to era. It thus tends to embrace a cyclical interpretation of history, in which one paradigm of conflict gives way to another, with the next paradigm not necessarily more stable than the last. Realism seeks neither to permanently pacify interstate conflict nor to escape it. Instead, realism seeks to manage interstate conflict, to keep it within acceptable boundaries through diplomacy and the wise exercise of power.

Nation-State System

This view of history leads realism to embrace a different view of the nation-state system than does idealism. Offended by this system's anarchical environment and the rogue options offered by unfettered sovereignty, idealism views the nation-state system with suspicion: as a principal source of war whose destructive impulses are best suppressed through creation of collectivist institutions. Idealism celebrates somewhat the alleged weakening of the nation-state brought about by growing external and internal constraints on national sovereignty. This weakening, idealism judges, will enhance opportunities for peace.

By contrast, realism appraises the nation-state system in less negative terms—indeed, in morally neutral terms. It views the nation-state as one type of social organization, an inevitable product of historical trends. Because realism regards conflict as the outgrowth of interactions among individual humans and social groups, it does not judge the nation-state as a unique cause of war. Although it acknowledges the growing importance of constraints on national sovereignty, realism is skeptical of the idea that the nation-state is disappearing as a potent actor on the world scene. Realism has a split view of this trend toward weakening of sovereignty: If states will be less capable of acting for the bad, they also will be less capable of acting for the good.

Indeed, realism views the nation-state as a positive political force in important respects, for the nation-state tempers social violence within its borders and allows for organized diplomacy on the international scene. Moreover, realism does not regard multilateral institutions as automatically an improvement over the nation-state system. It reasons that the health of such institutions is determined by the ability of their member states to cooperate in the first place, and that unhealthy institutions can do more harm than good—as was shown by the impotent League of Nations in the 1930s.

Military Power and War

Realism also disputes another central tenet of idealism: that military power and war are rapidly becoming outmoded in the post–Cold War era. Realism's judgment stems partly from skepticism about idealism's assertion that security issues have faded in importance and are being replaced by economics and other social issues. Security issues will always be critical to national governments; moreover, realism asserts, the issues now coming to the fore have security components of their own, and many wars have begun as a result of economic frictions. Realism notes that war will remain one instrument of national policy, and that a wholesale global disarmament is not under way. Indeed, it cites countervailing factors as important to the future: Several countries are bolstering their military power, modern forces are capable of inflicting immense damage, and emerging technology is increasing the lethality of even small forces. These trends, realism worries, may increase the propensity to violence. After all, history shows that aggression and war sometimes can succeed.

Realism views foreign policy not as a moral crusade on behalf of humanist visions[3] but as a vehicle for protecting national interests and safely managing an always-turbulent international environment. Endowed with a strong sense of pragmatism, realism argues that a nation's moral greatness is determined by its domestic accomplishments, not its foreign policy achievements. It endorses feasible efforts to promote international cooperation, but, first and foremost, it views foreign policy in defensive terms, as a vehicle to safeguard national sovereignty and vital goals. Larger endeavors are to be pursued only *after* this safeguarding has been achieved, not at the cost of self-abnegation.

Morality

In contrast to idealism, realism tends not to apply lofty moral standards in judging the behavior of nation-states. Critics accuse realism of being amoral, of downgrading excessively the empirical and normative role played by political values in shaping international affairs. Realist theoreticians dispute this claim as carrying a partially accurate analysis too far. Regardless of where the truth lies, realism's approach to morality undeniably is practical and utilitarian. It expects all countries to pursue their own interests, and it does not condemn self-interested behavior as inherently immoral. Realism assumes that interstate conflict is normal, not an abnormal outgrowth of flawed but correctable ethical values. Morality, it reasons, stems not from the denial of national interests but from a serious effort to prevent confrontation by harmonizing and balancing competing interests on the basis of legitimacy and fairness. Realism regards self-restraint as critical to the achievement of international stability and the avoidance of war. From mutual restraint, it reasons, can come political equilibrium, which is regarded by realism as a core factor in determining whether enduring peace is possible.

Owing to its search for equilibrium, realism sharply condemns states that blindly pursue acquisitive goals at the expense of the vital interests of other countries, viewing such behavior as the real cause of war. It also disapproves of states that seek absolute military security

---

[3] *Humanism* is a philosophical school based on respect for individual rights. It provides the foundation for democracy.

for themselves—an approach that can mean absolute insecurity for all others. Conversely, realism also disapproves of states that pursue accommodation to the point of appeasement—an approach, it argues, that can weaken prospects for equilibrium by suggesting to rogue states that no limits will be applied to fulfillment of their demands.

Foreign Policy

What realism seeks in the foreign policies of all countries is a balanced relationship between assertive goals and accommodation, and between firmness and self-restraint. It endeavors to pursue international harmony through diplomacy based on compromise and guided by standards of legitimacy. But aware that negotiation is conducted in a setting of conflict, it endorses the use of national power as critical to achieving a favorable outcome. When negotiation proves fruitless, it advocates use of military force. The willingness to use force for legitimate purposes, realism judges, can itself contribute to peace by creating powerful incentives for otherwise-malevolent states to exercise restraint.

Realism asserts that foreign policy is shaped largely by a state's geopolitical circumstances: to the point where domestic political values play only a contributing, not determining, role. Accordingly, realism is skeptical of the allegedly pacifying effects of democracy, and it argues that the moral self-righteousness being promoted by democratic states can exacerbate conflict when those states deal with authoritarian systems. Realism maintains that, for all states, including democracies, foreign policies are determined by national interests, which are shaped by a complex mixture of internal norms, self-serving goals, and external requirements. Realism thus is not blind to the influence of values, but it also endorses Henry Palmerston's dictate that there are no permanent friends, only permanent interests. In its judgment, peace is maintained by balancing interests, not by forming friendships; indeed, it suggests, friendships form only when common interests are upgraded or at least balanced on the basis of fair compromise.

Realism judges that prospects for stability are heavily influenced by the structural characteristics of the international system. It defines *stability* as the absence of unhealthy trends and dynamics that create a propensity for war, and *instability* in terms of the presence of those trends. The structural character of the international system provides the all-important environment in which foreign policies are shaped, and therefore plays a major role in determining whether the interactions of states propel the system toward stability or instability. Thus, some structural characteristics encourage the former, but others the latter.

ALTERNATIVE SECURITY SYSTEMS

Realism's judgments about the determinants of stability and a proper foreign policy can best be illuminated by offering the following conceptual scheme for organizing alternative security systems. Because the following alternatives are ideal types, reality will never identically conform to them; at best, it may only approximate them. These alternatives are abstract models that help bring the core features of international politics into sharp focus, thereby permitting them to be analyzed.

- **Collective Security.** In this system, which is marked by a formal alliance relationship among the member states, harmony exists and conflicts are resolved through peaceful diplomacy. The members are pledged to come to the defense of each other if one of them is attacked either by another member or by an outside power. Political consensus and common security horizons thus predominate.

- **Polarized and Depolarized Systems.** By *polarization* is meant a conflict-laden situation in which countries regard themselves in adversarial terms and interact closely enough to regularly and powerfully influence each other's behavior—much as planets in a solar system affect each other through mutual gravitational forces. In a polarized system, conflict and coercion predominate. The degree of polarization can vary, but the core feature is interstate rivalry and competition. In a depolarized system, countries have either harmonious or neutral relations: They do not view each other as adversaries, do not fashion organized security strategies against each other, and do not organize interstate subsystems to protect themselves from each other. A *depolarized system* thus is marked by a lack of intense friction and the absence of organized efforts to manage conflict through the exercise of coercive power.

- **Bipolar System.** As one type of polarized system, this model is marked by organized and opposing efforts to manage conflict through coercive power: Interaction is highly stressful, relations are adversarial, and interstate conflict is substantial. The two competitive blocs that make up the system may be either formal alliances or looser arrangements; they may be led by a single, dominant power or by several powers of equal stature; and they may be composed of any number of members. The key feature is that only two blocs exist, and their interaction defines the structural characteristics of the security system.

- **Multipolar System.** Similar to a bipolar structure, this system experiences organized efforts to manage conflict through coercion. Its distinguishing feature is that it is composed of more than two power blocs. The greater the number of competing blocs, the greater the degree of multipolarity. Whereas a bipolar system's dynamics are straightforward, a multipolar system's dynamics are very complex. Each bloc tries to promote its own interests but must confront the pressures of more than one actor. The result is a highly fluid pattern of relationships—and often great unpredictability and difficulty in pursuing goals.

- **Mixed System.** Because the international arena is composed of many states scattered across the globe, the entire system may not be dominated by a single structure. Instead, the international system may be broken down into regional subcomponents: One region may be a collective security system, another depolarized, another bipolar, and another multipolar. At no time is a single structure likely to characterize the entire world. A mixed system exists when no single structure dominates the global arena: when several different regional systems coexist with relatively equal weight.

Realism is primarily preoccupied with assessing situations in which there is no all-encompassing collective security system and high polarization exists. Realism does not view polarization as inevitable; when it does occur, realism endeavors to analyze its dynamics and to determine strategies for managing its conflicts. When stability is maintained among adversarial states in polarized settings, it occurs, realism argues, not solely because of diplomacy but also because a balance of power is preserved, one in which a relatively equitable distribution of military forces and other coercive assets denies any one system an incentive to commit aggression. In theory, a stable situation can be achieved through joint planning and coordination. Such a state of affairs is normally achievable only when interstate relations are harmonious. Because there is disharmony in a polarized setting, realism asserts, systemic outcomes—stable or otherwise—are normally the product of multiple, uncoordinated interactions, not of a cooperative central plan.[4]

A stable situation can emerge unintentionally, owing to supremacy-seeking nations that counterbalance each other through their competitive coalition-building dynamics. But this is not necessarily the outcome if physical assets are unequally distributed and natural alliance dynamics do not produce equilibrium. Accordingly, realism seeks stability through the wisdom of states with enough power to transform imbalance into balance by adding their offsetting weight to the disadvantaged side. Its hero is nineteenth-century Britain, which consciously sought to maintain a European balance of power by shifting its alignments whenever the situation demanded.

REALISM'S SECURITY-SYSTEM MODELS AND A DANGEROUS WORLD

The conceptual framework laid down by realism has important implications for analyzing whether a more dangerous world will evolve, and how this evolution might take shape. Even to realism, the current international system is not inherently unstable. What exists today is a mixed system that contains elements of different models regionally, with relatively low global polarization when judged by historical standards.

One important contributor to stability is the Western security alliance, which unites North America, Western Europe, and key Asian nations under the leadership of the United States, the globe's sole remaining superpower. In the Middle East, the Persian Gulf, and

[4]See James N. Rosenau, ed., *International Politics and Foreign Policy*, New York: The Free Press, 1969.

South Asia, polarization remains at traditionally high levels; but now, at least, the threat of war has receded. In Asia, polarization is fairly low, although this region has long been a hotbed of political conflict. The key region for determining instability is Eurasia, stretching from East Central Europe and the Balkans through Russia, the Caucasus, and South Central Asia. Given structure by the now-defunct Warsaw Pact during the Cold War, this region now lacks a collective security arrangement, and many of its governments are unstable. The former Yugoslavia aside, this region is not headed toward major polarization, for interstate friction is not at a high level. This region thus is best characterized as currently depolarized but moving toward polarization as a result of negative trends.

Because the post–Cold War era is only beginning to take shape, realism does not regard the current global situation as being in a permanent stasis, but instead as tentative. The threat of a more dangerous world, realism judges, will be determined by two factors:

- The degree to which polarizing interstate political conflict grows, thereby bringing about a weakening of existing community bonds and a slide toward greater polarization in key regions. Especially important is the outcome in Eurasia, for if the current depolarized setting there drifts toward polarization rather than toward collective security, the stability of the entire global system will suffer.

- If polarization occurs, the degree to which the dynamics of conflict management produce either stable security structures anchored on balance or unstable structures anchored on imbalance. Of particular concern are the negative consequences if a multipolar security system evolves, both within individual regions and across the globe as a whole.

Realism cannot predict whether conflict and polarization will increase in the years ahead. It does postulate, however, that ideological confrontation is not the only source of interstate conflict. In today's world, cultural and national interests and security dynamics remain even if ideological systems have passed away. Consequently, realism does not herald the disappearance of universalist rivalry between democracy and communism as the harbinger of global peace. The anarchical international system itself, realism argues, still

contains ample ingredients for strife that, depending on developments, could acquire growing importance in the years ahead.

Dynamics of Polarization

If polarization develops, realism offers insights on the dynamics of
how polarization often takes shape and on the likely consequences
for stability. According to realism, a bipolar system emerged in the
Cold War mainly because of two factors: the ideological confrontation between democracy and communism, and the global rivalry between two superpowers, the United States and the Soviet Union.
Because both contributors to bipolarity—confrontation and rivalry—
have faded, realism judges that the future may pose a trend toward
greater multipolarity.

Even in a world offering less clarity about ideology and power than
the Cold War did, the mathematics of coalition formation can create
incentives for bipolarity because countries, when confronted with
major uncertainty, tend to seek coalitions that provide the greatest
margin of military assurance. The search for assurance, in turn,
touches off a dynamic that tends toward bipolarity, especially when
two coalitions are growing to the point where no third coalition
could match either of them in power. Owing to its relative weakness,
a third coalition would be left vulnerable to invasion by one or both
of the dominant coalitions. At this point, a rush begins for all outside
powers to join one of the two dominant coalitions, with the result
that these two coalitions become stronger, and any likelihood of a
third coalition rapidly fades.

Military mathematics are far from the only determinant of coalition
formation, however, or even its most important determinant.
Political values matter greatly. As the importance of ideology fades,
states will turn to their national interests to provide a moral compass,
a development that will help erode the common bond of all-
encompassing values that is often needed to hold together two large
alliances of disparate members. In this situation, the sheer number
of nations on the global stage argues against the emergence of two
dominant blocs.

Especially because post–Cold War politics are taking shape regionally, the widespread geographical separation of regions also argues

against global bipolarity: A country located in one region often will be reluctant to extend security commitments to other regions unless those commitments can somehow aid its causes within its own locale. Indeed, the future plausibly might witness polarization among regions, which would propel the globe toward a multipolar system of at least five power blocs. Even within individual regions, bipolarity is constrained by the actions of the leaders of each bloc and the bloc's internal characteristics. A drift toward multipolarity can be brought about by a lack of common interests and the presence of complex political conflicts, or simply by the dictates of geography.

The potential emergence of greater multipolarity necessitates a concerted effort to understand its characteristics, especially because the last 45 years of bipolarity mean there has been no recent experience in managing the dynamics of multipolarity. Realist scholars offer differing interpretations; for the most part, however, they argue that multipolar systems are less structurally stable than bipolar systems: The competitive dynamics of bipolar systems tend to take the form of a stable balance of military power and, in any event, can be managed through relatively straightforward military strategy and diplomacy— especially when each bloc is led by a dominant power that can compel its junior partners to fall into line. Realism judges that the Cold War never collapsed into a full-scale military conflagration partly because it was tightly bipolar under the guidance of two superpowers, both of which led highly integrated military alliances.

By contrast, multipolar systems require far more complex and fluid policies that are susceptible to miscalculation. For example, whereas German Chancellor Otto von Bismarck was skilled at multipolar management, his successor, Kaiser Wilhelm, was ham-handed. This difference alone helped propel Europe to war in 1914. Moreover, the very nature of multipolarity lends itself to military imbalances that are destabilizing. A multipolar system is stable only when competing blocs are blessed with equivalent military assets in ways that check aggression by all of them. When imbalance prevails, the strong tend to devour the weak, or at least intimidate them into submission. Because three or more blocs exist, imbalance can easily occur, for a majority of blocs can join together to overpower the minority. Multipolarity presents an almost infinite array of permutations when the system is made up of numerous states, but only a small portion of these permutations is truly stable.

Military Imbalances

Realism judges that the incentives for multipolarity are further enhanced because, outside the Western Alliance system in today's world, worrisome imbalances exist in the military power of nations in the key regions. These imbalances are discussed in Chapter Six, but their core features merit note here. In East Central Europe and Eurasia, Russia, for all its troubles, remains far larger than any of its immediate neighbors, none of whom enjoys Alliance assurances. These neighbors, in turn, are mostly not in military balance with each other. For example, Ukraine will be stronger than Poland, which, in turn, will be stronger than its southern neighbors, the Czech Republic and Slovakia. Further to the south, Hungary will be stronger than Slovakia, but Hungary may be threatened by Romania and Serbia.

For this reason, the entire zone stretching from East Central Europe through the Balkans and Caucasus, and to South Central Asia is militarily unstable. In Asia, a tenuous military balance exists on the Korean peninsula, but China and Russia dominate the region elsewhere. Japan derives its military security from the United States, and other Asian nations are mostly small and vulnerable military powers. In South Asia, a tenuous balance exists between Pakistan and India; as India grows stronger, however, it will acquire supremacy over its neighbors. In the Middle East and Persian Gulf, military imbalance is also the rule. Israel remains the strongest regional power, but it defends itself alone against several Arab states that may still band together. To the south, powerful Iraq and Iran remain potent threats to the weak Arab sheikdoms that control the Persian Gulf oil fields.

Military imbalances will be of little consequence if key regions demonstrate harmonious interstate political relations, stable societies, and prosperous economies. But such a demonstration may not be forthcoming, so it is here that the newly emergent pessimistic literature becomes part of the equation.

THE SCHOLARSHIP OF INTERNATIONAL PESSIMISM

The literature of pessimism raises the prospect of increasing political and social stress in all key regions, which will compound the dangers ahead. Even if interstate frictions are not especially severe at the onset, a more multipolar system with military imbalances is worrisome enough because its structural properties are fragile. The climate of uncertainty and disorder that a multipolar system creates leads countries to act to perturb each other, thereby giving rise to fearful apprehensions and self-fulfilling prophecies. The act of adding a host of very real political and economic troubles affecting many nations and regions makes the risk of instability all the greater. The effect is to intensify the frequency and degree of interstate conflict, to increase the extent of polarization, and to narrow the scope for cooperation.

More countries will have more things to quarrel about and fewer reasons to work together. Minor powers will square off against each other more often, and major powers, themselves facing troubled relations with each other, will be less able to control them. Thus, the combination of structural multipolarity and tension-exacerbating trends threatens to produce a dangerous world.

The following works do not constitute the entire literature, but dominate it thus far. For convenience, this review divides them into three strife-specific categories: prophets of global anarchy and chaos, prophets of nationalism and ethnic strife, and prophets of economic troubles.[5]

Prophets of Global Anarchy and Chaos

- Zbigniew K. Brzezinski, *Out of Control: Global Turmoil on the Eve of the Twenty-First Century*, New York: Scribner's, 1993.

- Henry Kissinger, *Diplomacy*, New York: Simon & Schuster, 1994.

- Samuel P. Huntington, "The Clash of Civilizations?" *Foreign Affairs*, Summer 1993.

- Max Singer and Aaron Wildavsky, *The Real World Order: Zones of Peace, Zones of Turmoil*, Chatham, N.J.: Chatham House Publishers, 1993.

---

[5]The following review does not provide page and chapter cites for each book because key judgments are distributed throughout their contents. Major themes usually can be discerned by reading the introductory and concluding chapters. If more material is wanted, the reader is advised to read these books in their entirety.

Prophets of Nationalism and Ethnic Strife

- William Pfaff, *The Wrath of Nations: Civilization and the Furies of Nationalism*, New York: Simon & Schuster, 1993.

- John Lukacs, *The End of the Twentieth Century and the End of the Modern Age*, New York: Ticknor and Fields, 1993.

- Daniel Patrick Moynihan, *Pandaemonium: Ethnicity in International Politics*, New York: Oxford University Press, 1993.

Prophets of Economic Troubles

- Paul Kennedy, *Preparing for the Twenty-First Century*, New York: Random House, 1993.

- Alexander J. Motyl, *Dilemmas of Independence: Ukraine After Totalitarianism*, New York: Council on Foreign Relations Press, 1993.

- Jeffrey Garten, *A Cold Peace: America, Japan, Germany, and the Struggle for Supremacy*, New York: Times Books, 1992.

Prophets of Global Anarchy and Chaos

While acknowledging that the end of the Cold War may yield a stable global community, Zbigniew Brzezinski argues that unless present trends are reversed, worldwide disorder is likely. His central premise is that ideas play a critical role in determining the globe's political evolution. To understand how this role will be played out, the West needs to grasp exactly which ideas are being embraced. Whereas common values lay the foundation for global cooperation, dissimilar values pave the way to enduring conflict. As matters now stand, the world is witnessing a trend toward dissimilarity, not commonality.

Viewing the future through the lens of history, Brzezinski asserts that the nineteenth century gave rise to transcendent political ideology and mass politics, as well as nationalism, idealism, and rationalism. The result was a twentieth century of organized insanity, in which totalitarianism attempted to create coercive utopias, thus spawning megadeath, repression, and world war. The coming era represents a sharp reaction against this disastrous experience, not a global embracing of Western liberal democracy or its European philosophical foundations. We are entering, says Brzezinski, a "post-utopian" phase in which all millennial ideologies have lost their appeal, thus compelling social groups to fall back on their own interests and experiences for identity and meaning. With change taking place at ever-faster rates amid mounting economic interpenetration and social upheaval, the result is a global "crisis of spirit," reflecting a lack of common values.

To preserve global order, Brzezinski argues, assertive trilateral leadership is required by the United States, Western Europe, and Japan. Unlike some analysts, Brzezinski is not consumed with fear that the United States might fall into geopolitical rivalry with its principal Cold War allies. But he concludes that strong trilateral leadership from these three allies at present is not forthcoming and is not likely to be achieved unless policies among all of them are changed. To Brzezinski, the United States remains a peerless military power but is today so consumed by its materialist culture of the "permissive cornucopia" that it cannot provide a moral beacon or central authority. Western Europe and Japan are economic powerhouses, but they, too, are so inward-looking and self-centered that they cannot play the role of global leader. Overcoming this paralysis so that trilateral leadership can be forged for the new era is his principal recommendation.

Even if such leadership were to be offered, Brzezinski acknowledges, its effectiveness would hinge on whether it is accepted as legitimate across the globe. Especially absent efforts by the West to alter its own self-absorption in materialism, this legitimacy might not be granted: In many quarters, the West is not regarded as a model to be emulated. Communism collapsed in Europe not because Europe overwhelmingly preferred Western market democracy but because communism had become a grotesque political-economic failure that was cast aside by countries and ethnic groups seeking their own national identities. Self-determination thus is the dominant imperative, and the strains of transitioning to capitalism do not create the moderate political climate needed for liberal democracy to take hold. Europe's future thus is unlikely to be dominated by the progressive march eastward of the Western community and market democracy. Instead, the Continent likely will be divided in two, with a diffuse European Union to the west and a turbulent zone of undemocratic countries to the east.

Elsewhere, Brzezinski asserts, the world is witnessing a political awakening defined in material, psychological, and localist terms. The gap between expectations and realities is enlarging enormously, with starving spectators in non-Western countries looking with anger at insatiable consumers from Western societies that have lost their moral appeal. Thus, there is no consensus on behalf of common Western visions favoring cooperation and community-building.

Many countries resist the idea of falling under the West's tutelage, and some even look askance at the idea of cooperating with their neighbors for anything beyond normal trade relations. The trend is toward a dangerous dichotomy of outlooks, derived from different cultures and economic contexts brought into contact by modern communications. A global confederal structure is needed; instead, the resulting structure may be a jerrybuilt assemblage of regional conflicts, economic strife, xenophobia, new ideological conflicts, proliferation, power contests, great dissatisfaction, and mounting anger and frustration—a descent into anarchy.

In Europe, Brzezinski is doubtful that the then–European Community (now–European Union) or other collective institutions will permanently tame this long-turbulent continent. He argues that the EC will continue slowly evolving toward integration but will be too tangled in its manifold contradictions to unify Europe. In East Central Europe, Brzezinski forecasts continued efforts to achieve market democracy amid great strain. Farther to the east—in Eurasia—he foresees a geopolitical black hole: a vacuum of great potential instability and upheaval. Because the transition away from communism has only just begun, Brzezinski is quite doubtful that Russia will emerge as a liberal democracy anytime soon. At best, the chaotic economic situation will require Russia to follow the Asian model, whereby strong governmental control is used to establish a capitalist economy. Equally likely is a new kind of authoritarian statist nationalism, or even outright fascism bent on restoring the empire. Surrounding Russia is likely to be a cluster of unstable nations consumed by ethnic ambitions, raw nationalism, and vituperative hatred of each other. As Russia asserts dominance over these nations, Brzezinski says, it might well confront Germany for domination of East Central Europe, thereby setting the stage for the reappearance of an old economic-security rivalry that has often destabilized European politics.

In East Asia, Brzezinski argues, achievement of regional stability will depend largely on how major-power relations play out. Japan will continue to be America's closest partner, but Brzezinski worries about U.S.–Japanese trade frictions, which in the extreme could culminate in Japanese descent into mercantilistic nationalism and militarism. Short of this unlikely development, he concludes that Japan, owing to its own history and limited policy horizons, will not be able to play the role of a constructive regional leader. He thus foresees a region that does not integrate but is dominated by fluid multipolarity and purely national visions.

Brzezinski hopes that China will emerge as a constructive partner of the West, but he suspects that a more likely outcome is China as either a power-seeker in Asia or an authoritarian but capitalist leader of the Third World, offering an alternative to Western models. The result will be a region dominated economically by Japan but rendered tense by growing Chinese *assertiveness* (i.e., vigorous use of national assets to achieve foreign policy goals) in a situation dominated by the lack of a collective security structure. A stronger role by China, in turn, could trigger Japanese rearmament, thereby creating a tense security standoff between these two powers.

In South Asia, Brzezinski foresees Indian hegemony, and in the Middle East/Persian Gulf, he forecasts an impoverished, shapeless Moslem entity consumed by anger at the West but lacking sufficient political cohesion either to lift itself into modernity or to strike back forcefully at the West. The result will be a region of chronic instability, caught between the competing impulses of traditionalism and modernism.

Brzezinski's book primarily focuses on political issues and does not delve deeply into how future trends will manifest themselves in military affairs. Yet the implications of his analysis are obvious, for military rivalry almost inevitably comes in the wake of profound political tensions, which he foresees as mounting in virtually every major area of the globe. Moreover, Brzezinski envisions not only local conflicts but also restored military rivalry among the major powers if events deteriorate. Interestingly, he does not envision direct U.S. military rivalry with Russia or China, but he does foresee such a rivalry evolving indirectly if Russia squares off against Germany in Europe and if Russia and China fall into confrontation with Japan in Asia.

Beyond this, he worries that proliferation will produce more members of the nuclear club, including members in the turbulent Middle East, thereby further complicating management of the global power balance.

Brzezinski offers no specific insights on U.S. defense strategy, but his general points carry a powerful message. Fearing great upheaval in the years ahead, Brzezinski strongly endorses continued U.S. engagement and global leadership, and is opposed to isolationist withdrawal. His analysis asserts that the United States should remain a superpower, and that military strength can help increase U.S. global political muscle and reassure allies while leaving the country prepared for unfavorable developments. The rivals that the United States confronts, however, are faceless. Indeed, the principal risk is not that a hegemonic enemy will reappear but that a global system that is structurally unstable and prone to widespread tension and violence will emerge. His most important point is that the efficacy of American military power will be weakened unless military power is accompanied by a relevant political message. Absent such a message, he concludes, the United States will probably suffer an erosion of its influence abroad.

Regardless of how the future unfolds, Brzezinski asserts, the West should be prepared for major changes in the years ahead. If a peaceful global community is to evolve, common values will have to be fashioned out of today's discord, and, even then, a great deal of hard work and good fortune will be needed. Even as the United States seeks the best, he reasons, it should be prepared for something considerably less appealing.

Henry Kissinger's voluminous book is mostly a history of statecraft since the modern age was born in the 1600s, but it also contains powerful material on international politics and U.S. foreign policy for the coming era. According to Kissinger, the pursuit of national interests has been a fundamental feature of global politics for many centuries and is unlikely to change now. To him, history offers the lesson that although moral values matter, interstate tensions can be managed only if there is intelligent diplomacy based on realism. Such diplomacy, he asserts, must aim at crafting equilibrium according to shared principles of legitimacy.

Although Cardinal Richelieu inaugurated the modern age by creating the doctrine of state interests, Kissinger's heroes are Klemens Metternich and Otto von Bismarck. After using military power to crush their most dangerous enemies, both men exercised restraint and negotiated to create peaceful order with their neighbors. To Kissinger, Kaiser Wilhelm is the archetypical bumbling incompetent, who transformed peace into war through his own clumsy mishandling of European geopolitics. Adolf Hitler, in turn, is the satan of *realpolitik* because he used Germany's dominant position to pursue unlimited conquest.

Kissinger sees Joseph Stalin as a clever practitioner of *realpolitik* rather than a messianic ideologue. The Cold War started, he argues, partly because the Western powers failed to rise above their own illusions to perceive Stalin's true geopolitical motives. Owing largely to the U.S. ideological crusade on behalf of Wilsonian idealism, the United States was then unable to surmount its own self-righteousness to craft the *realpolitik* bargain that might have been available. Abetted by Soviet stodginess and vacillating U.S. behavior, a bipolar standoff resulted that lasted four decades, even though diplomatic reasoning says that it should have been settled long before.

Kissinger credits the U.S. commitment to Wilsonian idealism as a major reason for the West's cohesion during the Cold War, as well as for the World War II triumph over Hitler. But he also argues that the United States' sense of moral superiority led to twin undesirable impulses: the tendency either to take Wilson's principles too far or to withdraw entirely from global politics. These impulses, he argues, often got in the way of sensible geopolitical conduct as the twentieth century evolved. America's earlier penchant for isolationist detachment from distasteful global politics helped contribute to World War I. Indulgence in Wilsonian idealism then brought about the disastrous Versailles accord, which was followed by a second withdrawal into isolationism that helped give rise to Hitler. Kissinger blames the Vietnam debacle and other setbacks in the Middle East and Asia during the Cold War on the United States' inability to apply geopolitical restraint to its universalist principles. The United States, he concludes, is exiting the Cold War and the twentieth century with a dubious diplomatic record owing to its longstanding inability to handle the realities of power politics and geopolitical management.

Kissinger dismisses as naive the idea that the collapse of communism means that an era of global harmony is at hand. The ideological conflict of the Cold War, he reasons, is giving way to a more traditional era reminiscent of the eighteenth and nineteenth centuries in which nationalism will reappear as a dominant *raison d'être*. What will distinguish the coming era is that the international system will now stretch far beyond Europe to encompass the entire globe because communications and economic-strategic intercourse are becoming globalized. The result, he says, will be an insidious combination of fragmentation and globalization, the effects of which will be intensified by the accelerating pace of change in today's world. The result will be a propensity for disorder on a far larger scale than has been experienced before.

Kissinger forecasts that six powers will dominate: the United States, Europe, Russia, China, Japan, and India. No longer bound by Cold War constraints, all these states will now have much greater latitude to pursue their own interests, as well as the military and economic power to do so. Along with these major powers will come a host of medium-sized states and smaller ethnic entities, all of which will add further fluidity to an already-chaotic system. Kissinger does not predict an outright descent into multipolar volatility, but he does firmly assert that farsighted statesmanship will be needed to prevent this outcome. His fear clearly is that statesmanship will not be forthcoming, and the result will be the reappearance of the unstable and competitive old-style geopolitics that marked earlier centuries.

Kissinger acknowledges that the United States will not be able to control the globe, but he does view U.S. power as critical to realizing the hope that the lamentable past will not repeat itself. He does not call for a wholesale abandoning of Wilsonian values, but he does urge adoption of geopolitical realism[6] as a healthy counterweight needed to create a proper foreign policy, what Kissinger envisions as a combination of power politics and moral purpose that lays a foundation of geopolitical stability so that democratic values can spread. This foundation, he asserts, must be anchored on a neo-Metternichian search for equilibrium among the globe's most impor-

---

[6]A traditional, or realistic, *geopolitical relationship* implies that somewhat differing interests prevail in key regions and make inevitable a degree of incompatibility in agendas.

tant actors. The task ahead, he implies, is not to quickly proliferate democracy everywhere in the hope that doing so will bring permanent peace. Instead, the task is to patiently build peace through stability, thereby allowing democracy to slowly expand outward into regions where dictatorships have long held sway.

Kissinger is clearly worried that even this limited task will not be accomplished, primarily because he is skeptical that the United States will act with geopolitical maturity. He acknowledges that the impulse either to withdraw or to pursue moralistic crusades lies deep in American culture, but he also criticizes the policies pursued since the Cold War ended. He points a finger at the Bush Administration, but his sharpest barbs are reserved for the Clinton Administration, which he sees as tilting too far toward Wilsonian idealism and away from realism, especially in Clinton's policy toward Russia: The policy's total preoccupation with reform allegedly produces a failure to grasp the geopolitical agenda to be pursued by Moscow regardless of its government. For similar reasons deriving from the administration's alleged failure to grasp modern-day geopolitical realities, Kissinger is critical of current policies toward NATO, the European Union, China, and Japan. All these actors, he argues, are now being driven in undesirable directions by poorly conceived U.S. policies.

Kissinger lays down a host of policy prescriptions for the future, all reflecting his core philosophy of geopolitical management. He urges strong efforts to reconcile with France to preserve a healthy NATO and EU in lockstep with each other. Worried about the power vacuum[7] separating Russia and Germany, he calls for an effort to expand the Western community into Eastern Europe. He recommends respect for Russia's legitimate interests but also urges firmness against any Russian neo-imperial conduct aimed at restoring its old empire on CIS soil. In Asia, he is preoccupied with fear that unhealthy dynamics will lead China and Japan to begin throwing their weight around, thereby triggering instability across the entire region. He recommends a U.S. policy aimed at befriending China and continuing friendship with Japan, a policy with the goal of an equilibrium that will be reflected throughout Asia. In both Europe and Asia,

---

[7]A *power vaccum* is a situation in which security guarantees are absent and imbalances in physical resources—especially military resources—invite aggressive conduct.

Kissinger calls for a continuing U.S. presence and leadership role. But this role, he argues, must be imbued with a healthy dose of *realpolitik*, for blind idealism—especially if used as a smokescreen to cover disengagement—is a recipe for disaster.

Whereas Brzezinski and Kissinger foresee a complex of cross-cutting international cleavages, Samuel Huntington asserts that future world politics will be polarized by a clash of civilizations that will form the precedent for all other types of global politics. In advancing this view, Huntington repudiates the optimism expressed in his 1991 book, *The Third Wave*, which analyzed the march of liberal Western democracy into new areas. In his 1993 *Foreign Affairs* article, Huntington offers a sober pessimism that scarcely mentions liberal democracy as a key factor in pacifying global politics. What matters, he now asserts, is not political institutions but rather the cultural values and beliefs embraced by political organizations. His pessimism derives from an expectation that because such values and beliefs differ so greatly, they will provide the seedbed for widespread conflict, not peaceful consensus.

Indeed, Huntington predicts a future of stressful global politics. The fault lines will occur at geographical and "functional" points where the world's eight dominant civilizations meet. These civilizations are Western, Slavic-Orthodox, Islamic, Confucian, Japanese, Hindu, Latin American, and African. Huntington asserts that, if present trends gain force, these civilizations will find themselves far from being on similar wavelengths. Instead, they will confront each other from across unbridgeable chasms, the importance of which is magnified by the smallness of a world linked by modern communications. Precisely because dissimilar cultures have been brought into closer contact in a situation of growing interdependence but troubled futures, they are destined to clash more seriously than previously, when distance had a moderating effect.

He acknowledges that nation-states will remain the primary locus of governmental policy. Nonetheless, he asserts, affective bonds and growing economic regionalism will result in nations joining to form cultural power blocs that will act with unity of purpose on the global stage. For a variety of compelling reasons, including economic strife and religious rivalry, such power blocs are destined to confront each other in many places across the globe. The result will be a new form of world politics that replaces the old dominant nation-state rivalries. This new cultural politics among competing civilizations, Huntington acknowledges, easily could acquire strong military dimensions brought about by the ability of the various power blocs to gain access to modern weapons.

Most worrisome is his foreboding that global politics may take the form of "the West versus the rest," in which an outnumbered West will find itself besieged on all fronts by competing civilizations determined to modernize along cultural lines of their own, at the West's expense if necessary. Huntington points out that modernization is not the equivalent of Westernization. Indeed, he says, non-Western cultures face incentives to define themselves in terms of opposition to Western values as a device to mobilize their traditional constituencies on behalf of their own style of modernization.

Even short of this cultural polarization, he says, the U.S.–led West will find itself confronting a Russia-led Slavic-Orthodox civilization along a north-south axis in Europe stretching from the Baltic states into Romania. Concurrently, the West will face great stress in trying to deal with an angry Islamic civilization concentrated in the Middle East, North Africa, and the Persian Gulf. In Asia, the West will have to come to terms with growing assertiveness by the Japanese culture and the China-led Confucian culture. Meanwhile, the Slavic-Orthodox culture will confront Islam in Central Asia, and the Islamic-Hindu rivalry will continue apace in South Asia. The chief risk of collusion against the West, Huntington predicts, is an alliance between Confucian and Islamic cultures. He sees growing Chinese sales of military weapons to Arab countries as a forerunner of this new axis.

Besieged by many critics in the months after his *Foreign Affairs* article was published, Huntington is careful to point out that his thesis of clashing civilizations does not predict all the twists and turns of future international politics. What his thesis offers, he says, is a convincing intellectual paradigm: one capable of explaining the core structural features of the emerging global system. He presents a bottom-line argument for adoption of his thesis. There is no competing paradigm capable of outclassing it in explanatory power, and even if American scholars are repulsed by it, many foreigners, who understand their own conditions better than do Americans, see considerable value in it.

Although the Max Singer and Aaron Wildavksy book evidently was written as a counter to the worrisome portrayals offered by the pessimist school, it is mentioned here because it contains a strong dose of pessimism of its own. It argues that the world is becoming divided into two zones: a "zone of peace" in North America, Western Europe, Japan, Australia, and New Zealand, and an outside zone, a "zone of turmoil," encompassing the rest of the world. In the former zone, the authors assert, national security concerns as traditionally understood will diminish because those countries face no conceivable military threat to their existence or independence. Although ethnic subdivisions may push for greater autonomy, violence is unlikely to result. In the latter zone, war and conflict—marked by nationalism and ethnic strife—will continue as in the past. Many of the countries there, however, can be expected to make steady progress toward democracy and market economies. The result will be that the zone of conflict shrinks and the zone of peace expands.

Singer and Wildavsky argue that because the zone of turmoil lies outside the West's vital interest and does not threaten its national security, the West should try to avoid entanglement in it. The key exception is when upheaval triggers the further spread of nuclear weapons. When the United States does become involved, they assert, it should not seek "stability" for its own sake when doing so would involve a squelching of healthy and inevitable change. To deal with the zone of turmoil, they recommend the increased use of democratic multilateralism, including the UN. They assert that "the question of how we decide to intervene—which countries and institutions we rely on—will be more important than guidelines about when to intervene."

Prophets of Nationalism and Ethnic Strife

In his book, William Pfaff perceives the same lack of agreement on internationalist values cited by Brzezinski, but, unlike Huntington, he does not believe that the void will be filled by identification with cultural civilizations that transcend the nation-state. Rather, he believes the void will be filled by nationalism. He defines *nationalism* as an affective tie to one's community, based on deep emotions. It is marked not by identification with borders or governmental institutions but by blood loyalty, common history, defining myths, and shared destiny with a social group. To Pfaff, nationalism was the dominant force of the twentieth century, and it will dominate the twenty-first century as well. In some ways, he says, nationalism can be a positive force; indeed, it can form the bonds that keep a society together. But when it is defined in exclusionary terms and becomes the vehicle for determining aggressive policies of nation-states, it can also mutate in negative ways, thereby bringing great turmoil to the world scene. For this reason, Pfaff has a foreboding fear of the future, especially in Europe.

Pfaff argues that nationalism grew out of a nineteenth-century European reaction against the rationalism, universalism, and internationalism of the French Enlightenment. To him, nationalism is rooted in Romanticism: a philosophy that stresses the primacy of emotion over reason, of history over the modern future, of action over thought, and of the individual and group over transcendent movements. It is a vehicle by which individuals and groups assert their identity and self-control over political authorities and ideologies that would suppress them.

Acknowledging that nationalism has acquired a bad name in Western circles, owing to its association with imperial Germany and World War I, he points out that it once was regarded as a progressive force. It played an important role in bringing about the downfall of Europe's tradition-laden dynastic monarchies as well as the Hapsburg and Ottoman Empires. He asserts that it was instrumental in defeating Napoleon, Nazism, and Soviet communism. In its absence, he argues, Europe would have been swept over by some form of totalitarianism embracing universalist ideals as justification for coercive control. Winston Churchill, after all, was a nationalist at heart. Moreover, Pfaff observes that although nationalism can be militarily aggressive, its scope is normally limited to immediately adjoining territories. Continent-wide military imperialism, of the sort pursued by Hitler and Stalin, is the stuff of universalist ideologies, not nationalism.

Pfaff argues that U.S. observers are themselves so wedded to the Enlightenment that they fail to perceive how deeply nationalist values are held in many quarters today, even among the intelligentsia.

As a result, U.S. analysts have wrongly perceived the overthrow of Soviet communism in Europe as an endorsement of liberal internationalism, Western-style democracy, and market economies. In fact, he says, the upheavals of 1989–1991 were nationalist revolutions whose purpose was to cast off the yoke of Soviet control, not to embrace Western values. The social groups that fostered these revolutions were attempting to restore control over their own destinies: to be left free to choose their own form of government—perhaps democracy, but perhaps authoritarianism.

Pfaff asserts that nationalism has worldwide import, albeit in less strident terms than in Eastern Europe. It is relevant globally because nationalism was the vehicle by which Western imperialism was cast off in many regions. Moreover, many countries perceive the United States as an inherently nationalist power, one capable of asserting imperial domination of its own. As a result, nationalism is becoming a vehicle by which some countries define themselves in opposition to U.S. influence and intimidating control by the Western Alliance.

This is the case in Asia today, where Pfaff perceives that nationalism is growing. To him, Japan is the chief purveyor of nationalist values, which may yet be translated into an unhealthy force that could lead Japan to resume the quest for imperial domain. Fear of Japan, in turn, propels other Asian countries toward nationalism as a protective measure for warding off resurgent Japanese imperialism. Pfaff also worries about China, which might succumb to nationalist impulses in ways leading it to transcend its inward-looking stance and to begin to assert itself outwardly. In the Middle East, Pfaff sees nationalism as a reaction against the West's secular materialism, but he concludes that its effect will be diluted by the competing force of Islam, which is a universalist value system. To him, Islam is antimodern but essentially defensive, aimed at protecting against Western intrusion rather than attacking the West. Because the Middle East/Persian Gulf are composed of weak secular states that largely struggle against each other, Pfaff forecasts a divided region, incapable of unifying to the degree needed to assert primacy over surrounding territory.

Pfaff's principal worry is that nationalism will reappear in virulent form in Eastern Europe. In that region, he asserts, an unaggressive form of nationalism could have a healthy effect by stressing patriotism and communal loyalties. The trouble, he judges, is that amid great upheaval, nationalism can mutate in negative ways and become a vehicle for overcoming frustration and fear. It can become nativist, populist, exclusionary, and xenophobic: a primordial emotion of ethnic hate, not love. It can create a breeding ground for ethno-social mobilization under a dictator who offers war as a romantic expression of virility and a way to recapture a lost historical utopia.

Pfaff worries that this negative form of nationalism is already becoming well established in the Balkans and East Central Europe, unsettled regions where national identities cut across borders that have primarily been established through an accident of history. The upheaval of 1989–1991 swept away the Yalta agreement, which left the former Soviet Union in charge of these regions. Equally important, this upheaval also swept away the Versailles accord, which tried to establish order out of the chaos left behind by the collapse of the Hapsburg and Ottoman Empires. Because countries in these regions face imposing problems in trying to reestablish economic and political order, their societies are coming under great strain. The result is a trend toward angry nationalism that already has engulfed the former Yugoslavia and now threatens to spread elsewhere into the Balkans and Caucasus, and even into East Central Europe. If such a spread occurs, Pfaff reasons, it will not end there, for it could trigger a nationalist revival in Russia and even Germany. The outcome would be to propel Europe into an era of chronic turmoil and violence.

Fear of this downward spiral is the primary reason why Pfaff judges the West's failure to intervene in Bosnia as a strategic catastrophe. Arguably, Bosnia itself is not a vital Western interest, but the conflict there, he asserts, is becoming a model for the future. Nationalist-inspired ethnic aggression has been successfully launched, and the West's security institutions—NATO, the EU, the Conference on Security and Cooperation in Europe (CSCE), and the UN—have proven themselves too weak and indecisive to act. A bad precedent has been set, and Pfaff worries that before too long, it will come back to haunt the West.

Pfaff's chief prescription for Western security policy is that nationalism's growing primacy be recognized. The United States should abandon the illusion that liberal internationalism is the wave of the future or that most nations are now willing to copy its institutions or carry out its designs. Equally important, the United States should replace its naive faith in progress with a skeptical pessimism that recognizes the potential for reversal, disaster, and tragedy. Global chaos is not a predestined consequence of nationalism's upsurge, but it can be if care is not taken. The key is to recognize that the quest for global order must begin by acknowledging nationalism's powerful appeal and what is implied for the imperfectability of mankind.

Like Pfaff, John Lukacs offers a foreboding sense of nationalism's effect on future international order, but he conducts his analysis in a broader, geostrategic framework that focuses on interactions among the major powers. He primarily addresses Europe but discusses Asia; he ignores the Middle East entirely. To him, the modern age is ending because the legacy of World Wars I and II is finally being washed away. The end of the Cold War, however, does not translate into the triumph of liberal democracy. Rather, it means that a more traditional political geography is re-emerging. Equally important, the dominant political ideology will be nationalism, not internationalism. Indeed, Lukacs asserts, nationalism has been the story continuously since the nineteenth century. It dominated the twentieth century, and it will dominate the twenty-first century.

Lukacs does not regard the Cold War as having been a struggle between communism and democracy. Rather, he sees it as a contest brought about by the march of Russian national power into Central Europe, made possible by Germany's defeat in World War II. What has happened since 1989 is that Russian power has undergone a collapse, and that nation is now in strategic retreat. A political vacuum has been created in East Central Europe, and this vacuum is destined to be filled by Germany, which is now recovering its historic strength and dominant role in European security affairs. He asserts that the future will be determined largely by whether Germany and Russia can establish a new and satisfactory equilibrium.

Lukacs does not forecast Germany's return to military imperialism, but he sees that nation as steadily expanding its influence into East Central Europe and gradually distancing itself from the United States. As for Russia, Lukacs views that country in the context of its 1000-year history: a Slavic nation of authoritarian politics and imperial ambitions. The current strategic retreat goes beyond anything experienced before, yet Lukacs expects recovery in some form, albeit not as a liberal democracy or as a benign power. Fearing that dictatorship is more likely than democracy, he argues that Russia would be best off by restoring a constitutional monarchy. He quotes Bismarck's famous line that Russia is never as strong or as weak as it appears to be. In the end, he asserts, Russia will re-emerge in its traditional role and eventually will come up against Germany's eastward expansion. Conceivably, these two nations might maintain tranquil ties, but, equally likely, a tense relationship will be the outcome. After all, they have had trouble with each other at least since the eighteenth century, when Frederick the Great built Prussia and Peter the Great transformed Russia into an imperial power focused on Europe.

Lukacs asserts that Germany and Russia will encounter each other in East Central Europe and the Balkans, with the status of Poland and Ukraine being the most important determinants of the outcome. For many of the countries across this entire region, Lukacs sees troubles of their own making ahead. There, Lukacs dismisses the idea that parliamentary democracy will take permanent hold. He forecasts single-party leadership, strong central governments, and only partial conversion to capitalism. Above all, he forecasts the steady rise of nationalism as the dominant ideology. This nationalism, moreover, will not be defined in terms of benign and defensive patriotism but as exclusionary and extroverted, and will be aimed at power and domination. Contributing to this trend, he believes, will be a flaw in the West's own theory of democracy. When applied to East Central Europe and the Balkans, the premises of self-determination and majority rule will be translated into oppression of minorities.

In Asia, Lukacs forecasts a similar return to traditional geopolitics now that the abnormal Cold War is over. Again, nationalism will be dominant, and the key relationship will be between Japan and China. As with Germany and Russia, Lukacs acknowledges that various outcomes are possible, including enmity. But he raises the possibility that Japan and China might unite against the United States and Russia in a quest to establish control over Asia for themselves. Thus, Lukacs sees major-power politics returning on a global scale and in a traditional setting. Viewing the future, he regards it as feasible that Germany and Japan will remain in loose alliances with the United

States, owing to their rivalries with Russia and China. But he also senses the possibility that Germany will pull away from the United States if it draws closer to Russia, and Japan will do likewise if it draws closer to China. If so, the United States may see merit in building a close relationship with Russia, anchored in *realpolitik,* to counterbalance its former close allies. In any event, Lukacs offers the prognosis that the United States is destined to suffer a decline in its superpower role.

Lukacs worries that, if global anarchy and turmoil are the outcome, this development will owe to two dangerous trends. First is the institutionalized pressure for material and economic prosperity at a time when growth will be slow and uneven. The second trend is the populist inclination of nationalism. The former involves greed, the latter is a quest for tribal power. Lukacs recognizes that these two impulses are not incompatible and, indeed, can be mutually reinforcing. But he regards nationalism as the stronger of the two impulses, in both Europe and Asia. He especially dismisses the idea that economics has replaced power politics as the dominant force on the world scene. To embrace this idea, he says, "is stupid beyond belief."

In his book, Senator Daniel Moynihan predicts that ethnicity is on the verge of exploding into a major force in international relations, a force capable of causing great disorder in Eastern Europe and elsewhere. The effect is not to cause a reassertion of major-power rivalries but to fracture many existing nation-states, thereby spawning a host of civil wars and tribal conflicts. Smaller and smaller entities will claim "self-determination"—the right to their own states. These new states, in turn, will include minority groups within them that will, in turn, assert their own rights. Macro-conflict thus threatens to give way to a growing number of micro-conflicts, bringing about chaos of their own.

Moynihan argues that the United States has a poor track record in understanding ethnicity and developing policy toward it. The problem goes back to Woodrow Wilson, whose endorsement of universal self-determination was undertaken in ignorance of just how many and varied were the nationalities that could claim self-determination. Then–Secretary of State Robert Lansing regarded *self-determination* as one of Wilson's phrases that "will cause trouble in the future because their meaning and application have not been thought out." Lansing thus recognized that the destruction of the Hapsburg, Ottoman, and Romanov Empires was a mixed blessing because spreading disorder might come in its wake.   In recent years, Moynihan says, American failures to grasp ethnicity's influence accounts for the United States' inability to foresee the downfall of the Warsaw Pact, the Soviet Union, and Yugoslavia.   In the latter two cases, U.S. leaders found themselves calling for the preservation of existing states even after dismantlement had been decided upon by runaway ethnic forces.

Now that the ethnic genie has been let out of the bottle, Moynihan reasons, it cannot be forced back in, nor should it be, in many cases. Offering no simple remedies or single-minded policies, he asserts that "the challenge is to make the world safe for and from ethnicity." This means that the United States should seek to abate ethnicity's often-deleterious effects, for ethnic conflicts can affect the United States' own interests and the West's stability.   Moynihan recommends upgrading U.S. analytical efforts to understand ethnicity, including cases where its negative forces were contained in ways that controlled potential violence (e.g., South Tyrol between Austria and Italy, and Catalonia in Spain).   Although priorities will have to be set, he judges that Western military intervention in ethnic conflicts will become more frequent and, preferably, should be conducted under the UN flag.   The key to success, he implies, will be to use military force in ways that help produce political settlements among social groups whose hatreds run deep.   Bosnia and Somalia thus are not isolated cases but might presage the future, a future the United States had best be prepared for.

Prophets of Economic Troubles

This category of the pessimistic literature forecasts three different troubles: continuing poverty in undeveloped regions, failed market-democracy reforms in the former Soviet Union, and a weakening of the Western Alliance.   What unites the following books is a focus on uneven change in the world economy that allegedly will bring growing prosperity to some countries, little or no improvement to others, and backsliding for still others.   The common forecast is that disruptive effects will condemn some countries to wallow in frustrating discontent and will bring about new forms of competition that will strain relations among previously close Western allies. The implication is that economic dislocation will have negative strategic effects, thereby magnifying prospects for a dangerous world.

Paul Kennedy's book addresses the international turbulence that lies ahead owing to economic strife in underdeveloped regions. In his celebrated book of the mid-1980s, *The Rise and Fall of the Great Powers*, Kennedy forecasted imperial decline for the superpowers, the Soviet Union and the United States. In this new book, he emerges as a modern-day Malthus, a descendant of the famous British economist who in 1798 predicted that overpopulation would strangle global economic prosperity. Although Malthus was proven wrong when population growth slowed and industrialization came to the rescue in Europe, his dismal forecast is likely—says Kennedy—to be proven correct in the twenty-first century, as a burgeoning population interacts with a world economy that fails to operate for the benefit of all.

In making this statement about the world economy, Kennedy differs from David Ricardo and other classical economists who argue that entangling trade and financial relations can be an uplifting experience for all nations. His book nonetheless reflects mainstream thinking of many empiricist scholars (e.g., Lester Thurow) who analyze how the imperfect world economy actually does work, not how it should work in theory. Whereas most of these economists fret about the United States' prosperity, Kennedy's focal point for declinist forecasts is the fate of the Third World in an emerging world economy that allegedly will favor the strong but punish the weak. The core problem, he reasons, is that the world is filled with "weaklings": nations and societies that cannot control their own destinies.

Although Kennedy's book is mostly about economics, it usefully adds a new dimension to the pessimistic literature on future international politics. Whereas most writers focus on traditional power politics and ethnic nationalism, Kennedy tries to grapple with the issue of how economic turmoil will influence interstate political relations. He sees great trouble ahead. Whether Kennedy's analysis is fully on target may be arguable: even most pessimists engage in less one-dimensional hand-wringing than he. But if he is even partially correct, the international system will be subjected to far greater strain than that deriving from traditional interstate geopolitics alone.

At a minimum, if Kennedy is correct, economics will not act to heal wounds and reduce frictions growing out of the political arena. Indeed, economics might worsen things: If prosperity lessens political discord, poverty increases it—especially when only a few are rich, the rest are poor, and the system prevents the disenfranchised from improving their lot. In any event, the issue of how economics and politics will affect each other is one that merits close appraisal, for if politics comes from the barrel of a gun, economics provides the ammunition.

The heart of Kennedy's argument is that several negative trends are working together to cause grave economic problems in the coming decades. Of greatest importance is that a huge population explosion is taking place, largely in poor countries, which will enlarge the human race from about 5 billion today to almost 8 billion by 2025. Especially affected are the Middle East, Africa, South Asia, Latin America, and China. In many places, Kennedy argues, this demographic change will far outpace the expected slow rate of economic expansion, thereby making already-poor countries even poorer, or at least no better off. Many Third World states, he says, face a future of huge urban ghettos, overpopulated countrysides, weak manufacturing, and unproductive agriculture. Added on top are problems from environmental destruction, partly caused by Third World countries themselves, and from diseases, including AIDS. These bleak prospects, Kennedy asserts, will confront the rising expectations that are sweeping the globe, thereby producing great discontent.

Although the world economy is expanding under free trade and producing greater overall wealth than ever before, Kennedy argues, the principal beneficiaries will be already-prosperous countries and multinational corporations. These actors, he says, have the agility to compete and prosper in the high-tech global economy of the twenty-first century, but less-endowed participants are doomed to fall behind. Despite troubles of their own, the United States, Japan, and Western Europe are well situated to prosper or at least to not decline. As the East Asian "tigers" are showing, some Third World countries are displaying a strong capacity to adapt to the economic and technological realities of the emerging era. Many other countries, however, lack the cultural values, skilled labor force, managerial talent, middle-class society, economic infrastructure, and governmental institutions to prosper in a world economy that will be brutally competitive. Absent major improvements in these areas, Kennedy dismisses "policy gimmickry"—modern agriculture, industrialization, or export policies—as ready solutions for these countries.

The effect is that the world economy is producing not a rising tide in which everyone benefits but a new distribution of winners and losers, and some of the losers will be even worse off than before. Dismissing the idea that the gap between rich and poor will narrow appreciably, Kennedy forecasts a future world economy that will be at least as hierarchical as today's, and perhaps even more so. In his analysis, currently wealthy nations will retain their privileged positions, a small number of medium-sized countries will enter this privileged "club," a few will achieve moderate wealth, and many will remain mired in deep poverty. Moreover, the competitive dynamics of the world economy will establish prohibitive barriers to any country unable or unwilling to fully embrace the demanding requirements of the modern era.

He forecasts that greater economic hierarchy, in turn, will weaken the capacity of the international system to achieve political integration, much less global community-building. For regions that fall behind the economic power curve, the prospect is one of weakened national governments presiding over discontented societies and of frustrated countries that despise their neighbors—elements forming a breeding ground for immoderate ideologies and foreign policies, alliances among predators, and great resentment of the haves by the have-nots.

Kennedy expresses hope that wealthy countries will be sufficiently farsighted to join together to help the poor, but he expresses doubt that their aid will be massive enough or even can be adequate owing to the enormous problems facing impoverished nations with noncompetitive economies. As likely as not, he implies, wealthy nations will be fearful of draining entanglements with the unsalvageable, and, therefore, they will withdraw behind their own trading blocs: the EU, North American Free Trade Agreement (NAFTA), and the emerging East Asian bloc. Owing to G-7 (the group of seven nations that coordinates global economic policy) mechanisms, these blocs may wind up connected to each other in prosperous trade patterns, but the rest of the world—the preponderance of humanity—will be left on the outside looking in.

The negative effects, Kennedy says, will differ from region to region. Asia will be best off. But, interestingly, Kennedy is far less optimistic about China's prospects than are many observers. He judges that the Southeast Asian nations will not experience the economic transformation undergone by Korea, Hong Kong, Singapore, and Taiwan. He concludes that India and South Asia will remain economically inadequate owing to uncontrolled population growth, and that the Middle East will remain unable to achieve economic modernity owing to traditional Islamic values. He relegates Sub-Saharan Africa to chronic poverty because of weak governments, population growth, and a host of other troubles. Latin America, he believes, has somewhat better prospects but suffers from the legacy of the slow-growth 1980s brought about by overreliance on industrial autonomy rather than export growth. His principal question mark is the former Soviet Union and Eastern Europe, which are struggling to build viable economies and governments from the rubble of collapsed communism. He is hopeful for parts of Eastern Europe, but although Russia and its Commonwealth partners have major assets—natural resources and an educated population—he doubts their capacity to pull themselves up by their bootstraps anytime soon.

This economic-demographic downward spiral causes Kennedy to fear a quite troubled era in international security affairs. He does not argue that old problems will give way to new ones; rather, he judges that traditional power politics will survive in altered form and will be supplemented by new security stresses created by mounting economic turbulence. Such stresses, he asserts, will spill over into the military realm. The prospect is that demographically driven social unrest will produce political instability and regional wars. Economic nationalism with military overtones and ethnic aggression are obvious possibilities. Mass migration will create serious troubles, as will interstate friction brought about by trade policies that are seen as mercantilist and exploitative. In some cases, youthful populations with unfulfilled expectations will explode into violence and revolution. In other cases, political leaders will seek to channel domestic discontent into foreign adventures and conquests, especially when economic gains can be accrued at the expense of rival ethnic groups, religions, and races.

Kennedy offers no specific predictions about regional conflicts, but he notes that many nations facing bleak economic prospects will also be military powers. China and India, both nuclear powers with growing conventional arsenals, fall into this category. The poverty-stricken Middle East, he notes, is already a heavily armed camp and might be the next site of nuclear proliferation. Equally worrisome, nuclear-armed Russia, its Commonwealth neighbors, and East European nations all deploy large military forces, forces that will be ample to attack each other or to turn against states that do prosper in tomorrow's world economy. Implied is that regional wars are likely to sprout up in many places and with growing regularity. Whether these wars will threaten vital U.S. and Western interests is an issue not addressed by Kennedy, but he makes clear that the cause of world peace will definitely suffer serious blows. Global tranquility and order are among the least likely outcomes predicted in his book.

Alexander Motyl's book focuses on Ukraine, but its importance lies in its efforts to generalize about the prospects for market democracy in Russia and other republics of the former Soviet Union. Motyl endeavors to apply social science theory and models of political-economic development to the study of post-totalitarianism in formerly communist systems. Regardless of whether its judgments prove accurate, Motyl's book, hopefully, will be the forerunner of additional scholarly appraisals. Because the future of international politics will depend heavily on how the drama in the former Soviet Union plays out, the need for systematic understanding of this drama is all the more apparent.

Motyl offers a pessimistic portrayal of Russia's future as well as Ukraine's. He argues that totalitarianism and imperialism have bequeathed a legacy that bars the way to any early adoption of *market democracy* as this term is defined in the West. He further asserts that, if radical reform continues to be pursued in quest of a "Big Bang" transformation, the result almost inevitably will be temporary economic collapse and massive social disorder. Such a result, he says, will pave the way for a repeat of the Weimar Republic's disastrous descent into dictatorial fascism. He argues in favor of an evolutionary approach to reform, one that carefully transitions to a market economy and democratic government over many years. In the interim, he urges that the West not expect miracles from Russia, from either its domestic order or its foreign policy.

In putting forth these arguments, Motyl is within the mainstream of political science and sociology theory that has emerged over the past 30 years. Most Western economists trumpet the virtues of market mechanisms, but their abstract and self-contained microeconomic models often focus narrowly on supply-and-demand interactions between households and firms. Contemporary macroeconomic models are broader but still suffer from a similar limiting focus on purely economic inputs and outputs. Both types of models typically ignore the political and social foundations upon which economic order is based. Recognizing these drawbacks, Motyl draws on other disciplines and intellectual traditions to examine those foundations as they exist today in Russia, Ukraine, and other post-communist systems.

His analysis reflects two dominant conclusions that are offered by political science and sociology. The first conclusion is that the taking hold of market democracy on its own (i.e., it has not been implanted from above by an occupying power) owes to unique conditions and favorable circumstances. Especially important factors are a cohesive society, a politically dominant and entrepreneurial middle class, and functioning industrial and agricultural sectors. Moreover, even in successful cases, market democracy typically has evolved slowly in stages, as in the United States and Britain. This argument is advanced in many studies, but it is especially well-expressed in Barrington Moore's landmark book, *Social Origins of Dictatorship and Democracy: Lord and Peasant in the Making of the Modern World* (Boston: Beacon Press, 1993). The second conclusion is that totalitarianism, especially when implanted for many years upon a long-existing authoritarian order, leaves a deep imprint on any nation's society and economy. The effect is to sharply impede the pace at which revolutionary change toward market democracy can be safely conducted.

Both conclusions, Motyl asserts, apply to the former Soviet Union today, and they say a great deal about what cannot be accomplished quickly: Simply stated, Russia, Ukraine, and most other new countries in the former Soviet Union lack the social foundations for market democracy and are powerfully constrained not only by several centuries of czarist autocracy but also by 70 years of disastrous imperial totalitarian rule. The effect, he concludes, is to leave the future uncertain at best. He is not confident that a market democracy will emerge even in the best of circumstances; a new order cannot be built overnight, regardless of how eagerly this outcome is desired by the West.

Motyl lays down a normative post-totalitarian model of his own that is based on a sequential, not simultaneous, approach to building market democracy in the former Soviet Union. First, he asserts, a functioning state, rule of law, and civil society must be established. Then, a market economy can be created. In the final stage, and only then, can full-fledged democracy be adopted. This model leads him to favor interim governments that (1) embody strong central controls capable of preserving social stability; (2) can gradually enlarge market mechanisms while maintaining government ownership of key industries; and (3) slowly introduce democracy in a manner that does not compromise effective policy. The alternative of pell-mell radical reform, he asserts, inevitably will produce incapable government, runaway inflation, industrial collapse, and great social upheaval: elements forming a breeding ground for reactionary counterrevolution. Yet it is radical reform that Russia has been attempting and that has been unwisely urged upon Russia by the West. The result, judges Motyl, has been a steady march by Russia, Ukraine, and others to impending disaster.

Motyl fears for the worst in Russia. Even if the worst does not transpire, he urges the West not to expect a stable liberal democracy and market economy for many years. He urges the West to cooperate with Russia by allowing it to reform slowly, and he judges that the West's present ill-advised insistence on radical reform is based on a fascination with Russia that is destined for disappointment. He cautions that the West *should* expect Russia to maintain a strong army and to pursue restoration of its imperial domain, at least on the territory of the Commonwealth. He thus argues against a "Russia-first" policy that expects too much by way of partnership with that country. He argues in favor of a geopolitical Western foreign policy, in which the West would place primary emphasis on building market democracy in the more fertile terrain of East Central Europe (e.g., Poland and Hungary). The West would also build a closer relationship with Ukraine as part of an effort to prevent Russia from extending its imperial domain westward, where it could again threaten Europe. Behind this wall of restored containment, Motyl says, the West could patiently wait while Russia slowly and uncertainly inches its way toward a modern market democracy capable of a benign foreign policy and membership in the Western community.

Jeffrey Garten's book offers a survey of the Western Alliance's future in response to the economic and strategic changes that are allegedly eroding the common bonds that held this alliance together during the Cold War. Similar to members of the pessimistic school, Garten begins his book with the premise that the coming international era will be one of great strain and anarchical disorder in regions outside the traditional Western Alliance. A future of ethnic conflict, nationalism, economic upheaval, and regional conflicts lies ahead.

The principal hope for managing these tensions, Garten asserts, lies in cooperation among the "Big Three": the United States, Germany, and Japan. But will this cooperative leadership be forthcoming? Probably not as matters now stand, Garten judges. Surveying the trends, Garten concludes that the Cold War Alliance is destined to weaken: The future offers an era of "cold peace" among the three, brought about by growing economic competitiveness and declining security bonds among the principal partners. This does not mean that these three nations will fall back into the rivalry that led up to World War II. What does lie ahead is an era reminiscent of the 1920s: These three nations will lack the will and ability to join together on behalf of joint security-economic management. The world therefore faces an emerging leadership vacuum that will add further impetus to global disorder.

The Cold War Western Alliance, according to Garten, was a historical and strategic anomaly, one destined to fade away now that the Soviet menace is gone. The bond that held these three nations together, Garten says, was only partly the threat of communist military aggression. In addition, because Germany and Japan were both supplicants—defeated belligerents in World War II, outcasts guilty of enormous war crimes—the United States assumed the role not only of security provider but also of paternal sponsor of their economic rehabilitation and adoption of democracy. All three nations were willing to accept this superior-subordinate relationship, but the conditions permitting its continued existence have vanished. The United States is no longer willing to bear the unequal burdens of superpower sponsor and mentor. For their part, Germany and Japan are recovering self-identity and are no longer willing to act under Washington's tutelage. If Alliance partnership is to be maintained, it must be done on the basis of equality animated by common vision, not a parent-child relationship.

With no external military threat to unite them, these three nations are now being pulled apart by powerful forces whose influence seems destined to increase in the years ahead. One important but often-unrecognized factor, says Garten, is that their domestic ideologies are different in key respects. The U.S. system is anchored in individualism, which produces a uniquely American approach to federalism and capitalism. By contrast, the German and Japanese models are more communitarian and corporatist, thus yielding a greater fusion of government, economy, and society. As a consequence, U.S. policy often is the sum total of many uncoordinated actions, but Germany and Japan are better able to behave as unitary actors. The effect is not only to create an important gap between the United States and its erstwhile partners but also to leave the United States globally isolated: The German and Japanese models are more relevant to most other countries, especially to those emerging from totalitarian rule.

Another disruptive factor is that, at present, all three nations are inward-focused and thus are unable to pursue assertive diplomacies. Weakened by heavy Cold War expenses and its own questionable internal policies, the United States confronts major domestic problems in its economy and society. Its own economic dynamism fading, Germany faces the task of financing the expensive integration and rebuilding of its eastern region. For its part, Japan is exiting an era in which its priorities were focused on savings and investment. Laboring today on a shaky financial base, it must now undergo the difficult transition to a consumer society. All three countries face a prolonged period of domestic recovery during which their governments will be weak because of a lack of strong consensual support. Eventually, restored dynamism might permit assertive foreign policies, but for the coming years, all three countries will not be able to act with strength and vigor abroad.

Further narrowing the scope for collaborative action are differing interests in security and economic affairs. During the Cold War, the United States bore the principal military burdens of the Western Alliance. Although security requirements will be lower in the years ahead, they will be more weighty than is commonly realized. Because the United States is downsizing its defense establishment, its expected tendency will be to turn to Germany and Japan for help. This help, says Garten, is unlikely to be forthcoming. Both countries continue to be pacifist states with military strategies focused on defense of their borders, and they show little willingness to pursue demanding security missions abroad.

To the extent Germany and Japan are willing to act, says Garten, it will not be under Washington's tutelage. Nor will these two nations be willing to open their coffers to support U.S. military interventions in pursuit of national priorities deemed suspect by Berlin and Tokyo. For its part, the United States wants greater military burden-sharing, but it also wants to retain control. Moreover, especially for conflicts in which Allied interests are more at stake than U.S. interests, it will not be willing to expose its troops to combat in absence of Alliance partners, regardless of whether Germany and Japan are willing to pay the bill. The prospect thus is not for close security collaboration but rather for weak joint responses and constant squabbling, as has been witnessed in Bosnia.

In the increasingly important economic realm, the dominant reality is that these three nations are now competitors, not partners. They share a common interest in a rising tide of economic prosperity for all, but they place their own interests first. Their unique perspectives result in different policies for global economic management. Whereas U.S. recovery depends on a collaborative world economy, influenced by German and Japanese policies that promote imports of American goods and stimulation of their own economies, both Germany and Japan rely on export strategies to achieve domestic growth, and fear of inflation leads them to oppose stimulating policies aimed at appeasing the United States. The difference in perspectives is greatest in U.S.–Japanese relations, but it also is noteworthy in U.S.–German relations, which are further compounded by Germany's need to remain in lockstep with the European Union and France's insistence on agricultural protectionism. The scope for coordinated policies thus is narrow today. Unless all three countries can restore economic growth, it will not widen anytime soon. The prospect is for continued drift, if not outright friction, in the G-7 and the General Agreement on Tariffs and Trade (GATT).

Where are these negative trends headed? Garten acknowledges the possibility of a return to outright rivalry. He says that history could reappear, and that both Germany and Japan, motivated by increased nationalism, might begin acting in assertive ways not only in economics but in security affairs as well. This development could produce American animosity toward both and a three-sided battle for global supremacy. Alternatively, a new alliance could form in any of three different ways: either Germany and Japan against the United States, or the United States and Japan against Germany, or the United States and Germany against Japan. But barring major shortsightedness by all three countries, Garten does not foresee a downward spiral as Draconian as this.

What strikes Garten as most likely is a drift into three inward-looking trading blocs that are neither strategic partners nor rivals but are suspended in a never-never land somewhere in between. He forecasts that the United States will lead a NAFTA of the Western Hemisphere, Germany will lead the European Union, and Japan will lead an Asian economic bloc uniting the prosperous trading nations there. A common interest in prosperity and growing interdependence may enable these three blocs to maintain a modicum of cooperation in economic affairs and in protecting their own security. Highly unlikely is strong tripolar leadership and coordination in achieving common goals outside these three blocs. Garten does not spell out where this situation leaves the rest of the globe, especially turbulent Eurasia and the Middle East, where great turmoil lies ahead. But the worrisome implications are obvious.

If a solution is to be found, Garten judges, it must begin in an effort by the United States to restore not only domestic economic growth and social cohesion but also the global appeal of the American dream. Beyond this, Germany and Japan must realize their responsibility to play a constructive leadership role in global security and economics. The three nations must then fashion a new tripolar partnership aimed at designing coordinated policies for global management and reflecting U.S. leadership, yet establishing important roles for Germany and Japan. Such a partnership, Garten concludes, can be built if these nations surmount their current preoccupations by adopting a common strategic approach to international affairs. But achieving this goal will be difficult, and it may be time-consuming. Can post–Cold War global affairs afford the wait?

Although the answer to this troublesome question is not apparent, what can be said is that Garten's book is important because it is not alone. Indeed, an entire academic cottage industry has sprung up in recent years, composed mostly of political economists who forecast stressful troubles ahead in Alliance relationships caused by trade frictions and growing economic rivalry among the three nations. Examples are Lester Thurow, Robert Reich, Paul Krugman, Laura D'Andrea Tyson, Theodore Moran, and David Denoon. These analysts differ in their appraisals and prescriptions. Some argue that frictions can be resolved through the G-7 and GATT, others assert that the United States should pursue an industrial policy and managed trade, and still others predict a descent into mercantilism and rival trading blocs. What unites them is the belief that the security bonds holding the Western Alliance together are being weakened, to one degree or another, by growing economic strains. The implication is that, if international security affairs decline into instability, the Western Alliance may lack the vigor needed to restore order. Such development will add further weight to the reasons for pessimism about the future.[8]

A CRITIQUE OF PESSIMISM

The pessimistic school is made up of discordant voices with different messages, but its central theme is clear: Because worrisome trends are taking shape and gathering energy, a truly dangerous era lies ahead in world affairs. The reappearance of a single, powerful enemy is not the cause; rather, the cause is the out-of-control evolution of an unstable global system pulled apart by multiple pathological forces.

---

[8]See Lester Thurow, *Head to Head: The Coming Economic Battle Among Japan, Europe, and America*, William Morrow and Company, 1992. Also see Clyde V. Prestowitz, Jr., *Trading Places*, New York: Basic Books, 1988.

By calling attention to negative downturns that might occur abroad, the pessimistic literature serves as a useful counterweight to over-optimism, and it should be taken seriously in forming U.S. policy. Above all, it casts doubt on the heady forecast that the future international system will be harmonious, that dangers will be inconsequential, and that "high" politics will be replaced by "low" politics (i.e, a lack of security issues). In doing so, the pessimistic literature dispels the idea that the United States can relax its guard to the point that it will not have to embrace a national security policy and defense strategy worthy of the name.

Yet a reverse rush to judgment would be just as premature as was the eager embracing of the optimistic school. Both schools are subject to biases of their own, and neither school has a monopoly on truth or even a clear advantage in scientific research methodology. Indeed, both schools are trying to gauge an unclear future on the basis of incomplete data and imperfect models. The pessimists have laid out compelling hypotheses of the future, but the validity of these hypotheses is far from established. What the pessimists offer is a set of extrapolations based on negative trends, as yet only partially manifested, that are projected forward in time and are assumed to gather momentum, overpowering all countervailing forces in the way. This negative "tidal wave" may occur, but because its strength will depend upon many different negative events' all coming true, its occurrence is not predestined, especially in gigantic proportions.

Although the negative trends cited by this literature are gaining strength, they have not yet reached overpowering magnitude. Offsetting positive trends are also at work, and their energy is far from spent. Because the future will be determined by how these positive and negative trends interact, a sense of perspective is needed. The likelihood that market democracy will not be adopted everywhere does not mean it will be adopted nowhere. The fact that nationalism and ethnic rivalry are growing does not signify that they will always translate into war. Cultural antagonism does not necessarily become global cultural war. The reappearance of old geostrategic tensions does not imply that such tensions will explode into full military rivalries. The drift toward anarchy does not mean that all efforts to build community are doomed. A troubled world economy marked by deep poverty in many regions does not dictate that the pacifying effects of greater prosperity will be felt nowhere.

The mere appearance of negative trends, therefore, does not guarantee that their power will grow to fatal levels.

Nor do these trends lie outside the realm of human efforts to control, or at least diminish, their damaging effects. Fashionable argument today holds that nation-states are becoming impotent in the face of battering by external and internal forces. Realist theory reinforces this impression by arguing that the international system forges the parameters within which all countries are compelled to act. Nonetheless, governments everywhere will still retain a considerable capacity to shape their own destinies. In the years ahead, most of them will have powerful incentives to act in ways that prevent negative forces from producing a global disaster.

This is the case for the United States and the members of the Western community, all of whom have considerable leverage over international affairs. It also is the case for many states in Eurasia and the Middle East, where negative trends are expected to have the greatest influence. The presence of rogue states and the lack of communal bonds will limit the extent to which cooperation can be achieved, but this constraint does not mean that all governments will be rendered helpless. To the extent that states act constructively on their own and work together, the negative trends can be buffered and positive trends can be encouraged. For this reason and many others, the future continues to offer opportunity as well as danger. Its exact contours will be determined by how impersonal forces interact with the efforts of many countries to shape their surrounding environments.

Russia and China Critical

The pessimistic literature creates a visceral impression that the entire globe will sink into a dark void of major tensions. Critical to the outcome will be the political situations in Russia and China. Although market democracy might fail to take hold in both countries, even the pessimists are not forecasting virulent totalitarianism and global imperialism. Their common forecast is for post-communist authoritarian governments, mixed economies in which a fair amount of privatization will occur, and regional foreign policies that will assert national interests but that will not pursue universalist dreams.

A Russia and China of this sort may not be easy to live with, but these countries will not be bitter enemies of the West.

The pessimistic forecast is that unfavorable outcomes in Russia and China will cause military rivalry among the major powers to return in both Europe and Asia. Barring a complete rupture in political relations, however, this rivalry seems likely to be muted rather than explosive, and it will be controllable at affordable expense. The United States and its allies will need to take care to preserve a military balance of power in both regions. But unless events spiral out of control, they will not face the dangerous situation of opposing and highly primed military alliances directly confronting each other with offensive military strategies. The prospect is one of low-to-medium-grade military competition, not impending war. In this sense, the dark days of the Cold War seem unlikely to return.

Variable Level of Turmoil

Even if the pessimists are proven right, the level of turmoil will vary from one region to the next. The greatest worry is that Europe, formerly regarded as an island of stability, will become volatile owing to growing ethno-nationalism and a power vacuum in East Central Europe that produces interstate military rivalry and new alliances amid a multipolar setting. In Asia, barring the emergence of a confrontation between Japan and China, the prospect is less worrisome because Asia's nationalist ideology and power vacuums promise to be less virulent than Europe's. In the Middle East/Persian Gulf, resurgent Islamic fundamentalism and endemic poverty could produce great turmoil, but Kennedy and Huntington aside, most pessimists forecast a more muted outcome. The multipolar power structure of this region may produce tensions among the various countries, but a militarized Islamic alliance against the West is deemed far less likely.

The pessimistic literature has identified the multiple factors that could work together to make the future one of danger, not opportunity. But the pessimists themselves differ on how these factors and their interactions should be interpreted. A truly dark outcome for the entire globe emerges only if the worst is assumed for all factors. But this outcome seems unlikely if only because some negative trends may be mutually exclusive or may at least be rendered improbable by each other. Less-negative forecasts for all or even some of these factors yield a less pessimistic appraisal in several regions, if not in all regions. What the pessimistic literature has done is to identify the variables that could make for a dangerous future. However, it has not identified the exact way in which each of these variables will play out and the degree of danger that will confront the United States.

If the optimistic literature has a strength, it is the capacity to project a single integrated paradigm upon which further analysis can be built. By contrast, the pessimistic literature projects an overwhelming blizzard of negative events whose relative importance and interrelationships are hard to judge. What it offers is a deluge of information, not an elegant theory based on core foundations and a hierarchy of propositions. The pessimistic literature needs to be incorporated into a framework that accommodates focused thinking, not paralyzing confusion. A paradigm of pessimism is needed. Better yet, a paradigm that combines the best from the schools of both optimism and pessimism is needed.

Until a valid paradigm is established with neither unwarranted optimism nor overwrought pessimism, scholars will be unable to analyze where the international system is headed. More important, the U.S. government will be hard-pressed to forge a coherent national security policy and strategy. Policymakers may be left with an approach so intent on hedging against all bets that it lacks focus and direction. Equally worrisome is the prospect of a confused policy suspended among multiple judgments, endorsed by multiple constituencies. U.S. policy may evolve into reactive confusion that will increase as the credibility of the pessimistic school grows and the world itself becomes more turbulent.

Intensified research analysis on the future of global politics is an urgent priority. The various downturns that may lie ahead need to be better understood so that they may be better prevented. But *analysis*—the act of breaking a complex system down into component parts that can be more easily examined—will need to be accompanied by strong efforts at synthesis. We possess a sense of the component parts of an international system; what we lack is a clear grasp of how these parts are interacting and of how the entire global system is taking shape.

As the U.S. government endeavors to develop an understanding of emerging global politics, it will need to depart from the past practice of addressing only the present and the immediate future. In recent years, official attention has been switching in the right directions, and this effort should be intensified. Yet future forecasts should not be disengaged from the planning decisions of today. A key will be to assess how the present is influencing the distant future, for it is the near term that is most under the planner's control.

The quest for synthesis also will need to grapple with the dynamic interaction among military, political, and economic trends. If only military forces are examined, important political and economic developments may be overlooked; the future will not be shaped in a military vacuum. Important issues will be how politics and economics affect security affairs and how security arrangements influence political and economic trends. It is this interplay that will lie at the heart of future international stability and U.S. national security policy. Underlying social and technological trends must also be carefully evaluated because they will help to shape future international conflict.

The U.S. government will need to keep an open mind by constantly reexamining its premises and conclusions. Similar to all institutions, it is vulnerable to becoming locked into a single, simplistic paradigm for explaining the future, a tendency that is tantamount to putting on intellectual blinders: dangerous even when uncertainty is genuinely small and exponentially more dangerous when uncertainty is great. The recent past has been a warning sign in this regard, for the U.S. government was surprised by both the end of the Cold War and Iraq's invasion of Kuwait.

The best guarantee against fixating on one paradigm is to institutionalize alternative sources of analysis. Another guarantee is to adopt decision processes that promote searching debate. As Hegel observed, dialectical idealism—the counterpoising of alternative theses—is the most reliable vehicle for discovering the truth. The inbred pluralism of democracy fosters constant reevaluation. Executive organizations, however, typically take advantage of the opportunity only if an effort is made to encourage regular intellectual exchange.

The search for synthesis will need to be conducted below the surface of observable events. As argued above, tomorrow's world will be determined by interacting tectonic forces whose powerful dynamics are taking place beyond the sight of the casual observer. These dynamics may be operating in ways that seem counterintuitive to U.S. observers, who often reason by unconsciously making analogies with the recent past and with the United States' unique historical experience. To understand how counterintuitive dynamics can be misperceived, it is useful to remember that medieval astronomers who believed the sun revolved around the earth did so not because they were unobservant or stupid but because outward appearances conformed closely to the traditional theory. It took Copernicus to prove that reality was the reverse and that an entirely new theory was needed.

To understand future international affairs, policymakers must grasp the underlying causal dynamics actually at work, dynamics that might not conform to expectations or preferences. The next chapter provides a possible framework for the required synthesis of the components presented by the diverse analyses of the pessimistic school.

Chapter Four

PESSIMISTIC STRATEGIC SCENARIOS
FOR THE FUTURE

If the U.S. government is to begin assessing the implications of a dangerous world for its policy and strategy, it will need to bring the future into sharper focus. The pessimistic literature does not provide that focus but offers a panoply of alternative futures, none of them defined in crystal-clear terms and all seemingly of equal likelihood.

The manifold uncertainties ahead, including the real prospect of multiple major changes, make it impossible to build a single, credible estimate of the future. What can be done, instead, is to construct alternative "strategic scenarios" for planning. By *strategic* is meant a scenario that defines a distinct international security system with unique structural features (as discussed in Chapter Three). Within each system, many different subvariations might unfold, but the core structural features would remain constant.

TOWARD A SCENARIO-BASED FRAMEWORK FOR PLANNING

The purpose of this chapter is to develop alternative strategic scenarios for the future. It begins with a discussion of key variables to be considered, describes single-dimension scenarios, then develops multiple-dimension scenarios. It examines a multiple-dimension scenario that, from today's standpoint, appears to provide the best basis for planning. This chapter concludes with an appraisal of why even more-dangerous scenarios are not worth planning against.

Assuming a dangerous world lies ahead whose contours are unclear, this approach endeavors to assemble a limited set of different scenarios: Each scenario is coherent, is plausible enough to be taken seriously, and poses different implications for U.S. policy and strategy. The goal is not to eliminate uncertainty from planning but to establish manageable boundaries around that uncertainty and to bring emerging international affairs into relief. Scenarios offer multiple views of the future, thereby allowing the effect on U.S. policy and strategy of any one of these scenario's coming to life to be determined.

This methodology calls for the analyst to survey interacting trends, to cluster such trends, and to fashion several different scripts of how the future might unfold. Each scenario is to be analytically distinct from its partners—a separate view of the future with unique policy consequences—and must meet the criterion of feasibility. Highly implausible outcomes are rejected, thus leaving only plausible outcomes for serious study. Judgment plays a key role. The methodology of scenario construction is neither scientific nor flawless, but neither is it undisciplined. Realism and consistency can be demanded, and contradictory events can be ruled out. Techniques of inference and deduction can be employed, and formal rules of interpretation and criteria of evaluation can be enforced. Scenario-writing thus can aspire to analytical coherence and a strong measure of rigor. When it achieves these standards, it can offer valuable insights about the uncertain future, and thus can be a useful instrument for policy evaluation.

This section offers an exercise in scenario writing. The exercise begins with the postulate that, if a more dangerous world evolves, it will largely be a product of three interacting variables. A fourth key variable is U.S. behavior, which is treated as a constant here to simplify the analysis. This constant is that the United States will remain heavily engaged in international security affairs with a national security policy aimed at protecting its own interests and encouraging global order. The effect of American isolationism is not examined; the effect of isolationism would be to increase prospects for a dangerous world well beyond the scenarios examined here. The three variables are as follows:

- **The degree to which tensions increase within the three regions vital to international stability: Europe, Middle East/Persian Gulf, and Asia.** Measured in terms of political conflict, military competition, and propensity to violence, regional tensions are classified here on a scale of low, medium, high, and very high. Today, the greatest danger is posed by medium-level tensions in the Middle East/Persian Gulf and Asia (especially in Northeast Asia). Europe is classified as being at a low level of tensions. A "high" level of tension implies widespread instability and incentives for violence, but not continuing war; a "very high" level denotes an even more explosive situation, with war a regular occurrence.

Heightened regional tensions could manifest themselves in the same forms they do today, but they also could acquire new dimensions. In the Persian Gulf, Iraq and Iran will probably wax and wane as threats to the oil fields, but other dangers could arise: e.g., friendly oil sheikdoms that fall victim to domestic upheaval or growing Islamic fundamentalism in the Middle East. In Northeast Asia, the Democratic People's Republic of Korea–Republic of Korea (DPRK-ROK) confrontation could heat up; it also could give way to unification, to be replaced by regional rivalries among other powers across Asia. Europe could witness a back-and-forth dynamic of ethnic strife in the Balkans and many varieties of security tensions to the north. The specific nature of regional tensions thus is a variable; the constant is the tensions themselves.

- **The degree to which rivalry returns in Western relations with Russia and China.** Today, relations with these two major powers are tranquil. Future rivalry could take two forms: (1) moderate regional rivalry brought about by conflict in traditional geopolitical agendas, and (2) intense global rivalry (akin to the Cold War) brought about by emergence of virulent nationalism and imperialist policies by Russia and/or China.

- **The degree to which the Western Alliance suffers a loss of cohesion.** Today, both NATO and the U.S.–led alliance system in the Pacific remain cohesive. Loss of cohesion could take three forms: (1) reduced confidence that the United States' traditional Allies will cooperate closely with it in security endeavors outside Alliance borders, (2) weakened assurances that even traditional collective border-defense guarantees still apply, and (3) fracturing that brings about rivalry among former Alliance partners.

These three variables play a central role in shaping the basic structure of the international security system and in determining the extent of instability, which is the reason for focusing on them.   In
powerful ways, their interplay will shape the agenda confronting U.S.
policy and strategy in a dangerous world.   These variables do not
cover the entire globe and the full set of troubles that might emerge
in the future.   In particular, Sub-Saharan Africa, South Asia, and
Latin America are not addressed, although negative developments in
these areas could be important in their own right and could have
implications for U.S. national security policy.

Single-Dimension Scenarios

The process of scenario-writing begins by postulating "single-
dimension" downturns, downturns in each of the variables individu-
ally: (1) increased regional tensions, (2) renewed Western rivalry
with Russia and China, and (3) lessened cohesion within the Western
Alliance. Each of these pessimistic scenarios, in turn, offers subcases
with differing specific features but with structural characteristics
similar to those of the parent scenario. Postulated here are subcases
that do not exhaust the wide range of permutations and combinations that might occur but that do identify the dominant possibilities.
Most other alternatives can be incorporated within them.

Increased Regional Tensions. As argued by the pessimistic literature, the emergence of greater regional tensions would itself produce
a more dangerous world.   An increase in frictions in the Middle
East/Persian Gulf and Northeast Asia (e.g., Korea) would complicate
U.S. planning for such regions, which already are focal points of
American defense strategy.   Increased tension could be brought
about by a combination of negative political and economic trends
and would be amplified by further proliferation of nuclear weapons
and other instruments of mass destruction. Many possibilities in the
Middle East/Persian Gulf abound, including heightened tension with
Iraq and/or Iran, renewed Arab-Israeli rivalry, the spread of Islamic
fundamentalism and anti-Western attitudes, and the weakening of
pro-Western Arab governments. The same applies to Northeast Asia,
where increased tensions could stem from an even greater North
Korean threat to South Korea or from unification of these countries
that leads to increased regional tension with China and Japan. A re-

lated possibility is the spread of tensions southward, including into Southeast Asia. The nature and degree of increased tensions would matter hugely. For U.S. planning, however, the core effect would be the same: Greater dangers in both regions would mandate adjustments in current U.S. policy and strategy.

Increased regional tensions in East Central Europe and/or the Balkans could be brought about by many causes, including the spread of ethnic war in the Balkans and the Caucasus or an upsurge of tensions in Hungary's relations with its neighbors; the emergence of Ukraine as a rogue power that threatens its western neighbors; failure of market democracy in Poland and its neighbors, leading to anti-Western governments; and the emergence of unhealthy security dynamics brought about by the lack of collective defense assurances and fear of Russian military power, leading to self-protective military agendas, nuclear proliferation, and formation of new security alliances. These four alternatives, of course, are not mutually exclusive; indeed, all could occur at once. Their geopolitical effect would be to create a zone of great turmoil to the immediate east of NATO's current borders, but their effect on U.S. policy would depend on the specific dangers posed.

If the pessimistic literature is correct, a dangerous world almost inevitably would be marked by some degree of upsurge in regional tensions, the most likely being an upsurge in Europe, followed in probability by Northeast Asia, then the Middle East/Persian Gulf. Least likely is a huge upsurge in all three regions; however, this outcome is not implausible. Heightened tension in all three regions would be mounted by small-to-medium-size powers that would not pose a major military threat to the United States. The prospect is worrisome, nonetheless, because it would pose localized threats to areas that are important to Western interests while increasing the load on U.S. security policy, which today is anchored on the premise of managing tensions in only two regions.

If heightened regional tension would increase the challenges facing the United States, it at least would not pose the danger of renewed threats from major powers. Such threats can erode the structural foundations of the security system in ways having global repercussions, thereby threatening greater damage to international stability.

This danger could emerge in the event of renewed Western rivalry with Russia and/or China.

Renewed Western Rivalry with Russia and China. If rivalry with one or both of these countries evolves, the most probable cause would be their pursuit of traditional geopolitical goals on a regional basis, driven by nationalist agendas in Moscow and/or Beijing. As an illustration, an authoritarian government might emerge in Russia, and it might pursue a tough-minded Eurasian foreign policy, which might translate into establishment of a sizable military, coercive efforts to restore Russian control over the Commonwealth republics, and attempts to intimidate Poland and other countries in East Central Europe. The counterpart in China would be a pragmatic but uncooperative government that, through the vehicle of greater military power, begins pursuing an aggressive policy aimed at intimidating Korea, Japan, Taiwan, and countries in Southeast Asia. In this case, neither Russia nor China would behave as full-scale imperial powers or implacable adversaries of the West, but because of nationalist ambitions, their relations with the West would be marked by a fluid combination of normal diplomacy and limited confrontation.

A less likely but worse case would arise if Russia and/or China were to emerge as expansionist powers motivated by virulent ideology. In neither case would communism provide the motivation. Most probably, Russia would be motivated by an extremist ideology of fascistic nationalism brought about by the replacement of the current government with a right-wing dictatorship presiding over an economy of corporatist capitalism. China might be led by a regime that produces a uniquely Asian mixture of fascism, market authoritarianism, and communism. The outcome for both countries would be value systems that endorse vigorous imperial expansion through coercive military power and that discount cooperative diplomacy with the West. The result would be a high degree of confrontation with the United States and its allies in both Europe and Asia, as well as competitive rivalry on a global scale. The effect would be to draw U.S. policy out of its current regional emphasis and to mandate a greater focus on management of confrontational major-power relations on a global basis.

A Lessened Cohesion Within the Western Alliance. The withering of the Western Alliance would produce serious dangers of its own and would greatly complicate U.S. national security policy. Brought about by mounting economic frictions and lack of a common security vision, the weakened cohesion would be manifested most strongly by inhibited cooperation in managing security affairs. Alliances in Europe and Asia would continue to exist for traditional border-defense missions, but the U.S. military presence would be lower than now and integrated defense planning would decline. Most important, there would be a lack of cooperation in dealing with security affairs outside Alliance borders and an absence of willing partners to support U.S. activities of this type.

In Europe, the United States and its NATO partners would no longer be able to forge common policies for addressing events in either Europe or the Middle East/Persian Gulf, resorting instead to unilateral efforts and ad hoc coalitions of willing nations without contributions from common NATO assets. An unintended by-product might be conflicting security agendas that inhibit individual countries from acting successfully on their own. In Asia, a parallel development would be weakened U.S. alliances with Japan and Korea: Not only would these two countries decline to support U.S. security policies in the western Pacific and Asia, but they might also call for a sharp scale-down of the American military presence there. The United States thus would be compelled to base its military presence on islands in the western Pacific and to seek other partners.

Although the decline of cooperation for handling threats beyond current borders would be damaging in itself, the withering of Alliance cohesion plausibly might not stop at this point. The worst case is the emergence of outright adversarial relations between the United States and either Germany or Japan (or both). But a reappearance of the pre–World War II era seems beyond the outer limits of plausibility. A plausible case, however, is that Alliance bonds might erode to the point where Japan and Germany no longer place confidence in U.S. security guarantees for even traditional defense missions.

In Europe, an alternative is that the European Union might become so motivated by the quest for a separate European security pillar that it decides to sever its long-standing dependence on U.S. guarantees. The outcome would be that Germany or the EU, as well as Japan, elects to embark upon the course of military self-sufficiency, one result of which might be efforts to build greater conventional power-projection capabilities. This development could have a healthy effect by broadening the willingness of currently inward-looking Alliance partners to share the burdens of defense; however, if it was perceived as reflecting Germany's and Japan's neo-imperial agendas, the effect might be unhealthy—indeed, destabilizing. A more troublesome result might be decisions by Japan and Germany to cross the nuclear threshold, the effect of which would be the undermining of one of the international security system's most stabilizing features since the end of World War II. The consequences are impossible to know, but one almost inevitably would be to propel the world toward greater multipolarity, military competition, and political stress.

Together, these single-dimension scenarios provide snapshots of how a dangerous world might take shape and of how U.S. security policy might be affected. The scenario of heightened regional tensions would pose dangers similar to those encountered today, but of greater intensity and broadened geographic scope. The scenario of renewed rivalry with Russia and China introduces the risk of struggle with major powers on a global scale—a development fundamentally different from the situation encountered today. The scenario of diminished Alliance cohesion primarily would weaken the Coalition assets available to the United States; in the extreme case, it could damage international stability by leading to nuclear proliferation and other unilateralist military departures by Germany and Japan.

Shortcomings of Single-Dimension Scenarios

Each of these scenarios merits careful appraisal, because, at least somewhat, each is a plausible outcome of any drift to a dangerous world. Yet single-dimension scenarios offer limited analytic power because they focus on one development in isolation and therefore do not offer composite theories of how the overall international security system might take shape. In essence, they introduce variation in one factor while implicitly holding all other factors constant. The result can be tunnel vision: Even important events do not occur in isolation, but as part of a much larger mosaic of cause and effect. To the extent that all three scenarios are deemed feasible at the same time, moreover, the unintended result can be the portrayal of contradictory events and mutually exclusive outcomes. In the process, accuracy and relevance can be lost.

For example, the scenario of heightened regional tensions says little about Russia and China or the cohesion of the Western Alliance. Yet the nature and degree of heightened regional tensions will depend on Russia and China and on the Western Alliance: Ukraine is less likely to threaten neighbors to the west if it is menaced by Russia from the east, and Poland is less likely to build up its own military power if NATO welcomes it into the fold. Conversely, any increase of regional tensions in nearby areas might enhance the likelihood that China and Russia will emerge as rogue powers, but their emergence as imperial states might have the effect of suppressing regional tensions—how can Hungary try to expand its borders if it is under Russia's imperial sway? In any event, the Western Alliance might collapse if not faced with pressing security requirements. But will collapse occur in the face of mounting regional tensions and a resurgent Russia and China? Such interactions are critical, but their rich interplay can be ignored by single-dimension scenarios.

A related problem is that preoccupation with single-dimension scenarios can lead to flawed policy priorities by fostering overpreoccupation with one challenge at the expense of all others. For example, the scenario of heightened regional tensions implies a requirement for expanded U.S. involvement in the relevant regions. But does this involvement make sense if relations with Russia and China are forcing a confrontation? Is regional involvement even possible if U.S. alliances are decaying? If these alliances are eroding, should the first priority be to save them, rather than to rescue decaying regions? Can the United States even hope to retain sound alliances and cooperative relations with Russia and China if many regions are declining into chaos? Observers may disagree about U.S. priorities in any given situation, but single-dimension scenarios are not a sound vehicle for resolving such disagreements or setting U.S. priorities.

For these reasons, although single-dimension scenarios are a step in the right direction, they are not satisfactory solutions to the task of assessing the various forms a dangerous world might take. Any effort to address the future requires a comprehensive portrayal of the whole international system, not just part of that system. Comprehensiveness, in turn, requires analysis of the rich interplay of cause and effect and assessment of how the whole is made up of its parts.

Multiple-Dimension Scenarios

The need for composite portrayals of the future international system can be met by fashioning multiple-dimension scenarios that take into account the interactions of all three major variables discussed above. Table 4.1 is a matrix that presents a set of analytic options for the future international security system according to the way these three variables play out. The horizontal axis displays four types of regional tensions. The vertical axis displays seven combinations of Western relations with Russia and China, and cohesion within the Western Alliance. The result is a matrix of 28 different international security systems, each comprising unique structural features. These alternatives do not cover all permutations and combinations; they present a wide enough spectrum to portray the systemic alternatives that appear most likely to evolve and that are of greatest interest to U.S. policy and strategy.

In the upper left corner is the current international security system (A), which is dominated by moderate tensions in the Middle East/Persian Gulf and Northeast Asia, greater tranquility in Europe, stable relations with Russia and China, and a cohesive Western Alliance. Taking this system as the base case, one moves on the matrix horizontally and vertically toward alternatives of progressively increasing turbulence and stress, which portray options that assume future trends of the type cited by the pessimistic literature and that produce a more dangerous world with varying characteristics according to how these trends unfold. The combination of horizontal and vertical conditions determines the structure of the system as a whole and the overall level of stress created. In addition to the current situation (A), the horizontal axis displays three systemic alternatives of greater regional tension. Along with the current situation (A), the vertical axis displays six systemic alternatives.

The matrix has as its informing premise that all alternatives are not of equal probability: Some outcomes are far more plausible than others. To help distinguish among the varying likelihoods, the matrix assigns numerical scores from 1 to 4 for each horizontal and vertical alternative, with 1 being the least likely and 4 being the most likely.

Table 4.1

Future International Security Systems in a More Dangerous World
(illustrative scores)

	Regional Tensions			
	A (2)	B (3)	C (4)	D (2)
Relations with Russia and China, and Western Alliance Cohesion (illustrative scores)				
A (2)	4	6	8	4
B (3)	6	9	12	6
C (4)	8	12	16	8
D (3)	6	9	12	6
E (2)	4	6	8	4
F (2)	4	6	8	4
G (1)	2	3	4	2

NOTES: **Horizontal-Axis Regional Situations**

A.   Base case: The current international security system of moderate tensions in the Middle East/Persian Gulf and Northeast Asia, greater tranquility in Europe, stable relations with Russia and China, and a cohesive Western Alliance.

B.   High tensions in the Middle East/Persian Gulf and Asia (as opposed to today's medium-level tensions), coupled with the current situation in Europe.

C.   High tensions in the Middle East/Persian Gulf and Asia, coupled with high regional tensions (as opposed to low tensions today) in Europe, especially in East Central Europe and the Balkans.

D.   Very high tensions (beyond B and C) in all three regions, thus producing widespread turbulence and violence-promoting instability in all three.

Vertical-Axis Systemic Alternatives

A.   Base case: The current international security system of moderate tensions in the Middle East/Persian Gulf and Northeast Asia, greater tranquility in Europe, stable relations with Russia and China, and a cohesive Western Alliance.

B.   Harmonious Western relations with Russia and China coupled with a less cohesive Western Alliance.

C.   A traditional geopolitical rivalry with Russia and China, coupled with a cohesive Western Alliance. Russia and China, motivated by pragmatic ambitions that typically accompany the foreign policies of nations pursuing their self-interests, are postulated as pursuing aggressive regional goals.

Table 4.1—continued

NOTES: **Vertical-Axis Systemic Alternatives—continued**

D.   Traditional geopolitical rivalry of the West with Russia and China, coupled with a less cohesive Western Alliance.

E.   Confrontational rivalry of the West with Russia and China, and a cohesive Western Alliance. Russia and China, motivated by agendas of ultra-nationalism, are postulated as pursuing highly imperial and expansionist policies. The result is a high level of tensions in relations with the West, not only regionally but also globally.

F.   Confrontational rivalry of the West with Russia and China, coupled with a less cohesive Western Alliance.

G.   Confrontational rivalry of the West with Russia and China, accompanied by a fractured Western Alliance.

The score for each box is derived by multiplying the vertical and horizontal scores.

These scores are derived from the insights offered by the pessimistic literature. Other analysts could interpret the trends differently. Moreover, the scaling system and the technique of multiplying scores (rather than adding them) are themselves arbitrary. Operations research analysis accepts such methodology when there is great uncertainty. However, the scores are not the products of scientific techniques and must be interpreted as being illustrative, not definitive. For example, a score of 16 as opposed to 8 does not mean that the probability of occurrence is twice as great; it means that the probability is judged to be considerably higher. Even so, this methodology provides a crude indicator for separating the more probable from the less probable alternatives.

The implications are straightforward. The matrix suggests that the extreme alternatives can be regarded as low-probability events. Driving this conclusion are four judgments:

1.   The least-threatening outcomes receive low scores because a dangerous world is likely to witness a combination of heightened regional tensions and Western rivalry with Russia and China.

2.   Although regional tensions are destined to rise in a more dangerous world, they probably will not explode everywhere. The laws of

probability constrain the degree to which these tensions will both intensify and spread.

3. Although some form of Western rivalry with Russia and China may emerge, such rivalry probably will fall short of being highly confrontational. Traditional geopolitical rivalry implies military competition and some incompatibility of security agendas, but it does not imply a complete breakdown of collaboration or the outbreak of war.

4. The emergence of a more dangerous world will create incentives for the Western Alliance to remain cohesive. Some loss of cohesion is a serious concern; but even if a loss of cohesion occurs, this system is very unlikely to fracture to the point of undermining current collective defense guarantees. The real issue is whether these alliances will be effective enough to handle future international troubles.

As a result, a dangerous world seems likely to produce a more troubled setting than is envisioned by the least-stressful alternatives. Conversely, the most-troubled alternatives are unlikely to develop, because for them to do so would require the simultaneous unfolding of several low-probability events. Consequently, the closest scrutiny should be given to a limited set of middle-ground scenarios in assessing the implications for future U.S. policy and strategy. The following four scenarios are drawn from the cells of the Table 4.1 matrix that have the highest scores; they are sufficiently similar to their immediate neighbors to cover other scenarios that also have fairly high scores. Each of these four scenarios can be subdivided into several subpermutations and combinations; only their basic structural characteristics are discussed here:

- **STRATEGIC SCENARIO 1: Traditional geopolitical rivalry with Russia and China, high tensions in all three major regions, and a cohesive Western Alliance.** This scenario is assessed as the most probable for the following interacting reasons. If a more dangerous world evolves, the causal trends are likely to produce troubled relations with Russia in Europe and with China in Asia. But the outcome would not be full-blown confrontation because these two countries appear destined to pursue agendas driven by their national interests, not by universalist ideologies. Rivalry with these countries probably will be accompanied by high regional tensions in Europe, the Middle East/Persian Gulf, and Northeast Asia. Owing to endemic factors and to the ability of the major powers to achieve a modicum of cooperation, however, these regional tensions are unlikely to grow to the point of producing uncontrollable turbulence and rampant violence. This world would be characterized by moderate military competition among the major powers but not a high risk of war among them. The threat of regional conflicts would persist, but warfare would be the exception, not the rule.

- **STRATEGIC SCENARIO 2: Harmonious Western relations with Russia and China, high tensions in two or three regions, and a weakened Western Alliance.** This scenario postulates that market democracy reforms in both Russia and China will succeed at least to the point where both countries pursue benign foreign policies that allow for collaboration with the United States and its Allies. Even so, endemic frictions produce an upsurge of regional tensions in the Middle East/Persian Gulf and Northeast Asia, and perhaps in Europe, that could compel the Western Alliance to retain a sufficient level of cohesion to deal with the resulting problems. The outcome anticipated here, however, is weakened Alliance cohesion because of harmonious relations with Russia and China. This world would not be marked by military competition among the major powers, but regional conflicts would be an ever-present threat, including in Europe.

- **STRATEGIC SCENARIO 3: Traditional Western rivalry with Russia and China, high tensions in the Middle East/Persian Gulf and Asia, but not in Europe, and a cohesive Western Alliance.** In this dangerous world, the emergence of rivalry with Russia and China is accompanied by a different pattern of regional tensions from that envisioned by Strategic Scenario 1. Regional tensions in Europe abate or at least remain as they are today, owing to success of market democracy reforms in East Central Europe, the incorporation of countries there into the Western community, and containment of turbulence in the Balkans. An expanded NATO would face rivalry with a Russian-led Commonwealth, but at least the territory separating them would not be marked by local strife and unstable security dynamics. The risk of war would be that of a conflict between NATO and Russia, not that of ethno-nationalist aggression by the smaller states.

Regional tensions would mount, however, in the Middle East/Persian Gulf, owing to the spread of Islamic fundamentalism, assertive agendas by Iraq and Iran, renewed Arab-Israeli frictions, unstable Arab governments, and military proliferation. The risk of regional war would be higher than exists today, and conflicts might witness the use of nuclear weapons or other weapons of mass destruction. In Asia, regional tension also would grow, owing to aggressiveness by China, a widening role played by Japan, and troubled relations with Russia. A principal concern would be turbulence on the Korean peninsula, brought about either by an intensification of the current DPRK-ROK stalemate or by Korean unification that leads to trouble with China, Russia, and Japan.

- **STRATEGIC SCENARIO 4: Traditional geopolitical rivalry of the West with Russia and China, high tensions in all three regions, and a weakened Western Alliance.** This world is similar to that of Strategic Scenario 1, but with an important variation that brings about greater difficulty for the United States: the loss of cohesion in the Western Alliance to the point that, although traditional commitments remain in effect, both NATO and the Asian alliance lack the capacity for Coalition operations beyond current borders. The effect is to reduce the West's ability to manage stressful regional affairs and renewed rivalry with Russia and China.

ANALYSIS OF FOUR MULTIDIMENSION SCENARIOS

These four scenarios should be evaluated according to not only their different internal contents but also what they imply for the challenges posed to the West. To the extent that these strategic scenarios help define the most-likely forms to be taken by a more dangerous world, they suggest that, barring a sequence of multiple low-probability events, the United States is not likely to be confronted by a global nightmare. Regional tensions might increase, but not to the point of explosion. Relations of the West with Russia and China might deteriorate, but global confrontation is not the most probable result. The Western Alliance might lose cohesion but is unlikely to fracture. Above all, the deadly combination of heightened regional tensions, Western confrontation with Russia and China, and a weakened or fractured Western Alliance is very unlikely. Whereas these events are not beyond the realm of possibility, they are not among the more-probable outcomes if a more dangerous world takes shape.

HIGHER POTENTIAL FOR GLOBAL STRESS

Nonetheless, these four scenarios posit a significantly higher potential for global stress than exists today, and they illustrate the different ways such stress could be manifested. Scenario 4 is the most threatening because it forecasts deep trouble in all three variables, whereas the other scenarios posit trouble in only two, and they point to different combinations of difficulty. The scenario deemed most probable, Scenario 1, posits Western rivalry with Russia and China and heightened difficulties in all three principal regions, making the prospect of a still-cohesive Western Alliance a source of comfort. But how effective would this alliance be in handling these two very different forms of trouble? The answer to this question will determine how many allies would be available to help the United States as it goes about the task of dealing with this turbulent external environment.

Scenario 1 posits a high potential for interstate conflict in many forms, thus creating the ingredients for war. Geopolitical rivalry with Russia and China would not be conducive to war. However, periodic crises might occur, and regional war could be the outcome if diplomatic efforts are not managed carefully. All three regions would offer multiple combinations for wars launched by medium and small powers against neighbors and carried out in ways that threaten Western interests. This scenario thus offers the prospect of periodic but continuing violence on both a small scale and in ways organized by nation-states. Ethnic conflicts similar to those in Bosnia might become common, especially in Europe. Asia and the Middle East/Persian Gulf might see border skirmishes and full-scale invasions similar to those of the recent Gulf War. Looming over this situation would be the prospect that powerful Russia and China periodically might resort to force to pursue their regional agendas. In a dangerous world of this sort, military power would count heavily.

Although organized violence might not be the rule, it would not be the exception.

The United States would face no hegemonic threat comparable to that in the Cold War or World War II, but it seldom would be able to relax its diplomatic and military guard. Almost regularly, it would face the prospect of conflict or war breaking out somehow, somewhere: one time in Europe, the next time in Asia, the following time in the Persian Gulf. Not all these conflicts would merit commitment of U.S. forces, but many would call for U.S. diplomatic involvement, and some would require military intervention. Meanwhile, the United States would, in fact, be concerned that negative global political dynamics could coalesce in ways producing an alliance of several rogue states hostile to Western interests. Such global tensions likely would wax and wane. At their worst, the result would be to leave U.S. foreign policy in anxious abeyance.

The Need for Individual, Sensible Policies

These four scenarios, moreover, are not grounds for a casual dismissal of extremely bad outcomes. The pessimistic literature offers worry that xenophobic nationalism and fascism might take hold in Russia, and perhaps a form of it in China as well. This literature also voices concern that a combination of poverty, ethnicity, and cultural antagonism could produce very high tensions in all three principal regions. It also provides arguments that the Western Alliance may atrophy even in the face of dangerous international trends. These outcomes may be unlikely. However, the disasters of World Wars I and II were low-probability events in the years preceding their outbreaks. The forecast that these outcomes will not occur is based on the postulate that governments will pursue sensible and responsive policies to prevent their occurrence. Yet history shows that sensibility is not always the course chosen, especially by governments preoccupied by other problems and by societies under great stress. The implication is that U.S. policy and strategy should include strong efforts to safeguard against such outcomes, and that the United States should understand the steps that must be taken if the worst does occur.

Even if the worst does not occur, the four most probable strategic scenarios would themselves pose far greater international stress than exists today. Moreover, the structural characteristics of these four alternatives differ a great deal not only when compared with today's world but also in relation to each other. All would mandate a different U.S. policy and strategy than is being pursued today. Each, however, would require a unique response. Thus, no single policy and strategy would suffice for all four scenarios.

Yet common themes stand out. The first common theme is that of renewed traditional geopolitical rivalry with Russia and China in three of the four scenarios. The second theme is that of a still-cohesive Western Alliance, albeit with uncertainty about the ability of NATO and the Pacific alliance to handle new security troubles. A third theme is that, in one way or another, regional tensions are likely to prevail in a more dangerous world regardless of how relations with Russia and China unfold. The exact nature of the regional tensions, however, is a variable: A situation of moderate tensions in three regions is different from heightened tensions in two of them. Whereas the former situation poses troubles of widespread geographic scope, the latter creates troubles of greater intensity in a more limited setting.

Specific Dangers Different from Today's

The most important conclusion is that the international settings posited by these four strategic scenarios are not only more stressful than today's situation but also offer specific dangers quite different from those perceived today. The immediate aftermath of the post–Cold War world has been regional tension in the Middle East/Persian Gulf and Northeast Asia against the background of stable relations with Russia and China. Many contemporary forecasts suggest that, if conditions worsen, the chief danger is intensified frictions in the two current regions of greatest worry. The estimate offered here is that, although tensions in both regions might increase, increased tensions may not be limited to the two regions alone. Regional tensions may rise in Europe if current negative trends gain momentum. Equally important, relations with Russia and China may take a downward turn if market democracy reforms fail.

This combination of Western rivalry with Russia and China, coupled with tensions in all three regions, is what could make the future world considerably more dangerous than today's. Moreover, this combination could pose the greatest demand for a fundamental alteration of U.S. policy and strategy. The act of handling tensions in two regions is a manageable proposition, especially if these regions already are the focal points of U.S. action and remain so for the foreseeable future. The act of dealing with three stressful regions as well as strained relations with Russia and China is something else again but may be the reality even if the Western Alliance remains cohesive—doubly so if this alliance itself were to falter.

Thus, even international outcomes well short of the worst case could confront the United States with serious troubles, not because one or two especially severe dangers intensify but because multiple dangers emerge, each of a moderate but still-serious nature. Together, these dangers would pose a collective impact in a highly complex setting, one that requires the United States to juggle many balls at once—far more than now. This future is very different from the one commonly expected today.

Possibilities in Unincluded Regions

As discussed above, all four strategic scenarios ignore events in Sub-Saharan Africa, South Asia, and Latin America. Negative developments in these regions might not be fundamental to the future international security system, but this does not mean that they will be unimportant. Turbulence in all three secondary regions could damage global stability by drawing in the major powers or by having a ripple effect in the three regions of primary importance. This especially is the case for South Asia, where the Indo-Pakistani rivalry could contribute to nuclear proliferation, affecting not only Persian Gulf politics but also relations among the United States, Russia, China, and Japan. Sub-Saharan Africa has faded in importance with the Cold War's end, but it seems likely to remain mired in poverty and stressful local political conflict. Latin America apparently has better prospects for democracy and economic prosperity, but regional tensions will persist. Latin America will remain important to U.S. policy because vital U.S. interests are involved there. Developments in these three regions thus merit consideration as factors of at least secondary importance in assessing the implications of the four strategic scenarios.

More-Stressful Scenarios

Although these four scenarios are deemed the most probable, more-stressful scenarios nonetheless are plausible if the international situation veers even more sharply toward instability than is envisioned here. Such outcomes thus should not be entirely discounted in contemplating the implications for future U.S. policy and strategy. What seems highly improbable is any full-scale fracturing of the Western Alliance, a judgment that owes to the assumption that the United States will remain engaged in global affairs and to the likelihood that economic frictions among the United States, Japan, and Western Europe will not grow to the point of having major negative consequences for Alliance security commitments. If either of these conditions is violated, the probability of a serious fracturing would increase substantially.

The likelihood of confrontational rivalry with Russia and/or China is assessed as lower than in the four strategic scenarios owing to the judgment that, even if relations with the West worsen, both countries will pursue pragmatic policies driven by their national interests. Yet the future plausibly might see one or both countries succumb to extremism and chauvinism. Another plausible development is the emergence of extremely high tensions in one or more of the three principal regions. Either development, or both at the same time, would confront the United States with security challenges more severe than are envisioned by the four most-probable scenarios. For this reason, they need to be considered in judging the implications of a dangerous world for U.S. policy and strategy.

FUTURE DIVERGENCE FROM IDENTIFIED SCENARIOS

Conceivably, the future will witness scenarios radically different from those identified in Table 4.1, with entirely new geopolitical axes and their own dangerous characteristics. The likelihood of these scenarios increases the farther analysis looks into the future. Their likelihood may be quite low 10 years from now, but higher 20 years hence, and even higher 50 or 100 years from now. Their likelihood also increases to the extent that traditional causes of conflict (geopolitics and ethnic nationalism) are replaced by entirely new causes: for example, economic rivalry and cultural antagonism. New sources of

conflict can give rise to new patterns of interstate rivalry and accommodation, potentially quite different from those experienced
today.

Different Rivalries and Power Blocs

If economic rivalry comes to play a dominant role, a quarrelsome
relationship plausibly might develop between the United States and
its current close allies: Western Europe and Japan. Out of this sea
change could come global politics of a fundamentally new nature yet
reminiscent of earlier times: an entente between the United States
and a democratic Russia aimed at containing either an antagonistic
China or a unified Western Europe or an assertive Asian coalition led
by Japan. If culture and race become dominant causes of conflict,
the outcome might be a world divided into competing regional blocs:
an alliance between North America and Europe in confrontation
with a united Islamic world or China or a unified Slavic bloc. In this
multipolar world, China and the Islamic world might join forces to
combat Russia and the West. Many other permutations would be
possible. The far-distant future might also witness countries such as
India and Brazil rising to play more important roles in international
affairs, thereby creating further multipolarity and interregional tension. One ultimate possibility is that of eight regional power blocs,
all pursuing their own interests and maneuvering against each other,
regularly changing alliances of convenience when circumstances
dictate.

All these scenarios of new power relationships are worth keeping in
mind. After all, few observers in 1984 would have dared predict the
way international affairs took shape in 1994. If an upheaval of this
magnitude is possible in only ten years, even more fundamental alterations are feasible over two decades and more. As history shows,
when the international security system has broken free from stasis
and is being propelled forward by powerful new forces, truly structural changes are possible. Evolution can give way to revolution,
thereby producing consequences that surpass even the most vivid
imaginings of those present at the creation.

Barriers to Different Power Blocs

The barriers to fundamentally different power relationships anytime soon also need to be recognized. For the period ahead, the alliance uniting the United States, Western Europe, and Japan might wither, but it is unlikely to crack in ways producing polarized relations. All three participants have absorbed the valuable lessons of working together, and they have too much experience in the dreadful consequences of internecine warfare to allow any drift into rivalry short of true cataclysm. During World War II, militaristic Germany and Japan formed an alliance of convenience against the United States, but the outcome was a crushing defeat that impressed upon them the importance of not making the same mistake twice. For its part, the United States has learned the geopolitical advantages of having Germany and Japan on its side; even if economic frictions with them intensify, the United States is likely to cling to this alliance—doubly so if the rest of the globe is turbulent.

Arguably, the Western Alliance could fracture as a result of rising economic frictions and eroding security bonds. However, in a dangerous world this collapse would have to occur before tensions with Russia and China grow to the point of giving this alliance renewed strategic reasons to hold together. This sequence is not implausible, but it seems improbable because, at the moment, relations with Russia and China are far more tenuous than the Western Alliance's internal cohesion. Regardless of the sequence, a fracturing of the Western Alliance could occur only in the event of colossal policy failures among the key participants, failures of the sort scrupulously avoided for the past 45 years. All these factors do not ensure that this triangular alliance will remain sufficiently strong to manage the external troubles of a dangerous world, for a loosening already is under way and may gain momentum. But the incentives are quite powerful against a wholesale decline that would produce rivalry.

Similar skepticism applies to the idea that the United States will form a condominium with either Russia or China. Talk of a U.S.–Russian strategic partnership is heard in some quarters. Although some forms of cooperation will be achievable, full partnership could occur only if Russia fully democratizes, and successful democratic reform seems improbable in the unhealthy situation of a dangerous world. Especially if Russia emerges with an authoritarian government and a neo-imperial foreign agenda, cool Russian relations with Europe and Japan would bar the way to close partnership. The United States would have little to gain by befriending Russia at the expense of its traditional friends, and Russia would have little to offer for the favor. Similarly, the United States has reasons for achieving harmonious relations with China, but little incentive to align with China at the expense of Japan as long as Japan remains in the Western fold. Barring an Asia turned upside down by renewed Japanese militarism, U.S.–Chinese relations in a dangerous world likely will be conflictual, not strongly cooperative.

Nor would Europe and Japan stand to gain by joining with an imperial Russia at the expense of their main protector, for Russia itself would be a primary threat to both of them. The same calculus applies to the idea of Japan's aligning with China in Asia. Indeed, a dangerous world most likely would lead Europe and Japan to forsake a freewheeling game of shifting coalitions in favor of the safe shelter offered by the United States. The principal risk is not that a unifying Europe and Japan will act as did Bismarck, but that they will seek to maintain too low a profile by handing off security burdens to the United States. In any event, the most-probable outcome is not that one or another Western partner will ally with Russia or China, but that the Western Alliance will find itself in rivalry with Russia in Eurasia, and with China in Asia.

Plausibly, Russia and China could be drawn together if both face rivalry with the Western nations. Especially if Russia recovers its balance and China becomes an economic and military powerhouse, an accord between them would better enable both to pursue imperial agendas in their respective regions. But owing to their own imperial policies, their conflicting ambitions in Central Asia would inhibit them from drawing too close and, indeed, would probably produce polarization between them. During the Cold War, communism was an insufficient common bond to hold these two historical rivals together; in the years ahead, nationalist ideologies are likely to be no more bonding. The principal risk is not alliance between them but rather stiff rivalry in Eurasia and, maybe, war.

A Chinese alliance with a unified Islamic Middle East is more probable, and it would complicate problems for both Russia and Europe. But how unified will Islam become, and exactly what cement would bind this alliance for anything other than mutually profitable trade in weapons and other commodities? After all, China and Islam do not share a common culture or flourishing economic relations or similar strategic aspirations. China and most Middle East countries think primarily in regional terms, which militates against closely coordinated policies. In all likelihood, China would not be willing to extend itself in the Middle East and Europe on behalf of Islam, and Islam would be reluctant to underwrite China's ambitions in Asia, especially since Islamic nations in Asia might be victimized by a powerful China. If China and an Islamic Middle East draw together, their relationship likely will be fleeting and tentative, not deep and enduring.

As for India and Brazil, today both are underdeveloped countries. Even if they achieve far greater economic and military status, their geographic isolation will inhibit their ability to influence global politics. India is cut off from Eurasia by the Himalayan Mountains and hemmed in by China. Brazil is located in the southern part of the Western Hemisphere, far from the focal points of world affairs. Their primary destiny is that of acting as regional powers, with India dominating South Asia and Brazil holding sway in South America. India could wield larger influence by aligning with Russia against China and the United States, and by building a nuclear arsenal. Brazil could help or hinder U.S. aspirations in Latin America. In these ways, their behavior will be relevant beyond their regions, but neither will possess the leverage to tip the global power balance. A world of eight powerfully competing regions is most likely decades away. For the years immediately ahead, the dominant prospect is that both South Asia and Latin America will play marginal roles in global affairs.

For all these reasons, global affairs for the coming decade or two are likely to be marked by a fairly high degree of structural continuity so that entirely new power relationships are improbable. Therefore, if a more dangerous security system evolves, it will emerge because Russia and/or China fall into polarized rivalry with each other and with a still-existing Western Alliance, and because regional tensions in key places intensify for reasons of their own. Change outside these parameters is possible, but it is far less likely than change within them.

SUMMARY

The four strategic scenarios thus provide a frame of reference for defining what can be expected. This does not mean, however, that the current international system will give way to only one of these scenarios and that permanent stasis will then ensue. An equally plausible outcome is that the current system will yield to more than one of these scenarios, as one is replaced by another in response to the dynamics of tectonic change. For example, the process might begin with Scenario 3 (tensions in the Middle East/Persian Gulf) accompanied by rivalry with Russia and China, then transition to Scenario 1, owing to an upsurge of tensions in Europe coupled with some cooling in the two other principal regions. Scenario 1, in turn, might give way to Scenario 4, through weakened cohesion in the Western Alliance.

Many other combinations can be imagined. Within each scenario, fluid change bringing about a shifting pattern of subvariations is possible. For a time Russia might be a rival of the West, only to be replaced or accompanied by China. For a time, the Middle East/Persian Gulf and Northeast Asia might be the most unstable regions, only to be replaced by a suddenly turbulent Europe. Political cooling in one region may be accompanied by rising heat in another, then followed by a swing backward in the reverse direction. The same can be said for relations among the major powers and, for that matter, in the Western Alliance. No single causal process can be identified as destined to control the sequence of events. Regional tensions and major-power rivalry could arise for separate reasons. Their appearance also could be interactive. But either one might presage the other, and each could take many different forms.

The key point is that at various stages over the coming two decades, different international situations might apply. One security system might appear for a few years, then vanish into history, to be replaced by a new system having unique characteristics but frequently changing specific features. Depending on the pace and extent of change, all four of these strategic scenarios—or even different scenarios—might be encountered. If so, the United States may be compelled to respond by fashioning a new policy and strategy several times over.

This prospect of frequent change is fully as important as the scenarios themselves in gauging the implications for U.S. planning, which are discussed next, in Chapter Five.

IMPLICATIONS FOR U.S. NATIONAL SECURITY POLICY

For a dangerous world to begin taking shape, a world that is worse than that of today, will have important implications for U.S. national security policy, especially because the current approach is not based on the expectation of something worse than the world of today. Indeed, to the extent optimism is still embraced, the expectation is that things will get better and that U.S. security problems will lessen. Yet the opposite could be the case: as analysis peers ever farther into the future, worrisome uncertainties grow.

Because so many different negative trends could unfold, the exact implications will depend on the specific situation. However, certain basic judgments will apply irrespective of what transpires. What parts of U.S. policy and strategy should remain the same, and what should change? How can the United States best contain the negative international forces at work today? And how can it best prepare for a future that may be less bright than that anticipated only a short while ago? These questions are addressed in this chapter, which begins by discussing the need to recognize the dangers ahead. It then presents the need for a coherent strategic concept and goes on to analyze the ways and means of a national security policy.

RECOGNIZING THE DANGERS AHEAD

Four Speeches

The first step toward deep, sound thinking for the United States is to sharpen its perceptions by recognizing that the post–Cold War world might soon become a more troubled place, a possibility the U.S. government may have yet to recognize. During September 1993, important foreign policy speeches were given by President Clinton, National Security Council (NSC) Adviser Anthony Lake, Secretary of State Warren Christopher, and UN Ambassador Madeleine Albright. Rejecting neo-isolationism in favor of continued U.S. engagement abroad, all four speeches spoke of the dangers that remain in international affairs. For example, President Clinton cited ethnic and religious wars, nuclear proliferation, small conflicts that grow large, terrorism, repression of democratic consciousness, hunger and disease, and environmental neglect. The other speakers offer similar lists. Yet these statements do not reflect a comprehensive theory of the troubles ahead if a dangerous world evolves.[1]

All four speeches can be read as conveying the impression that the scope of future dangers will remain limited, and that the vast opportunities ahead will far outweigh the troublesome threats. These speeches mention future threats, but their discussion is brief and general, often vague enough that the audience is left hard-pressed to decide exactly where these threats might be manifested and who will be the enemies. To critics, generalities of this sort can imply a lack of detailed focus and serious intent: a few throw-away lines added to calm the overly worried rather than a forceful statement of views that are deeply held and fully understood. Until emerging international troubles are perceived for what they are, they cannot be acted upon.

The Clinton, Lake, and Christopher speeches barely mention the role to be played by military forces in carrying out U.S. national security policy in peacetime. All imply that peace is brought about by the steady outward expansion of democracy, market capitalism, and free trade. None points to a major role for military strength in fashioning peace or even in laying the security foundations that allow market democracy, Western community, and a collaborative world economy to take hold. All implicitly portray the idea of a balance of power as though it stands outside polite discourse and is a legacy of a dark past, something to be banished if at all possible. The implication is

---

[1]These speeches were presented within a few days of each other in early fall 1993 and were intended to establish the Clinton Administration's position on national security policy. Presented at the United Nations, Clinton's address was broad-gauged and dealt mostly with U.S. policy for the United Nations. Christopher's address focused mostly on the Middle East, and Albright's speech dealt with U.S. defense policy. Lake's address at Johns Hopkins University came closest to establishing an overall strategic concept, which he called "enlargement."

that military power is a sword to be kept in a scabbard, to be extracted and used only when diplomacy fails, not a positive instrument to be employed in peacetime for the promotion of healthy community-building goals. Only former Secretary of Defense Les Aspin discussed the positive relationship between military power and peacetime goals in any depth; however, his voice was not heard as loudly as the others.

To be sure, Clinton and his top advisers were clear in their intent to keep NATO alive, to meet U.S. security commitments to Japan and Korea, to honor other treaty obligations, and to vigorously defend vital U.S. interests when necessary. They firmly rejected retrenchment and disengagement. Their support of a "Partnership for Peace" initiative in Europe suggests a willingness to extend security commitments and defense cooperation, along with economic and political ties, to former Warsaw Pact adversaries (see the "Steps Toward an Alliance-First System" subsection of this chapter). What stands out in their speeches is not indifference to military security but an effort to downgrade security's once-preeminent status in U.S. foreign policy by relegating it to a supporting role behind diplomacy and economic relations. This stance may be an appropriate response to the post–Cold War world that exists today, but it does say something about the limited extent to which looming dangers are seen as lying at the center of official American international visions.

Arguably, an upbeat portrayal is justified because the world today is less dangerous than during the Cold War, when a nuclear exchange and global conventional war were constant threats. Moreover, a dangerous world is not yet upon us. The need for perspective, nonetheless, works both ways: The relative difference between yesterday and today does not mean that the contemporary scene is tranquil in an absolute sense.

The more important issue is whether the Executive Branch, in the privacy of its own councils, understands the true extent of the troubles that might lie ahead and that might have to be headed off with concerted action before they grow out of proportion. If the Executive Branch does not possess this understanding, then U.S. national security policy has a problem embedded deeply in its own design that will manifest itself as the global system begins sliding toward instability. This policy will lack the intellectual components needed to accomplish its most basic purpose, that of warding off international troubles. How can serious troubles be warded off if they are not even perceived as being important during the germinal period, when they may still be prevented?

The Aspin Bottom-Up Review

Thus far, the one attempt to categorize future troubles and to formally draw implications for U.S. national security policy and military strategy has come from former–Secretary of Defense Aspin's *Report on the Bottom-Up Review*.[2] In this document, Aspin cites four dangers as central to future defense planning:

* The spread of nuclear, biological, and chemical weapons

* Aggression by major regional powers or ethnic and religious conflict

* Potential failure of democratic reform in the former Soviet Union and elsewhere

* Potential failure to build a strong and growing U.S. economy.

This categorization scheme is a step forward in the right direction, and it responds to several of the national issues that immediately come to mind. Nonetheless, closer scrutiny suggests that it can be interpreted as a laundry list of troubles rather than an intellectually rigorous theory of future global security affairs if the pessimists are proven correct. Neither this list nor its supporting arguments offer a philosophical inquiry into the nature of the international system and where it is headed. Will this system be fundamentally unstable or stable? Are these four dangers isolated and self-contained or do they represent an array of other dangers that might emerge? Is the purpose of U.S. defense policy to squelch these dangers alone or is the purpose also to address more deeply seated dynamics to preclude producing different dangers? The answers to these questions are not evident.

------

[2]Secretary of Defense Les Aspin, *Report on the Bottom-Up Review*, Washington, D.C.: Department of Defense, October 1993.

Furthermore, this list offers an odd combination of apples and oranges. Whereas the first two dangers are symptoms of underlying causes, the last two dangers deal with causes themselves, and the final danger refers mostly to the U.S. domestic situation, not the international arena. Do the causes produce the symptoms? Are they related at all? Also, only the second danger refers directly to the threat of military conflict. The other dangers refer to different, pre-conflict phenomena. Are they assessed as likely to produce military conflict? If so, how and where? Aspin's supporting analysis provides some answers, but not enough to address these issues.

Beyond this, are these the only two symptoms and two causes worth worrying about? Its own lack of a core theory notwithstanding, the pessimistic literature points to a wider spectrum of symptoms and causes. For example, it cites the danger of peacetime military competition among the major powers brought about by anarchical conditions, the lack of a collective security framework, and rekindled geostrategic rivalry. It also cites the risk of military confrontation between civilizations brought about by economic failure not in the United States but in the world economy, thereby leaving the Third World poverty-stricken.

Other examples could be cited, but the key point here is that DoD's list of dangers seems narrow and reflexive. It also comes across as somewhat superficial, possibly raising the wrong issues. Is the risk that democracy will fail in Russia or that Russia, regardless of its government, will again pursue an imperial foreign policy that will threaten vital Western interests? What of China? Does it count for nothing in the list of dangers? Is the United States worried about democracy's failing there, especially since China is still a communist country? Is the risk that nuclear weapons will proliferate or that these weapons will be used in peace, crisis, and war? Why do nuclear weapons proliferate? Does proliferation occur because rogue states gain access to a supply of fissile materials? Or does it happen because anarchical conditions leave countries uncertain of their security, thus begetting heightened demand, including demand among neutral states and even friendly countries?

The difference is critical, for it implies that dissimilar approaches must be taken to prevent further proliferation. If supply is the problem, then physical restrictions on access to nuclear materials are the answer. If demand is the driver, then security reassurances for some countries, not punitive measures, are the answer.

The intent here is not to unfairly criticize any official speech or document. The Bottom-Up Report is the best national security and defense strategy document yet produced by the Clinton Administration. By discussing international dangers in relation to U.S. national security goals and defense strategy, it does a good job of justifying the new force posture and program. Where it falls down is in its ability to assess external dangers from a core theory of future international affairs. This is an important shortcoming to be remedied in future documents. If the world does begin descending into widespread chaos of the sort envisioned by the pessimists, something more sophisticated will be needed than former-Secretary Aspin's four dangers.

TOWARD A NEW STRATEGIC CONCEPT

The U.S. government can prepare for a more dangerous world by understanding how key national security goals and priorities might have to change. At the moment, U.S. policy appears intent on pursuing the kind of agenda deemed appropriate for the international system of today: fundamentally stable, marked by isolated troubles that require management but perhaps evolving toward a permanently peaceful era. How must this approach change if the global system begins sharply veering toward instability? If the pessimists are right, this question might have to be answered sooner rather than later.

Above all, a dangerous world mandates articulation of a coherent strategic concept to guide U.S. national security policy and military strategy. By the term *strategic concept* is meant an intellectual construct that lays down a set of interlocking core premises and postulates whose function is to project a vision into a void. It defines U.S. perceptions, establishes values, and points toward desired destinations. It also endorses a scheme of objectives and priorities, articulates a relationship between ends and means, and, by specifying what can be afforded, establishes a framework for gauging the spectrum of possible options. A good example is the strategic concept laid down by ex–Secretary of Defense James Schlesinger in the mid-1970s, a time when the growing need for clarity was being frustrated by great ambiguity. Schlesinger did not resolve all debates, but by sharply focusing strategic thinking around a few powerful ideas, he cut through the confusion to provide a sense of direction and purpose.[3] Something similar may soon be needed.

An argument is made that in today's world of uncertain trends but little immediate danger, a strategic concept is not needed by the United States, cannot readily be fashioned, and will not command consensus. Presumably, enlightenment must be provided by the outside world before the United States can clarify its own thinking: The United States should be content to improvise, muddle through, and pursue multiple uncoordinated actions with no unifying logic. There can be little room for argument about the unsuitability of this stance in a dangerous world. The country will be better off if a strategic concept is in place before the political-military troubles of the future are fully upon it.

Enlargement

The closest approximation to a strategic concept comes from National Security Council Adviser Anthony Lake's address to the School of Advanced International Studies at Johns Hopkins University. In his address, Lake outlined a national security strategy of "enlargement" with four components. The first component, he said, is to strengthen the existing community of Western market democracies. The second component is to foster and consolidate market democracy in countries endeavoring to adopt this ideology. Especially important is successful reform in Russia, but hope is also held out for eventual progress in China. The third component is to minimize threats from outside the market-democracy community by containing and isolating rogue powers. The fourth component is to undertake humanitarian interventions when the situation calls for this step.

As acknowledged by Lake, this strategy is anchored in a modern-day version of Wilsonian idealism that postulates that the character of a

---

[3]See James Schlesinger, *DoD Annual Report*, Washington, D.C.: U.S. Government Printing Office (GPO), for fiscal years 1975, 1976. For a detailed analysis of Schlesinger's strategic concept, see Richard L. Kugler, *Commitment to Purpose: How Alliance Partnership Won the Cold War*, Santa Monica, Calif.: RAND, MR-190-FF/RC, 1993.

nation's domestic order strongly influences its foreign policy. Hence, this strategy views the spread of market democracy as a device for taming the world and transcending the evil forces of traditional power politics.   Its chief departure from Wilsonian idealism, maintains Lake, is its recognition of constraints on the United States' ability to carry out the full design.   The overarching goal of enlargement, Lake asserted, must not drive the United States into overreaction; priorities will have to be set and distinctions made. Exactly how and where the United States will strike a proper balance were not made clear by Lake.

The feasibility of this strategy will depend on how it is received by foreign countries—by whether they regard it as projecting a compelling moral vision, common goals, and respect for their viewpoints. The inner logic of universal acceptance of enlargement itself is not inevitable.   As outlined by Lake, the strategy can be interpreted as dividing the world into three camps: those countries that already are members of the Western community, those eager to join, and those malevolent rogues that want to remain outside for illegitimate reasons.   Yet the world is not so easily divided into the "good" and the "bad."   States pursue their own interests, and some might want to remain outside the Western community for understandable and valid reasons.

Some foreign governments (e.g., in Eastern Europe) are reacting warmly to the idea of enlargement. But as this strategy's visions become known, others may react with a standoffish or even disdainful attitude. Less inclined to perceive the Western community as a purveyor of ethical standards and material wealth for all, they may adopt a cost-effectiveness calculus that leads them to prefer peaceful relations from the outside. Beyond these states, there will be genuine rogues that reject both market democracy and the Western community, and they can be expected to work hard to prevent enlargement from taking hold.

Enlargement in a Dangerous World

Irrespective of this strategy's selling points in today's world, it will have to be heavily altered if a dangerous world unfolds. Modest enlargements will still be possible in selective cases, but wholesale enlargement will no longer be the central organizing concept of U.S.

policy. Emphasis will shift to the more mundane task of protecting U.S. interests and the Western community from the dangerous forces lurking beyond Alliance borders. Indeed, the United States might have to struggle just to keep the Western Alliance in Europe and Asia together, for one of tomorrow's dangers might be the collapse of this alliance.

An updated form of containment must be emphasized for dealing with events outside the Western community. It will not be containment of a new hegemonic threat but, rather, control of the turbulent forces of anarchy, nationalism, economic strife, geopolitical rivalry, military competition, regional war, and ethnic conflicts. How successfully such turbulent forces can be controlled will largely determine whether the lid is kept on a dangerous world or whether severe conflict and instability give way to chronic violence and war. Success in this regard, in turn, will also determine whether and to what extent market democracy and peaceful conduct spread beyond the Western community and into new regions.

Systemic Containment

Perhaps an appropriate title for a new strategic concept would be "systemic containment" or, alternatively, "peace through global stability." Regardless of the title, the United States would remain heavily engaged abroad. Its core task would no longer be one of prosecuting democracy's inevitable victory. Market democracy would continue to be promoted as a worthy goal, but it would take its place alongside a host of other less idealistic objectives. A philosophy of "first things first" would be adopted, recognizing that before a worldwide community of market democracies can be built, a peaceful foundation of global stability must first be laid. The building blocks of this foundation would include not only economic ties and shared political values but also well-managed security relationships, carefully prepared defenses, and a willingness to deal firmly with adversaries.

Under this concept, the United States would still aspire to progress, but it would recognize that progress comes slowly, in evolutionary phases rather than as instant gratification. It would aim for enduring peace, but it would acknowledge that conflict and war will always exist. It would not try to escape history; rather, it would aim at "nudging" history along in the right directions without loudly proclaiming its own moral supremacy. It would accept its own role as a superpower leader, but without assuming unfair burdens and implausible agendas. The United States thus would seek an optimal mix of activism and restraint that reflects feasibility and affordability. It also would carefully preserve its reputation for effectiveness in security management, a reputation that will be key to dealing with a dangerous world. It would reconcile itself to constant struggle and periodic reversals but would not abandon the hope that has come from Cold War triumph.

An Enduring Strategic Concept

Implied here is a reasoned balance not only between optimism and pessimism but also between idealism and realism, a balance that will compel the United States to abandon both premature hope and sour skepticism in favor of a firm understanding of what is happening abroad. Opportunities and dangers will have to be recognized for what they are and kept in perspective. The United States also will be compelled to adopt a new form of hard-headed realism while setting aside Wilsonian imperatives without discarding the visions of idealism that provide an important framework of goals to be attained. Required here is recognition that realism and idealism can be made to work together by being synthesized. Realism can become a vehicle by which international commitments are effectively carried out, thereby allowing for purposeful idealism to be embraced, with confidence that its goals can be attained. In essence, realism provides the road map and idealism, the destination.

Regardless of its exact intellectual framework, a sophisticated and enduring strategic concept will be needed. The act of building a coherent strategic concept will require the blending of many ideas, most of them representing an upgraded combination of competing views that offer only partial insights. Therefore, a strategic concept that is intellectually sound and politically salable will not come easily. But if a dangerous world beckons, it will have to be developed.

THE WAYS AND MEANS OF NATIONAL SECURITY POLICY

If a dangerous world evolves, the chief problem confronting U.S. policy will be managing great turmoil, much of it taking place in areas outside the Western community and beyond the scope of traditional Cold War interests. Principally involved here are East Central Europe, the Balkans, and Eurasia, as well as emerging trouble spots in Asia and the Middle East/Persian Gulf. What is to be the U.S. stance toward turbulence in these regions, and what is implied for its concrete goals and priorities?

An attempt to address these tough questions must begin with a far-sighted appraisal of American interests. Serious analysis easily dispenses with the canard that an interest-based policy allows for a retreat into a neo-isolationism now that the Cold War has been won. It also rejects the idea that the need for domestic economic renewal justifies wholesale cessation of involvement in international security affairs. If there is a case to be made for disengagement, it arises only if the world is a safe place and will remain safe afterwards. By its very existence, a dangerous world invalidates this case; it poses threats to U.S. interests, thereby pulling U.S. policy toward becoming involved assertively to protect those interests.

Early in the twentieth century, the United States experimented with a policy of domestic growth and international isolationism. The indirect consequence was the outbreak of two world wars, followed by eventual U.S. intervention at great human and material cost. The United States partly repeated the same mistake after World War II, and the consequence was the outbreak of the Cold War, with its four decades of great risk and high cost. These experiences showed conclusively that the United States has vital overseas interests and that it must diligently safeguard them in peace to prevent their being threatened by war.

In World Wars I and II and the Cold War, the United States came perilously close to strategic disasters that would have gravely compromised its security and prosperity, and perhaps its ability to exist as a liberal democracy. How would the world appear today had the German Army not exposed its right flank to French counterattack as it swept into France in August 1914? What would have happened had Hitler not stopped outside Dunkirk in 1940, or wrongly shifted air strategy in the Battle of Britain a few months later, or misplayed his invasion of Russia in 1941? And what if Stalin had invaded defenseless Western Europe anytime between 1945 and 1950? The fact that Western Europe today is democratic and allied to the United States rests on these narrow military events, all of which easily could have taken a different course had luck not intervened. This history is a sobering reminder of the risks that can accompany a policy of remaining aloof from foreign troubles until disaster stares the United States in the face.

The specific dynamics that produced these three conflicts have passed into history, but the looming prospect of a dangerous world means that the underlying causes of global catastrophe have not gone away permanently. Although these conflicts took the form of military confrontation with hegemonic powers, it should be remembered that these powers arose in response to turbulence with deep undercurrents of the type that may be taking shape today. Moreover, enemies were able to commit aggression partly because the Western powers failed to create a stable security framework that blunted enemy designs from the outset. A dangerous world is unlikely to recreate the underlying causes and hegemonies of earlier conflicts, but it may give rise to equally troublesome mutations. The need to prevent new mutations is reason enough for a U.S. policy of engagement.

Even if only strategic interests are allowed into the calculus, neo-isolationism and economic self-absorption are impossible today for two powerful reasons that did not exist a century ago. First is that some countries, including potential adversaries, will possess the nuclear weapons and missiles to destroy the United States. Especially in a dangerous world, this grim reality compels a heavy U.S. overseas involvement to ensure that these weapons are never used against it. The second reason is that 10 to 20 percent of the U.S. economy will be heavily involved in international trade and commerce. Owing to its dependence on a healthy world economy, the United States will not be able to attain domestic recovery and enduring prosperity if international security affairs are unstable: An unstable security environment damages prospects for a healthy world economy and, beyond that, can compel an expensive rearmament that drains money away from domestic investment. International stability is thus a necessary condition for domestic recovery. In a dangerous world, stability can be ensured only if the United States takes powerful steps to preserve it.

U.S. national interests are determined by more than geopolitical imperatives, economic profits, and military calculations. The propagation of democratic values qualifies as a weighty national interest. Granted encouragement of humanitarianism is one contributing motive, but something more tangible is involved than trying to better the lot of mankind or wanting other countries to mimic U.S. values as an end in itself or in response to a sense of historical destiny. Liberal democracy can best flourish in the United States if it also is prospering abroad, especially in countries dealt with regularly and in regions where U.S. geostrategic interests are at stake. Adoption of liberal democracy by other countries does not guarantee perpetual peace, but it does help tilt the odds in favor of peace. It can encourage cooperation in economics, security, and a host of other endeavors. For both reasons, support for the expansion of market democracy makes sense as a practical expression of U.S. interests.

This constellation of interests makes the real national security issue not engagement versus disengagement but determining how far U.S. heavy involvements should extend geographically. Should the United States erect a barrier around the Western community as it exists today, seeking insulation from the turbulence that may engulf areas outside this community? Or should it extend itself beyond this geographic line, becoming heavily entangled in what could become a geopolitical quagmire? Key decisions about U.S. national security policy in a dangerous world will be driven by the choices made between these two alternatives.

Erecting a Barrier

A case can be made for erecting a barrier and hiding behind it. After all, the Cold War ended with the United States in firm control of the regions most vital to its interests: Central Europe, Japan, and Korea in Northeast Asia, and the Persian Gulf oil fields. The Western Alliance and the economic G-7 network form an armature around these regions, thereby drawing key countries into a cooperative bond with the United States. Loss of these regions would be a strategic disaster to U.S. vital interests; provided they are safeguarded, most important U.S. security and economic requirements arguably could be met even if the rest of the world plunges into chaos. Also, these regions seemingly can be protected at affordable cost even if economic times are tough, which adds more merit to this policy.

Extending Geopolitically

Powerful counterarguments pull in the other direction. One argument is that U.S. interests are following the spread of democracy and economic ties with countries in the zone of turmoil are expanding. A second argument is that if the United States can tame this turmoil and draw former adversaries into its orbit, its long-range situation will be further solidified even if costs must be paid in the short run. A third argument draws its inspiration from history, noting that World War I began in the Balkans, that Europe plunged into World War II because of a power vacuum in East Central Europe, and that Asia's descent into World War II began with Japanese aggression in areas originally judged peripheral. By extension, this argument reasons that even if it wants to defend only vital regions, the United States should not repeat the mistakes of its ancestors, who failed to see how events in distant trouble spots could spread outward if not checked.

A fourth argument is that many key U.S. allies do not embrace limited geostrategic horizons and are themselves marching outward in ways that compel the United States to follow or, better yet, lead the way. For example, the European Union may admit the European Free Trade Association (EFTA) states and some East European countries during the coming decade. Because WEU security guarantees will be extended to these nations, NATO will be hard-pressed not to follow suit even if it prefers to defend only its current borders. A similar situation may arise in Asia if Korea unifies and U.S. allies in Northeast Asia join common cause with democratic states in Southeast Asia.

The fifth argument perhaps is the most powerful. It asserts that the world is changing in ways that blur old geographic distinctions and prevent the drawing of lines and building of barriers. This argument rejects a policy of insulation because insulation allegedly will not work. Postulating that even strong barriers will be porous, it asserts that if external turbulence erupts, the Western community will be negatively affected in many ways, including finding its military security threatened. How, this argument asks, can NATO hope to barricade itself from a malevolent Russia, virulent ethno-nationalism in the Balkans, and a new nuclear-armed security alliance in East Central Europe? How can Japan be insulated if a unified Korea acquires nuclear weapons, China seeks military suzerainty in East Asia, and Russia returns to an imperial course? And how can the weak Persian Gulf oil sheikdoms be insulated if Iraq and Iran become expansionist military powers, and if Islamic fundamentalism sweeps over the rest of the region? Because the answers are self-evident, this argument holds that barrier-building will work only when international conditions are sufficiently tranquil to make it pointless. When external conditions are turbulent, insulation will fail because it seeks to avoid problems that cannot be avoided, not solve them.

This argument further asserts that a policy of barrier-building may have the opposite of its intended effect unless it is abandoned the moment its contradictions become apparent. This argument reasons that, if insulation is attempted, the most-exposed members of the Western community will be drawn outward in an effort to control external turbulence. Especially affected are likely to be Germany and Japan, the most prominent U.S. Alliance partners in Europe and Asia. If they are, one of two developments will occur: Either the Western Alliance will respond to the imperatives of these powerful members or it will fall apart because these two countries will withdraw to pursue their own destinies. In the former event, a policy of insulation will have merely proven short-lived. In the latter event, it will have failed in fundamental ways, for it will have created even worse turbulence than it sought to avoid.

If barrier-building will not work, the reason owes heavily to the emerging interests and requirements of U.S. allies. This realization gives rise to another policy option with appeals of its own: devolution. *Devolution* is handing off to allies the task of grappling with external turbulence. The attraction is that the United States would be allowed to avoid the weightiest burdens of the coming era. For all its surface appeal, however, devolution breaks down when its own internal contradictions are exposed: In a dangerous world, it relies too heavily on the performance of allies, whose efforts are likely to be flawed in ways that could come back to haunt the devolver.

Security alliances worked during the Cold War because they had a superpower—the United States—to lead them. In the absence of such leadership, alliances of all kinds tend to fall into impotence even when the task is simply one of protecting borders. This especially is the case when they are composed of a large number of small or medium-sized powers unable to form consensus behind a single plan. This being true, what are the reasons to believe that U.S. allies will act wisely and forcefully if they are entrusted with the responsibility of trying to solve complex problems beyond their own borders? Will Germany and its West European partners mishandle turmoil in East Central Europe, the Balkans, and Russia? Will they worsen the turmoil to the point where the United States must become involved, but too late to make a difference? Will they trigger wars that the United States will have no choice but to fight, on unfavorable terms? Will the same happen if Japan and Korea are left to their own devices in Asia? And what of far weaker Arab partners in the Persian Gulf? The obvious answers to these questions suggest that devolution may bring more trouble than it is worth.

Over 20 years ago, Harvard professor Stanley Hoffmann wrote that the Cold War left the United States caught in a chain gang, vulnerable to its disasters and unable to escape. For different reasons, his apt analogy may apply to a dangerous world, for a new chain gang might be taking shape, one created by the ineluctable logic of policy analysis. If a dangerous world takes shape, U.S. interests will compel the United States to stay heavily engaged in international security affairs, because they cause a high premium to be placed on protecting the existing Western Alliance and economic community, but they do not permit blindness to events outside. Because external turmoil will not confine itself to its origins, the superpower cannot hope to hide behind barriers built along the borders of its alliances. Nor can it have faith in the option of devolving primary responsibility onto its allies. The result is to leave the United States still in the leadership role, chained to a new security agenda of strong imperatives, complex undertakings, sobering risks, and uncertain consequences.[4]

The primary aim of a U.S.-led policy for projecting security involvement outward is to help contain the turbulent instabilities that might otherwise sweep over important regions beyond the Western com-

---

[4]See Stanley Hoffmann, *Gulliver's Troubles; Or, The Setting of American Foreign Policy*, New York: McGraw-Hill, 1968.

munity's borders. One risk is that this effort might fail even after considerable expense. A more worrisome risk is that, by virtue of entanglement in intractable problems, the United States will become exposed to painful reversals or worse consequences. Yet the potential risks and costs of passivity could be far greater. Global stability would be left hostage to dynamics pointed toward great upheaval and conflict, with the potential to severely damage the Western community's security, prosperity, cooperative instincts, and democratic values.

This logic does not mandate an indiscriminate plunge into all zones of turmoil created by a dangerous world. U.S. interests will condition what priorities are set and restraints exercised. Not being able to spend more money than it can afford alone will set limits on what the United States can attempt. Some problems will be so intractable and explosive that it will be best off staying aloof from them; other problems will be amenable to resolution by its allies or will turn out to be less serious than contemplated by pessimistic scenarios. Yet, the United States will be unable to turn a blind eye toward areas that are truly critical; for problems that genuinely threaten international stability, it will not be able to huddle behind barriers or expect its allies to accomplish what it shuns. For these reasons, the logic of policy analysis points down a path that is almost impossible to avoid.

An Activist Policy

Assuming the United States decides in favor of an activist policy, it will need to look beyond the United Nations and other international agencies to handle a dangerous world. In the immediate aftermath of the Cold War's end, considerable emphasis was placed on the UN, CSCE, and similar bodies but is giving way to a sober realization that these institutions are not a global cure-all. They likely will be even less efficacious in a dangerous world, especially if they are not led by an assertive U.S. policy that will bring them to life. They are an *aid* to constructive American leadership, not a substitute for it.

These institutions will continue to have their uses, especially in such areas as peacekeeping, monitoring of arms control accords, and pursuit of truly common causes. But they can work effectively only when there is widespread consensus on the international agenda. Even when the problems being addressed are fairly minor, these in-

stitutions can become paralyzed when participating countries disagree on policies and programs, or are unwilling to contribute their
fair share. More important, these institutions can become irrelevant
when the major powers do not share a common strategic direction.
This lack of common purpose was the reason why these institutions
were not powerfully effective during the Cold War, and it will be the
reason why they are only marginally effective in dealing with a dangerous world.

Because international institutions likely will be a partial solution to
problems, the United States will be required to act as a global superpower. It will not be allowed the luxury of subordinating its role to
that of multilateral bodies that remove the responsibility for authori-
tative national conduct. The United States will be compelled to pursue global stability through a policy that begins with a unilateral
willingness to employ power on behalf of purpose. It will then need
to work with other countries and institutions that share this purpose
and to deal firmly with actors that are opposed.

To carry out this agenda, the United States will need to fashion an
integrated stance toward the three variables discussed in preceding
chapters: the Western Alliance, Western relations with Russia and
China, and growing regional tensions—variables that are so inter-
related that they should be viewed as parts of a whole, requiring
coordinated stances that produce overall coherence and prevent
ineffectiveness or running afoul of each other. If a dangerous world
emerges and the U.S. objective is to deal effectively with it, its goals
and priorities in relation to these three variables in all likelihood will
need to be different from those being embraced today.

From "Russia-First" to "Alliance-First" Policy

Current policy places great emphasis on creating a friendly partnership with a reforming Russia in the hope that this partnership will
contribute decisively to a stable world and the global triumph of
democracy. The realities of a dangerous world most likely will not
permit partnership with Russia to be the centerpiece of U.S. policy.
Indeed, an unreformed Russia may emerge as an adversary and rival.
Even if Russia is not the problem, it probably will be too self-involved
to play a leading role in solving the world's troubles. The United
States therefore will have to look elsewhere for influential friends,

and it will not be able to count on warmly cooperative relations with Russia to ameliorate the problems posed by mounting regional strife. As of mid-1994, the idea of an enduring strategic partnership with Russia was already fading. The prospect of a dangerous world does not eliminate all grounds for cooperation with Russia, but it does further narrow those grounds, and it creates the prospect of outright competition with Russia in some areas.

Priority will need to switch away from singular focus on collaboration with Russia toward a rekindled emphasis on maintaining and refurbishing the Western Alliance, at a minimum to preserve the current capability to defend Alliance borders and to promote cooperative economic policies. But beyond these traditional missions, the demands of a dangerous world will require reformed alliances that can project powerful involvement outward, into regions where instability threatens. What is often called a "Russia-first" policy today thus will give way to an "Alliance-first" policy for tomorrow.

Under this approach, U.S. alliances would be restored to the centerpiece position in its national security policy, but they would play vastly different roles than during the Cold War. The act of transforming alliances so that they can export security will require new policies to be forged for fair burden-sharing, distributions of roles and missions to be altered, and effective decisionmaking to be instituted. Decisions in these crucial areas must reflect the changing distribution of power within alliances that are acquiring greater independent power and for which the United States is no longer willing or able to carry most of the load alone. An equitable balance of influence and responsibility will have to be achieved at the same time that the capacity for effective action is being preserved.

Achieving these goals will not be easy in a dangerous world with characteristics that could erode Alliance cohesion and prevent even imperative reforms. If this Alliance system were to weaken or merely prove unresponsive to new challenges, the United States would be left far less able to cope with a dangerous world. If U.S. alliances were to collapse entirely in the face of great outside turbulence, the result could be a geopolitical tragedy of immense proportions; if U.S. alliances can be made relevant, U.S. burdens will be far lighter and its prospects for achieving global stability far brighter.

Steps Toward an Alliance-First System

Critical to this endeavor will be reform of NATO. This process was initiated at the landmark NATO Summit of 1994, in which important departures were laid down: "Partnership for Peace" and Combined Joint Task Forces. The former called for expanded military ties with European states outside NATO; the latter called for flexibility in creating command arrangements for Western military operations not mounted by NATO. Yet these measures are only small steps in the right direction; they will need to be accompanied by a multiyear effort to reconfigure NATO so that it becomes capable of projecting security and military power outward. As this effort unfolds, it should be accompanied by measures to encourage the emergence of a European security identity under the EU/WEU, but one that preserves the transatlantic bond and helps invigorate NATO, not replaces it. The result will be European allies that work with the United States because a reformed NATO will serve their goals and interests.

Forging a New U.S.–European Bargain. A primary mechanism for building a new NATO thus would be the forging of a new transatlantic bargain between the United States and its European partners, one aimed at reorganizing the West so that it can deal with the East. Under the new bargain, the Europeans would underwrite a stable leadership role for the United States that reflects U.S. interests, responsibilities, and resource contributions to NATO and Europe. In return, the United States would commit itself to an enduring presence in Europe as well as to strong support for European unity within NATO. The United States would still lead NATO, but more influential roles would be gained by the principal allies: Britain, Germany, and France. The United States and these nations would cooperate closely in employing NATO and the EU/WEU to help foster security and democracy in regions outside current Alliance borders. The strategic goal thus would be to reinvigorate NATO so that it can halt Europe's slide into crisis and restore the Continent to the kind of stability needed for progress to occur.

Forging New U.S.–Asia and U.S.–Middle East/Persian Gulf Bargains. Comparable steps will be needed in Asia and the Middle East/Persian Gulf, but they must reflect political realities there. Appropriate U.S. efforts already are under way in both regions; the agenda ahead is to intensify those efforts. The forging of a new trans-Pacific bargain is needed, similar to the U.S.-European bargain, that enables the United States to work with Japan and other key allies to export security and thus stabilize the entire region. As in NATO, this bargain will need to reflect balanced roles and responsibilities for both the United States and its allies. Creation of a large, multilateral Asian alliance similar to NATO is many years away, owing largely to reluctance to accord Japan a leading role. Yet the future may offer opportunities to broaden U.S. bilateral alliances with Japan and Korea so that they can play larger regional roles.

In Southeast Asia, the initial steps toward collective security are being taken. The challenge will be to channel these efforts in a direction that encourages cooperation with the United States and its alliances in Northeast Asia. In the Middle East/Persian Gulf, protection of Western access to Gulf oil remains the dominant strategic priority. The task will be to build upon the successes of Desert Shield and Desert Storm by drawing the Arab sheikdoms into a stronger collective security pact under U.S. leadership while encouraging Arab-Israeli reconciliation in ways that achieve greater security collaboration with the United States.

The alliance measures envisioned here are security initiatives, but they would have to be accompanied by comparable transformations in economic policy aimed at halting the erosion of recent years. Arguably, a peaceful world allows the United States, Japan, and Europe to fall into strategic economic competition with each other, i.e., not the healthy competition of the marketplace but national rivalry borne of self-seeking imperatives. A dangerous world prohibits such a disastrous outcome by potentially lowering the prosperity of all and definitely damaging the security of all by preventing them from cooperating on the new agenda. The overriding security imperatives of a dangerous world thus would compel strategic policies aimed at surmounting economic friction to achieve cooperation in the security realm as well. The goal would be collaborative prosperity for all, so that needed security policies could be crafted to prevent a dangerous world from becoming calamitous.

The cornerstone of a new U.S. national security policy for a dangerous world thus would be restored and transformed alliances with Europe and Japan, along with other Asian partners and friends in the Middle East/Persian Gulf. These renewed alliances would rest on

two reinforcing pillars: security collaboration and economic cooperation. The strategic purpose of these alliances, however, would be
very different from that of the Cold War, when the purpose was self-
protection. In a dangerous world, the purpose would be to radiate
security and democratic community outward, thereby not only
warding off new threats to Alliance members' safety but also promoting stability in turbulent regions beyond their borders in ways that
enable their own values to take hold.

A new U.S. security policy for a dangerous world thus would avoid
the temptation to bypass global management by seeking solutions in
Moscow. Above all, it would not sacrifice core interests of existing
U.S. alliances to curry favor from Russia. Instead, it would establish a
conceptual anchor in its alliances: Using them as a principal foundation, it would endeavor to project activist involvement ever farther
outward. When feasible and appropriate, new market democracies
would be added. But the goal would not be expanded membership
for its own sake, especially when new members might dilute Alliance
effectiveness. Instead, the goal would be a steadily enlarging zone of
stability, security, and democratic prosperity to create a widening
geostrategic buffer for the Western Alliance and greater safety for
neighboring democracies and to steadily shrink zones of turbulence.
To draw an analogy, U.S. policy would aim to push the wolf away
from its doorsteps and steadily drive him backward into the woods.

The rationale for this policy is to combine practical geopolitics with
idealism. The United States' most reliable partners are its closest allies, not countries that were formerly bitter adversaries and that, in
the best of circumstances, will become full-fledged democratic partners only many years from now. Its first priority, therefore, should
be to support the aspirations and requirements of its allies.
Outward-looking U.S. interests tend to be most vital in the regions
immediately adjoining its Alliance borders, and the best candidates
for market democracy and benign foreign policies tend to be
reforming nations located there, especially in East Central Europe,
Southeast Asia, and parts of the Middle East and Persian Gulf. U.S.
assistance efforts would be focused on such countries, particularly
those that express need for U.S. support on the basis of reciprocity,
and would employ the help of its allies. Other countries would
receive help when U.S. interests dictate, when the cost is affordable,

and when assistance would be effective. Nonetheless, U.S. priorities would be decided by a philosophy of "first things first."

Russia and China in U.S. Policy

Although no longer centerpieces, Russia and China would continue to figure importantly in U.S. policy, but differently than they do today. In the best case, in which one or both countries emerge as peaceful democracies, a substantial partnership with them will be possible, and zones of security responsibility can be established. In essence, Russia and China could be encouraged to promote cooperative democracy around their peripheries. By dampening regional tensions, the combination of their democratic zones and the Western Alliance might work together to bring far greater stability to a dangerous world than would exist otherwise. In the worst case, confrontational global hostility with Russia and China would create a far less tranquil situation, and U.S. policy toward them would reacquire many of the features of the Cold War: containment, deterrence, and organized defense planning.

The most likely case in a dangerous world is a traditional geopolitical rivalry with quasi-authoritarian governments in Russia and China, brought about by their pursuit of tough-minded but pragmatic policies guided by their national interests. If the West is faced with the Slavic and Confucian equivalents of Gaullism,[5] close partnership with Russia and China would not be feasible. But deep animosity need not be the outcome. A political equilibrium marked by an ever-shifting pattern of limited rivalry and limited cooperation is an achievable goal. Permanent peace and community with Russia and China would not be gained, but the likelihood of war would be low, provided security issues are managed competently.

If equilibrium is the goal, a mixed U.S. policy would seem appropriate. It would embody a combination of inducements and pressures, levers needed in combination to deal with Russia because use of one lever without the other is likely to fail. Owing to Russia's history and fears of encirclement, heavy-handed Western efforts to coerce that

---

[5] *Gaullism* denotes an especially boisterous and vocal promotion of the national interest à la Charles de Gaulle in France.

nation in ways that violate its legitimate interests would produce a vengeful backlash. Yet experience has also taught that appeasement does not work; indeed, appeasement tends to encourage Russia's aggressiveness. In the troubled years ahead, it may damage prospects for democratic reform by suggesting Western willingness to acquiesce to a hard-line Russian foreign policy. What applies to Russia also will apply to China if that country pursues an aggressive foreign policy. For both countries, a balanced Western approach, embodying firmness and restraint, makes best sense in a dangerous world.

If both nations continue to pursue market democracy, their efforts would receive Western help. Yet if market democracy is not the outcome, both countries would receive the fair treatment normally accorded to sovereign states, provided their foreign policies are responsible and their domestic policies meet humanitarian standards. They would be welcomed participants in negotiating security affairs and economics in Europe and Asia. Political conflicts would be resolved through bargaining and fair compromise, not with threats or use of force.

Success at achieving equilibrium would depend partly on whether common ground can be found between the United States and these two nations. A more important variable would be the stances adopted by Russia and China toward the United States' closest allies—Germany and the European Union in Europe; Japan and Korea in Asia—as well as toward the small and vulnerable states along the borders of Russia and China. In Europe, the key zones are East Central Europe, the Balkans, and the territory of the former Soviet Union. In Asia, Taiwan and Southeast Asia would be key. Because Alliance commitments and democratic values would place sharp limits on the flexibility of the United States to tilt toward Moscow and Beijing, equilibrium could be achieved only if Russia and China show restraint toward their neighbors.

The search for equilibrium thus could not take the form of Western acquiescence to empires reconstituted through coercion or to "zones of special influence" as this term is understood in the language of *realpolitik*. Such conduct by Russia would be inappropriate not only because it tramples the rights of neighboring states but also because it rearranges the political geography of Europe, raising the specter of a renewed Russian military threat to the Western Alliance and its friends.   Especially to be avoided is formation of a new Commonwealth of Independent States (CIS) military bloc led by Russia and equipped with an offensive military strategy and force posture oriented to projecting power westward.

Key to avoiding this outcome will be Ukraine's success at keeping its independence from Russian domination. If Ukraine were to fall under Russian sway in ways leading to a unified CIS military bloc, NATO would quickly be pulled eastward and compelled to admit new members and create counterbalancing military arrangements. Almost inevitably, the result would be a redivision of Europe into two camps, a new confrontation along the Bug River, and a renewed Cold War. A similar outcome could unfold in Asia if China were to extend its political control and military presence outward. To avoid these outcomes, political equilibrium requires that Russia and China respect Western geopolitical interests, as well as the rights of neighboring states granted by the UN charter, international law, and other agreements.

Legitimate Equilibrium

What would constitute a legitimate equilibrium? It would be initiated by providing guidelines for shaping the military establishments of Russia and China. Both countries can be expected to be sizable military powers, but their forces would be based within their borders and would be subjected to limitations that reduce the threat posed to neighboring states and U.S. interests. Both countries would be called upon to honor arms control agreements and to embrace defensive military strategies and commensurate force postures. Ruled out would be capabilities to project overwhelming power that would permit either country to conduct sweeping invasions through neighboring regions. Also, both countries would be discouraged from proliferating military bases far beyond their territory in ways that would enable prompt deployment of offensive forces.

In Europe, a legitimate equilibrium would take the form of the following security structure: A still-cohesive and modestly expanded NATO and EU (e.g., inclusion of the Visegrad countries); a band of neutral but secure countries in East Central Europe and the Balkans; and, to the east, a loosely integrated Commonwealth of Independent States led by Russia. Within the CIS, member states would be allowed whatever degree of sovereignty and independence is sought by their governments. The Baltic states and Ukraine would remain free and outside Russia's orbit. In Asia, a legitimate equilibrium would enable China to play an influential role. However, Japan would remain a leading power, Korea would retain its freedom, and other states along China's periphery would enjoy sovereignty and independence from outside coercion. Most important, China would act in ways that respect the security of its neighbors and the geopolitical interests of the United States and its closest allies.

The concept of legitimate equilibrium would also govern the policies of Russia and China in other regions. Both countries could be expected to play influential and, it is hoped, constructive roles. In any event, the United States would not be prepared to acquiesce to malevolent and destabilizing conduct by Russia and China, especially in the Middle East/Persian Gulf. The essence of a traditional geopolitical relationship implies somewhat differing interests in key regions and makes inevitable a degree of incompatibility in agendas. In a dangerous world, the United States could not rely on partnership-like cooperation from Russia and China in assisting its policies and should expect periodic opposition from them. In both the regions of their involvement and the nature of their conduct, the concept of legitimate equilibrium would be violated if they were to sell offensive weapons to regional adversaries of the United States, or to forge provocative alliances, or to encourage destabilizing conduct by local powers.

In the event of illegitimate conduct by Russia and China, U.S. policy would call for stiff resistance and counterpressure. Aggressive counteraction would be mounted when either country showed disrespect for legitimate Western interests, proper codes of conduct, and the need for fair compromise. Pressures could be applied through political means, including public exposure, mobilization of world opinion, encouragement of opposition, and withdrawal of support for diplomatic agendas deemed important by them. Economic sanctions also could be employed, including denial of access to Western aid, markets, technology, and technical assistance. Military force would be available, but it would be regarded as a last resort for use only in political extremity.

Against the background of a forthcoming but firm diplomacy toward Russia and China, the Western Alliance would always endeavor to maintain stable balances of military power in Europe and Asia. In doing so, the West would draw a sharp distinction between balance of power as a situation and as a philosophy. It would endorse the former and disavow the latter. That is, it would aspire to military balance as a situational state of affairs that helps encourage political stability, but it would refrain from manipulative conduct designed to intimidate or coerce. The goal would be to promote a calm atmosphere and to avoid suspicion and competition.

The Western Alliance would avoid creating new forms of military containment, deterrence, and defense. It especially would refrain from fashioning new geographic lines of confrontation and from seeking military supremacy, a threatening offensive posture, a competitive edge, or coercive control over Russia and China. Instead, the West would acknowledge the reality that Russia and China will remain militarily strong and that this strength will have political overtones. Accordingly, the West would maintain military forces whose defensive capabilities roughly match the strength of Russia and China in critical dimensions. The intent would be to fulfill Alliance security commitments, to create overall equality, to reassure vulnerable states of their security, and to dissuade Russia and China from malevolent conduct. Russia and China, therefore, would reappear in U.S. national security planning as countries to be influenced in a dangerous world.

U.S. Approach to Regional Turbulence

These policies for U.S. alliances and relations with Russia and China provide the framework for shaping the U.S. approach to regional turbulence in Europe, Asia, and the Middle East/Persian Gulf. Critics today allege that U.S. policy in this arena is confused, erratic, and caught between conflicting impulses: intervening when involvement is unwise and refraining from intervening when detachment is shortsighted. In a dangerous world and with limited resources, the United States will definitely require a focused policy that sets its priorities straight and calls the right shots, which will require that humanitarian values be supplemented by a keen-minded sense of geopolitics.

Although the ideal goal would be to eradicate regional turmoil through democratic reforms, economic prosperity, and effective social policies, such cures are unlikely to be attained because of the multifaceted causes of turmoil in a dangerous world. Common sense dictates that efforts should be launched to suppress the destructive impulses of virulent ethnic nationalism, cultural antagonisms, economic greed, and atavistic irredentism. Common sense also dictates, however, that these efforts may prove largely fruitless. Yet, if the United States cannot save regional hot spots from themselves, it can hope to prevent them from consuming the rest of the world. Predominant emphasis will have to be placed on containing such turmoil and on preventing it from escalating in size and geographic scope, thereby drawing in a widening radius of nations, including the major powers. This admittedly is a pragmatic agenda of limited horizons, but it is the one that best corresponds to irreversible realities.

Obviously, prevention of nuclear proliferation ranks at the top of U.S. priorities, followed by control of conventional proliferation and competitive military rivalries. Yet this military agenda must be accompanied by a political strategy that reflects sensible priorities and goals. U.S. policy should focus most heavily on regional conflicts that menace vital Western interests, seriously threaten escalation, or threaten to set dangerous precedents. Within individual regions, U.S. efforts should aim at dampening political polarization, multipolar dynamics, cross-border aggression, and untrammelled civil war. Equally important, the United States should aspire to prevent turbulent regions from infecting each other and from becoming either the cause of major-power rivalries or the stage for playing out such rivalries.

The act of keeping local turbulence isolated may be more important than halting the turbulence itself. Although some forms of regional turmoil are gravely threatening in themselves—e.g., aggression against the Persian Gulf oil fields or North Korean use of nuclear weapons—the risk for the majority of cases lies in their propensity to trigger a chain reaction of escalations. Such a process can begin when local turbulence spreads outward to contaminate an entire region and several major powers then intervene but fall into conflict themselves because of incompatible agendas and larger rivalries. The combination of regional turmoil and major-power antagonism spreads to other regions, thereby triggering even greater struggle among the major powers.

The principal risk is not that a single crisis explodes into world war with blinding speed but that a slower-motion descent evolves over a period of months and years. The ultimate outcome can be an unstable international system racked by multiple regional conflicts amid a setting of deep antagonism among the great powers: a system poised to re-create 1914's disaster on a global scale. The stage for World War I was set by 20 years of limited crises that never led to war but bred frustration and anger.

What may matter most for the United States is the ability to regularly break the chain, thereby preventing small problems from becoming far bigger ones in a global setting whose destabilizing dynamics are not fully understood. Doing so today is not especially difficult because the firing mechanisms for escalation are not yet cocked. Tomorrow may prove another story if a dangerous world appears on the scene: Tensions almost everywhere can create multiple paths to escalation if they are somehow brought together, if rivalry among the major powers is overlaid on seething regional tensions in Europe, Asia, and the Middle East/Persian Gulf.

Breaking the chain does not imply that the United States and its allies should steer clear of involvement in regional crises. A hallmark of sound superpower conduct in a multipolar era will be the ability of the United States to husband its resources and pick its involvements carefully. Impulsive interventions that lack geopolitical reasoning may bring unnecessary casualties, squander domestic consensus, damage America's reputation, and produce negative consequences. Intervention may be needed to protect Western interests, to resolve local conflicts, and to prevent escalation from occurring. Each situation must therefore be judged on its own merits.

Mandate of Skill at Crisis Management. What the future will mandate is great skill at crisis management, guided by diplomacy and military strategy that grasp not only the local issues but also the larger ramifications. Bosnia has been difficult enough in itself, but it would be far more difficult if it had evolved in a setting of troubled Western relations with Russia: The principal difference between

1914 and now is that the major powers had big stakes in the Balkans then; as yet, they do not have equivalent stakes today.

Even if some crises are purely local affairs, first and foremost their management will require clear goals that are then used to shape and coordinate all actions that flow from them. Experience shows that success is achievable even in difficult situations when the goal is clear; failure often results when the objective is blurred. The U.S. goal will vary from situation to situation: to carry out an agreed-upon peace accord, to enforce an accord against opposition, to rebuff an adversary, to protect an aggrieved party, or to enforce international codes of conduct.

A second component of crisis management is making all policy actions work together under the mantle of a coherent strategy to achieve the desired end. Regardless of the instruments chosen, they must form an integrated whole and offer the prospect of a successful outcome in an acceptable period of time. The actions must be feasible, effective, capable of sustaining the consensual support of all who participate, and affordable in ways ensuring that the gain will be worth the cost.

Coherent Relationship Between Means and Ends of Crisis Management. The statement that crisis management requires a coherent relationship between means and ends may seem trite, yet history shows how easily this standard is violated and the tragic consequences. Bosnia is a classic example. From the outset, the Western nations were unclear about their own Balkan interests in ways leaving them torn between involvement and detachment, and between advocacy and neutrality. As a result, they intervened enough to get themselves entangled but not powerfully enough to resolve the situation. Accompanying this half-hearted involvement came a paralyzing debate over objectives, with some arguing for a compromise that partly rewarded Serbian aggression and others favoring full restoration of Bosnia's territory.

Out of this debate came a muddled compromise. The Western nations pursued a diplomacy animated by ambitious goals, applying powerful economic sanctions against Serbia. But they also displayed great reluctance to apply military forces for anything beyond humanitarian aid. Peacekeepers were sent, a large airlift was mounted to deliver food and medical supplies, and NATO warplanes patrolled the skies to keep the Serbian air force on the ground. Although air strikes against Serbian ground targets were threatened, they were launched late and in limited ways, and the Western powers declined to give weapons to the outgunned Bosnians. As a result, Western intervention provided some succor to the Bosnians but did little to staunch Serbian aggression.

Lacking the military resolve to carry out their ambitious political agenda but unwilling to scale back that agenda, the Western nations experienced a dispiriting setback: In the face of mounting but impotent Western outrage, ethnic cleansing escalated. Not only did Bosnia steadily disappear from the map as violence spread across the entire area, but the Western nations suffered a loss to their reputation.

The need to balance means and ends will be important for purely local crises; it will be doubly important for management of crises that have broader ramifications. The risk of escalating crises and runaway multipolar dynamics leading to unintended war may become the most worrisome characteristic of a dangerous world. No single problem will be fatal in itself, and no single country will pose the overwhelming menace of Nazi Germany or the former USSR. What will bring about potential fatality is the combination of several unstable regions and medium-grade rivalries among major powers that interact with the effect of pouring fuel on smoldering coals. The consequence can be higher levels of political tension than need be the case, but the larger danger is that of an explosive war of vastly greater proportions than dictated by the spark that initially sets it off.

Summary

In summary, the U.S. national security policy sketched here is less appealing than the vision of global market democracy, close friendship with former adversaries, and permanent peace that remains popular in many quarters today. But it has the advantage of being in contact intellectually with the realities of a dangerous world. It also has the advantage of laying down goals and priorities that are internally consistent and that add up to a coherent whole. Equally important, this policy is feasible and affordable even as the United States focuses on domestic renewal. It stands a reasonable chance of succeeding in ways that are crucial. To be sure, it will require sustained commitment, effective action, and painful sacrifice. But that is the price of superpower leadership in a dangerous world, and it may be the price of survival in the way the United States wants to survive.

This policy calls upon the United States to maintain and upgrade its existing alliances, to manage relationships of traditional geopolitical rivalry with Russia and China so that a peaceful equilibrium is preserved, and to control regional strife so that international stability is not endangered. Although this may not be an inspiring vision to some, it will allow the United States to protect its vital overseas interests without sacrificing its domestic agenda. It will also give the international system—or at least its critical parts—a chance to cope and to survive the storms of a dangerous world. In the meantime, it offers the opportunity to continue nudging forward the cause of democracy, market capitalism, and peaceful community. It does not allow the United States to escape history, but it does provide a vehicle for safe passage through history's next phase in ways that keep alive hope for slow progress.

If a policy and strategy of this sort are mandated by the situation, a critical issue will be whether the United States is able to muster the resources and internal consensus to carry them out. The resource equation will be heavily influenced by the exact requirements that evolve, but the health of the U.S. economy will also play a critical role. If growth remains slow, lack of federal revenues, budgetary deficits, and competing priorities could all conspire to prevent commitment of adequate resources to the U.S. international agenda. But if sustained growth is achieved, a great deal more will be affordable. Domestic economic recovery thus will continue to be a key variable in the ability of the United States to play the strategic role required by a dangerous world.

Internal consensus must also be labelled as an uncertain variable for the future. The disasters of the early twentieth century dispelled the earlier public opinion that disengagement and isolationism are viable options. The United States established a good track record for constancy of purpose during the long Cold War. Even the Vietnam setback did not produce a wholesale swing into withdrawal. By the early 1980s, the United States was leading the Western Alliance toward strategic resurgence. Yet in recent years, preoccupation with domestic priorities has led to some slackening of American internationalism.

This trend by no means is destined to accelerate, yet the record also suggests that the American people and government become most committed to internationalism when a moral crusade beckons and slacken off when the cause is less clear. For good or ill, the future may offer no compelling ideological causes. It will require a policy aimed at protecting U.S. interests and allies, and at advancing U.S. democratic values and the cause of global stability. But these goals may lack emotional appeal, and there likely will be no single mortal enemy to galvanize anger and focus U.S. efforts. In the final analysis, the kind of dangerous world envisioned here will require the United States to act as a *traditional geopolitical power*: a nation aware of its values but not on a global crusade, and willing to exert power in situations that are sometimes clear but are often ambiguous. Will the American people and their government be able to muster this kind of political maturity? The answer will determine the United States' ability to carry out the policy and strategy required by a dangerous world.

Even if the United States does its part, success for this policy is by no means ensured. This policy requires farsighted cooperation by U.S. allies, as well as respect for the dictates of equilibrium by Russia and China even as they pursue their interests in sometimes-unfriendly ways. It also requires strong efforts by beleaguered regional states to solve their problems for themselves. If these requirements are not met, then an even less ambitious U.S. policy will have to be forged. But if other states do their part, success can be attained and global stability will be the better for the effort.

Perhaps something better can be fashioned. But if so, what? At issue here is not superstructure, for the policy offered here is not a fixed blueprint but a flexible creation whose specific features can be altered. At issue here is the underlying foundation: this policy's core strategic concept, goals, and priorities. Also at issue is relative performance, not expectations of perfection. As with any approach, this policy's objectives will not be fully achievable, but the policy is robust in the sense that even partial success may be sufficient for U.S. purposes. Again, would an alternative policy provide better results or equivalent results at lower cost? The daunting realities of a dangerous world make the task of designing a superior national security policy far from easy.

Equally daunting is the task of forming both a superior military strategy and a force posture. Before the policy and posture can be formed, we must examine the fundamentals that will guide their formation. Chapter Six analyzes the fundamentals of military power in a dangerous world.

THE ROLE OF MILITARY POWER IN
A DANGEROUS WORLD

The degree to which strategic scenarios of instability and violence may occur will be influenced by the distribution of military power in tomorrow's world. Although forecasts of the military future are rendered unreliable by profound political uncertainty in an era of drastic change and upheaval, and by hard-to-decipher interactions of economic trends with technological developments, such efforts are not futile. Certain fundamentals provide usable guidelines for forecasting.

Three variables especially will shape the military distribution and its implications:

- **The level of armaments.** The widespread availability of large and well-equipped military forces—nuclear forces for some, but conventional forces for many—will provide the physical ingredients for aggression. The converse will temper aggression.

- **The nature and degree of military competition among neighboring states.** Competition typically emerges when one or more countries prepare their forces to carry out offensive military strategies and others develop counteroffensive strategies and forces of their own. The result is an action-reaction cycle leading to the emergence of power-projection forces arrayed against each other. The absence of competitive rivalry promotes stability; its existence promotes instability.

- **The degree to which competitive rivalries are marked by a relative balance or imbalance of military power.** Balance exists when forces are equally distributed in ways that deny both sides confidence that aggression will succeed. Imbalance exists when forces are unequally distributed, thereby allowing for confidence that aggression can succeed. Military balance enhances political stability; imbalance weakens it.

This chapter maintains that, if a dangerous world evolves in the form of the strategic scenarios discussed in Chapter Four, intensified military preparedness will accompany that evolution. Nuclear proliferation might accelerate, and many states will endeavor to deploy strong conventional forces capable of meeting the demands of a troubled time. Growing access to modern technology will enhance the capacity of these forces to wage war and to pursue more diverse political agendas. Consequently, the military dimension of security affairs will acquire even greater importance than it has in today's world. U.S. national security and defense strategy will be confronted with challenges that are both greater than and different from those being experienced today. To identify the specific challenges, however, requires that each of these three variables be examined closely.[1]

This chapter begins by discussing the dynamics of military competition and force imbalances in general. It then discusses nuclear force trends. The heart of the analysis is the subsequent assessment of conventional force trends in Europe, Asia, and the Middle East/Persian Gulf.

THE DYNAMICS OF FUTURE MILITARY COMPETITION

Political Conflict–Military Competition Cycle

Military downsizing has been pursued in Europe since the Cold War ended. However, complete disarmament is not in the offing. Most states are planning to retain large and modern forces that can carry out major combat operations. Traditional border-defense missions are being emphasized, but awareness of the need to be prepared for handling crisis-management situations is leading to a growing emphasis on other missions, ranging from peacekeeping to sizable offensive campaigns. Elsewhere, major downsizing is *not* occurring.

---

[1]Data for current military forces are consistent with the International Institute for Strategic Studies' *The Military Balance* for 1992/1993 (London: Brassey's); future estimates are my own and are based on multiple unclassified sources.

In Asia and the Middle East/Persian Gulf, great attention is being given to the possibility of nuclear proliferation. Even as this debate occurs, the pace of conventional proliferation already is picking up and may intensify in future years. Indeed, many countries are planning to bolster their forces in response to growing economic resources, expanding access to new technologies, pressures to adjust forces to new doctrines, and mounting concern that the future will bring instability to their regions. This global situation provides the backdrop for gauging the military future if interstate political relations deteriorate.

Even today, the anarchy of the international system creates awareness that states rely primarily on their own efforts to achieve security. The resulting sense of isolation and vulnerability that may pervade the many regions lacking collective security guarantees is cause for taking a prudent stance toward defense preparedness, and will be doubly so when international tensions run high: Political conflict can stimulate military competition, which can cause further political tensions. Although budgetary constraints, diplomacy, and arms control accords will have a moderating effect, the incentives to field powerful forces will grow for the simple but compelling reason that a dangerous world mandates such a response.

At a minimum, the quest for defensive sufficiency amid great uncertainty will propel policies in this direction, and the tendency to plan conservatively by maintaining a margin of safety will add further momentum. Some countries—perhaps more than a few—will not be content with a defensive strategy. If they pursue aggressive foreign policy agendas, they will be motivated to pursue offensive strategies and maintain forces capable of major power projection. Potential victims will be compelled to react, thus begetting intensified competition. Surging military rivalry, in turn, will heighten political tensions. Budget constraints and common sense should prevent an upwardly spiraling action-reaction cycle that can end only in explosion. Yet any significant trend toward intensified military rivalry could itself become a powerful, independent variable propelling the march toward a dangerous world.

The exact outcome will depend on how international political trends are manifested. If regional tensions grow, the small and medium powers occupying the affected regions, such as those in the Middle

East/Persian Gulf, Asia, and Europe, will be the ones to rely on strong military forces. But the extent of military competition will be shaped by the degree of political tension in each region. Renewed Western rivalry with Russia and China will affect the major powers, and the outcome will be heavily influenced by the degree to which Russia and China develop power-projection capabilities. In the event that the Western Alliance loses cohesion, the capacity for collective military action will decline. The result, however, might not be disengagement and disarmament but, instead, a drift toward re-nationalized defense policies, unilateral action, and reliance on ad hoc coalitions of the willing. The combination of increased regional tensions, renewed major-power rivalry, and weakened Alliance cohesion could lead to intensified military preparations across the board.

Technological Influences

Future military dynamics also will be shaped by the technological revolution already taking place and seemingly destined to sweep over the globe in the coming decades. Today, only the United States, NATO, and Russia possess the full set of modern communications and intelligence systems that provide up-to-date information on military events almost everywhere. Tomorrow, if new technologies are distributed worldwide, many additional countries will possess these systems and the access to information they provide. Accompanying this revolution will be access to better sensors and munitions. Such technologies will yield weapons of far greater precision and lethality, opening the door to new forms of warfare. Desert Storm might be the forerunner of high-technology conflicts dominated by information, long-range targeting, sophisticated operations, speedy maneuvers, intense attrition, and rapid outcomes.

Imbalance of Resources

Will the outcome be military balance or imbalance? The outcome will be a variable, subject to the interplay of many factors, including U.S. policies and those of other countries. What can be said is that the physical means to build military power—population, money, material, industry and expertise—are not equally distributed, because countries—both globally and within the regions most likely to be the focal points of military rivalry—do not have equal resources.

The natural state of affairs thus is not balance but, instead, imbalance brought about by a panoply of small, medium, and large powers.

Perhaps countervailing dynamics that result in the formation of coalitions with offsetting power will achieve balance. Yet, as noted in Chapter Three, no immutable law of nature dictates this outcome: Indeed, political factors can impede or even prevent it. If the outcome is balance—globally and within key regions—it will owe as much to an improbable accident of nature as to concerted policies pursued by many countries with conflicting agendas. Most likely, a mixed future of balance in some areas but imbalance in others lies ahead. If a dangerous world evolves, it will be accompanied by enough imbalance to make the international system all the more precarious and to make warfare all the more likely.

The continuing prospect of war does not translate, however, into an expectation that the military confrontations of the future will be similar to those of the present. Because the threat of global warfare is not likely to reappear, regional conflicts will continue to predominate. Yet, the combination of cataclysmic political upheaval, a sequence of ever-changing security systems, and newly emerging military imbalances seems likely to produce new forms of regional conflict.

This forecast does not imply that current regional confrontations will pass from the scene (although this could happen). It does mean that additional conflicts might appear, and that the scope for change broadens as analysis peers ever farther into the distant future. One or two decades from now, defense planners may be worried about different wars, in different places, against different enemies, and fought for different reasons. If so, tomorrow's military agenda may bear little resemblance to today's, as the nuclear relationship between the United States and the former Soviet Union illustrates.

NUCLEAR FORCE TRENDS

United States and Russia

The nuclear relationship between the United States and the former Soviet Union was critical in shaping the Cold War. Present trends suggest that a nuclear relationship between the United States and

Russia will be less central to security affairs in the era ahead, provided the two countries do not again fall into full-blown global confrontation. Even if muted geopolitical rivalry emerges, it most likely will not be played out through the vehicle of intense nuclear competition. To be sure, both countries will remain nuclear superpowers. If they are anything less than close partners, their arsenals will be shaped in relation to each other, and some competition will always exist. Moreover, their nuclear force levels will be far smaller than they are now but still sizable. The second Strategic Arms Reduction Talks (START II) accord permits triad postures (i.e., ballistic missiles, aircraft, and nuclear submarines) of about 1000 launchers and 3000 warheads apiece; if additional agreements are reached, each side seems likely to retain several hundred launchers and 1000–2000 warheads. Even so, the great change of the post–Cold War era seems destined to hold firm, with both countries viewing their nuclear arsenals as instruments of self-defense, not as means for prosecuting their international security agendas. Provided this remains the case, nuclear competition will be replaced by accord on the need for stability at the lowest possible force levels.

The United States and Russia currently agree that stability and equality should be the guiding concepts, and emerging trends are not pulling them away from these concepts. The United States will continue to honor commitments for extended nuclear deterrence coverage of its allies in Europe and Asia, although growing confidence in Alliance conventional defense prospects translates into diminished reliance on nuclear weapons to deter nonnuclear aggression. Provided this confidence remains intact and new nuclear threats are not encountered, the old Alliance doctrine of flexible response, which allowed for willingness to cross the nuclear threshold in the initial days of fighting, will increasingly give way to a new doctrine of defensive last resort, as is already manifested in the U.S. decision to retire most of its tactical nuclear arsenal. The new doctrine will acquire greater importance as precision-guided conventional weapons become available in ever-greater numbers, thereby further reducing reliance on nuclear targeting plans.

Similar to the United States, Russia has a powerful incentive to avoid intercontinental nuclear war. Its stance toward tactical nuclear war is less clear. During the Cold War, the former USSR's huge conventional posture seemed to obviate any need for early resort to nuclear weapons, provided the threshold was not crossed first by NATO. The major downsizing now under way in Russia reduces this conventional margin of safety, but the end of the Cold War also lessens the risk that Russia will fight a theaterwide war in Europe or elsewhere.

Yet Russia's new military doctrine does not rule out major war. It allows for military operations not only in defense of Russia's borders but also in pursuit of vital interests beyond those borders. Moreover, this doctrine has embraced NATO's old formula of flexible response, which permits Russia to initiate nuclear escalation if conventional operations are failing. This self-appointed right to escalate applies not only to nuclear-armed opponents but also to nonnuclear adversaries that are allied with nuclear powers.

What is meant by this formulation cannot yet be discerned, and it may amount to little more than rhetoric for domestic consumption: Apart from nuclear-armed China, Russia today faces no major military threat to its borders and it will retain far greater conventional power than its Eurasian neighbors. Yet this formulation may signal a more meaningful shift toward tactical nuclear weapons as compensation for having smaller conventional forces. If so, the cause of nuclear stability will suffer.

Proliferation

The question mark about Russia aside, the chief threat to stability comes from the mounting prospect of proliferation. In addition to the United States and Russia, the nuclear club includes Britain, France, and China—all of which deploy small or medium-sized arsenals intended for national defense. Ukraine has 176 MIRVed ICBMs (multiple independently targetable reentry vehicle–carried intercontinental ballistic missiles) on its soil plus 564 bomber-carried cruise missiles, but it does not exercise operational control over them. Under pressure to join the START Treaty and Non-Proliferation Treaty (NPT) accords, it has pledged to yield them over the coming 3–7 years. A few other countries possess (or are rumored to possess) nuclear warheads and at least primitive delivery systems, but none deploys the combination of many warheads, missiles, and bombers that are needed to form a full-fledged arsenal.

The looming risk is that this situation will change in the years ahead through proliferation by several states. China probably will become a major nuclear power by deploying more ICBMs and possibly SSBN/SLBMs (nuclear-powered submarines armed with ballistic missiles). Many observers fear that serious nuclear arsenals also will be developed by Israel, Iraq, Iran, Libya, India, Pakistan, North Korea, and others. If these states join the nuclear club, then pressures will mount for others to do likewise.

The incentives will be highest for countries that do not benefit from Western collective security guarantees, because they do not enjoy nuclear deterrence coverage from Alliance partners. For these countries, prudent defensive intent alone could be motive enough for a decision to go nuclear—especially if such weapons are acquired by neighboring adversaries. In the extreme case, proliferation thus could spread outward to countries that, in today's environment, are not regarded as potential candidates for this step. Therefore, although the Middle East/Persian Gulf and South Asia are the regions looked upon as the most likely sources of proliferation today, in tomorrow's world, other regions could become candidates as well.

Asia is a particular concern. The fear that North Korea may become a nuclear power and China may increase its arsenal may motivate Japan, South Korea, and Taiwan to enter the nuclear club. Although such motivation is reduced because all three are aligned with the United States, these countries would be unlikely to hesitate to join if American security assurances were doubted. Europe, too, could become a focal point because a power vacuum has emerged in East Central Europe since the Cold War's end, depriving several countries of security assurances. Ukraine today is the test case. If this power vacuum persists amid mounting turmoil, other countries have the industrial technology and political skill to acquire nuclear weapons for themselves. The greatest shock to stability would be nuclear acquisition by Germany, a likely signal that Germany is drawing away from NATO to again play a freewheeling role in Central Europe.

Even if the worst fails to transpire, the nuclear club could expand by two- or threefold. Although few countries are likely to acquire intercontinental arsenals capable of striking the United States, even short-to-medium-range delivery systems would pose a grave threat to regional stability. Adding further danger is that, whereas current nuclear powers are states that strive to maintain the status quo, some new nuclear powers may seek to upset the political status quo and may be inclined to use nuclear weapons not only for self-defense but also on behalf of aggressive foreign policy agendas or for outright military conquest or even genocide.

How much proliferation will occur is uncertain. Efforts are under way to strengthen NPT controls against it, and most states share the commitment to physically prevent the spread of nuclear weapons through the International Atomic Energy Agency (IAEA) and other mechanisms. Yet aversion to proliferation is not universal. Possession of nuclear weapons has attractions of its own: Nuclear weapons can provide instant status and recognition far beyond what normally are possible, can offer a major upsurge of military power, and can be a viable way not only to bully vulnerable neighbors but also to hold larger powers at bay. Awareness of proliferation's negative effects comes only when the likely counteractions of other states are taken into account. Their Cold War experience causes Western countries to view nuclear weapons through this lens, a perspective not necessarily shared by all other states.

Proliferation is driven not only by stressful interstate relations that give rise to a perceived need for nuclear weapons even in the face of international disapproval but also by access to production technology. As more states acquire modern industrial economies, access to nuclear materials and production facilities will grow. Recent experience shows that international controls can be circumvented. The key issue will be whether these states will want to avail themselves of the opportunities at their disposal, a decision that will be based on a political and strategic calculus. Owing to destabilizing political and economic trends, the risk of widespread proliferation will increase if a dangerous world evolves—more so if ethnic hatreds and ultra-nationalism give rise to an upsurge of political extremism that damages prospects for international cooperation and self-restraint.

If proliferation occurs, it will become a cause, not merely a consequence, of a dangerous world by further exacerbating interstate frictions. Whereas control of proliferation is most needed when political tensions are high, it is least easily accomplished in this situation. If one state circumvents NPT controls, other states gain greater political latitude for doing so. Access to nuclear weapons, in turn, tends to further polarize political relations, especially when neighboring states already harbor deep distrust for each other.

Widespread Proliferation

If widespread proliferation occurs, international security affairs will be propelled toward greater instability and higher volatility. Even in peacetime, regional dynamics will be marked by greater political stress and military competition. In theory, nuclear weapons can dampen the propensity to crisis. But they can do so only if these weapons are distributed to all participants in balanced ways that promote mutual deterrence and are controlled by rational actors.

The most worrisome risk is that nuclear weapons will come to be held by irrational, rogue powers surrounded by vulnerable neighbors. Yet even if rationality and balance prevail, mutual deterrence works only if the arsenals of adversarial powers are capable of withstanding surprise attack and then retaliating. Unfortunately, second-strike deterrence is far harder to achieve than merely deploying a nuclear arsenal that can be used for a first strike. Vulnerability to surprise can create compelling incentives for preventive war even for prudent-minded governments.

For these reasons, widespread proliferation means that the frequency of crises likely will increase. If so, the potential consequence is a regional nuclear war, and perhaps more than one. Beyond doubt, this development would add a new dimension to military conflict in the coming era, and it would confront U.S. defense planning with a different type of challenge than is being faced today.[2]

Other Instruments of Mass Destruction

The spread of other instruments of mass destruction would have similar negative consequences. Gas warfare and biological warfare are mounting concerns, and the necessary capabilities are more easily acquired than nuclear weapons. As was shown in the Persian Gulf

---

[2]See Marc Dean Millot, Roger Molander, and Peter A. Wilson, *"The Day After . . ."* *Study: Nuclear Proliferation in the Post–Cold War World*, Volume II, *Main Report*, Santa Monica, Calif.: RAND, MR-253-AF, 1993.

War, there are worrisome signs that some countries are becoming willing to use both instruments against their neighbors. Like nuclear weapons, these weapons' use is not restricted to the battlefield: They can be employed by organized military forces and by terrorists, not only against military forces but also against vulnerable urban areas.

CONVENTIONAL-FORCE TRENDS IN EUROPE AND EURASIA

Although public attention is focused on nuclear proliferation, an equally important drama is unfolding behind the scenes as many countries plan their future conventional forces—the forces that primarily will be called upon to fight the wars in the future. Bosnia shows that even brutal attrition war is not outmoded, and the Persian Gulf conflict illuminates the advantage of having well-equipped forces capable of carrying out modern doctrine. Indeed, the world may be entering an era in which offensive strategy and forces will dominate the defense and some conflicts can be won quickly and decisively. If so, this development will have major implications if a dangerous world evolves: It will enhance the incentives for resorting to force.

At a minimum, emerging trends in conventional armaments expand the opportunities for war. One reason is that the ongoing revolution in technology is making conventional weapons more lethal and affordable so that small forces might be able to accomplish great victories. This possibility negates the earlier belief that massive armies are necessary for major campaigns. In the future, even small countries may be able to think big if they succeed in capitalizing on weaponry trends. Equally important, modern ground forces can move longer distances faster than in the past, and airpower is closer to realizing its long-awaited promise of becoming a strategic instrument in itself. Naval forces, too, are developing a better capacity for blue-water operations and distant projection. As a result, states will become more able to apply military force against countries that once were deemed too distant to worry about.

Today, Western forces have the edge in modern equipment, and they will retain that edge somewhat in the future. But whereas this advantage enhances their confidence in future conflicts, it does not always guarantee success; history shows that victory and defeat are determined by more than equipment. Nor does the West's modernity edge imply that the worldwide propensity for violence is somehow reduced, especially when conflicts are those in which Western forces will not be involved. Even if regarded as outdated by the West, the current weapons of other countries are capable of inflicting immense destruction, especially when used against each other.

What matters in war is not the absolute level of modernity but the *relative* level. Armies with older but functional weapons can overpower forces with obsolescent systems. Over the coming years, moreover, many countries can be expected to acquire modern arsenals of their own. Their equipment may never match that of the United States, but this does not mean that they will be uncompetitive on the modern battlefield. To the extent that a growing number of states become competitive, the risk of war will mount.

For all these reasons, global conventional military trends always merit close scrutiny, especially if a dangerous world evolves. The following questions must be asked during such scrutiny: What is the situation today and where does it seem headed? What are the implications for the overall level of force, for the prospect of competitive rivalries, and for whether balance or instability will be the outcome? This review will address these questions region by region. It begins with Europe. Fashionable consensus that other regions are becoming more important than Europe notwithstanding, the military and geopolitical balance there will have a key bearing on the global picture. Whereas a stable Europe will have a calming effect worldwide, an unstable Europe marked by renewed military competition will have an outward ripple effect toward instability. The analysis will then consider Asia, especially the emerging balance of power in Northeast Asia, and will conclude with a discussion of the Middle East/Persian Gulf. The situations in these three regions do not define the globe, but they will shape the globe's military superstructure.

Europe—NATO

In Europe, NATO today is the Continent's premier military organization. Combining the power of 16 nations under U.S. leadership and an integrated command, it will remain so provided it retains its cohesion and adapts to the new era. NATO exited the Cold War with a multinational posture in Europe of about 80 divisions, 5200 combat aircraft, and 550 major naval combatants.   This total included 330,000 U.S. troops, with 5 Army division-equivalents, 500 combat aircraft, and the 6th Fleet in the Mediterranean. Heavily concentrated in Central Europe, NATO's posture was also distributed along the arc stretching from Norway to Turkey. About 60 percent of this posture could be considered modern and ready; the remainder—primarily along the southern flank—is less well prepared.[3]

With the goal of retaining sufficient forces for the new era, a major downsizing is now under way. Ground forces are being reduced by about 33 percent, and sizable numbers of remaining units are being transferred into reserve status. Air forces are being reduced by about 25 percent, and naval forces are being pared by about 15 percent. U.S. forces in Europe are being reduced by about two-thirds. All these reductions will leave NATO with about 53 mobilizable divisions, 4000 combat aircraft, and 470 major surface combatants: still an impressive total. Future plans call for readiness and sustainability levels attuned to the new situation, and for a slow-paced but, it is hoped, adequate modernization. If defense budgets fall below required levels, emphasis probably will be placed on modernization at the expense of the other pillars. NATO thus intends to retain its qualitative edge in modern equipment and technology.

NATO's strategic contribution to European and global stability will be determined by its future military horizons. At the moment, NATO is an alliance for defense of its own borders; its emerging plans for force downsizing and reconfiguration reflect this continuing mission. Yet NATO's borders are unlikely to be directly threatened in the coming era. The principal threats to stability will lie outside, in the unstable geostrategic regions stretching from East Central Europe and the Balkans through the Middle East and Persian Gulf. At issue is whether NATO will develop the military forces and political consensus to enable security intervention in these areas.

NATO's present capabilities for power projection are not nearly as impressive as those for border defense, but an effort is under way to

---

[3]For more detail, see Richard L. Kugler, *U.S.–West European Cooperation in Out-of-Area Operations: Problems and Prospects,* Santa Monica, Calif.: RAND, MR-349-USDP, 1994.

improve them. Current military assets are defined primarily by NATO's Rapid-Reaction Force (RRF), which totals 10 divisions, 360 combat aircraft, and comparable naval forces. In theory, this force is large enough to conduct a mini–Desert Storm, but the reality is less impressive. The RRF is drawn from 10 different nations and thus lacks a cohesive central mass. Also lacking are the command structure, mobile logistics, transport assets, and war reserve stocks to project this force outside the NATO area and sustain intense combat. What this posture offers is a smorgasbord of assets from which small portions can be selected *à la carte*, thus providing flexible diversity at the expense of mass. In essence, NATO today is capable of projecting about 1 ground corps and somewhat larger air and naval assets, which are enough for a modest single mission (e.g., peacekeeping) but are not sufficient to fight a major war or to address two smaller contingencies at once.

The improvement efforts now under way are multifaceted. Under prodding from NATO headquarters, numerous West European nations are trying to strengthen their forces for power projection. Although Britain and France today are the best prepared, both are pursuing measures to strengthen their current capacity to project about 1 division and 1–2 air wings apiece. Also trying to improve are the three Low Countries, but each will be capable of deploying only small forces: about 1 brigade and 1 air squadron apiece. Key to the future will be Germany, whose Cold War focus on border defense results in today's capacity to deploy only 1–2 battalions abroad. Current German plans aim for a larger capacity of 1 division and 1–2 air wings. If all these plans are carried out, NATO forces will improve slowly.

Improvements also are being registered in NATO's command structure. NATO previously relied on the integrated command for all operations. This approach required hard-to-reach unanimous consent for the launching of missions outside NATO's borders. To provide greater flexibility, NATO has now embraced a plan to fashion Combined Joint Task Forces for these missions, which will enable coalitions of the willing to form quickly and to draw upon common NATO assets in such critical areas as planning, intelligence, communications, transport, and logistics. Impetus will be added by emerging efforts to assemble a West European Union (WEU) force and to build the Eurocorps, both of which will be available for border defense and power projection, under either NATO or another agreed-upon command. When these measures are accomplished, NATO will have greater flexibility. It will be able to act under the integrated command or in ad hoc fashion and to respond when U.S. forces are committed or when only West European forces are involved.

Impetus also will come from emerging efforts to draw closer to East European nations that want to associate with NATO. Most affected will be the Visegrad nations of Poland, Hungary, the Czech Republic, and perhaps Slovakia. Under the recently adopted "Partnership for Peace" plan—which is aimed at better enabling East European forces to conduct a range of missions, including crisis management, with NATO forces—NATO will engage in planning, exercises, and other defense cooperative activities with these and other countries. Over the long term, the plan will improve the NATO forces' capability to operate in East Central Europe. This trend will accelerate if the Visegrad nations achieve their goal of formally joining NATO and thereby gaining Article 5 assurances that NATO will defend the borders of new members, and it will be obligated to adjust its military posture accordingly.

Such concerted action requires a coherent strategic plan, and strategic plans are hard to form in the absence of a clear destination. Previous NATO improvement measures have benefited from a known destination. The ultimate political and military goals of the current effort have not yet been defined. NATO thus has determined its strategic direction—outward and eastward—but it has not yet decided exactly where it wants to travel. Until it does so, its defense planning will be uncertain and will be rendered more so by a lack of consensus within the Alliance.

Therefore, although NATO is not a major military power in regions outside its borders, if a dangerous world emerges and Europe is threatened, the odds for a stronger NATO response will increase. But another weighty issue will loom large: Will the pace of improvement be fast enough to meet the growing security challenges and expanding commitments? The answer to this question will have an important bearing on whether Europe remains stable or plunges into instability. Because Europe lacks other credible collective security institutions, a militarily potent NATO is needed even today to help contain turbulence and lessen power vacuums outside the Alliance's current borders. If this type of NATO is not created, turbulence will be less contained, power vacuums will not be filled, and Europe's stability will suffer—all the more so in the event of a dangerous world.

Eurasia—Russia

Russian military power also will be important to shaping security arrangements in Europe and on its periphery. If a dangerous world evolves, this power may be part of the problem, not the solution. Even if Russia reappears as a potential menace, the degree of threat will depend on its foreign policy: a traditional geopolitical agenda will be far less troubling than xenophobic nationalism. Regardless, Russia will never again be able to field the huge Cold War army of over 200 divisions that threatened to overrun all of Europe as well as other regions, aided by a dominating presence outside the USSR's borders and by the Warsaw Pact.[4] But the more limited capacity to pursue aggression around Russia's periphery—the "near abroad," including East Central Europe—would be a formidable security problem in itself. Russia appears likely to acquire this capacity, not now, but in the years ahead.

The forecast that Russia may reappear as a military power of at least regional potency flies in the face of contemporary expectations and is inconsistent with Russia's current condition. But it is not inconsistent with the atmosphere of a dangerous world, which would elevate Russian insecurity and fears of encirclement. Nor is it at odds with Russia's rich tradition of military prowess and amply demonstrated capacity to rebound from reversals, nor in today's atmosphere with the military plans for recovery that Russia already is laying down. To paraphrase Bismarck, Russia is never as strong or as weak as it appears to be. Both aspects must be kept in mind.

On paper, Russia today still has a large and well-equipped conventional posture on its soil of about 90 Army divisions, 3700 combat

---

[4]During the Cold War, the Soviet Union had a population of 270 million and spent 15 percent of its gross national product (GNP) on defense. Russia has a population of 150 million and will spend only 6–7 percent on defense.

aircraft, and a sizable navy. Three powerful constraints, however, bar the way to fully using this force to carry out an external agenda along Europe's periphery. The first constraint is that only a portion of this force is based in the western military districts around Moscow: 30–40 divisions and 1300 combat aircraft. Most of the rest are deployed in the Siberian Far East and, short of laborious effort to move them westward, are not available for use in the "near abroad." Even if this effort were mounted, the process would take months and would require use of rail and transport assets that are badly needed to help shore up the faltering Russian economy.

A second, equal constraint is the lack of Russian forces based on foreign soil. Russian forces no longer are deployed in Eastern Europe; although a presence is still maintained in the Baltic states, it is slated for elimination. As a result, Russia no longer is capable of launching short-warning military operations in the heart of Europe: Indeed, it is barred from direct physical access to Europe by Belarus and Ukraine. Where Russian forces are still deployed outside Russian soil is in the southern republics of the Commonwealth. Deployed in the Caucasus are 12 divisions and 330 combat aircraft. Deployed in the five republics of Central Asia are 14 divisions and 850 combat aircraft. Most of these forces are jointly controlled by Russia and the host republic under Commonwealth auspices and, today, provide Russia with powerful levers for intervention in the internal affairs of the host states. Whether these republics distance themselves from Russia and take over forces on their soil or become more tightly integrated into the Commonwealth in ways that lead to a perpetual Russian presence will determine the future of the Eurasian security order.

The third and perhaps most important constraint is that the Russian military at home and abroad has suffered a catastrophic decline in readiness since 1991. Unit manning is far down, owing to poor recruitment and reduced draftee inductions. Reports suggest that enlisted ranks are now no larger than the officer and noncommissioned officer (NCO) corps. If true, losses of this magnitude can cripple an army. Combat training is negligible. Army units report little money for exercises. Air force units evidently are not flying enough to ensure safety, much less combat proficiency. The Russian Navy mostly is confined to port. Maintenance has declined badly. Some weapons (e.g., tanks) can withstand periods of poor care, but sensitive equipment items (e.g., electronics) require constant care and are unusable when proper standards are not met.

Procurement and modernization have fallen off because of declining funds. Whereas major weapons were annually produced by the thousands during the Cold War, today only a few are being procured: not enough even to compensate for normal obsolescence and attrition. Morale is bad and cohesion is worse, owing to low pay, inflation, poor housing, job insecurity, and declining status for the military in Russian society. Evidently, the sense of decay and pessimism has spread from the enlisted ranks to the officer corps, thereby threatening the wholesale loss of personnel with critical skills. Beyond this, Russia's defense industry is evaporating because of the ongoing economic upheaval as the transition to capitalism is pursued. Because the military-industrial sector was bloated during the Cold War, some loss can be absorbed; after a point, essential assets are lost, thereby constraining any quick recovery.

As a result, the Russian military today is not capable of large-scale offensive combat operations or a vigorous modernization effort. Yet Russian military power should not be entirely written off, especially for limited endeavors. Russian forces today are active in Tajikistan, Moldova, and Georgia. They still guard Russia's borders, airspace, and offshore waters. If used in small numbers (e.g., company and battalion level), Russian Army units can be employed for proactive missions: either to maintain domestic order or to coerce neighboring foreign governments. Beyond this, evidently, the Russians have kept up the readiness of 3–4 airborne divisions, 2–3 other divisions, and several tactical air regiments. Some other lower-readiness units probably could be upgraded quickly by reassigning personnel from other units and by focusing training funds on them. These forces provide Russia with a strategic reserve of at least modest proportions.

Russia, therefore, has military options. Much will depend on the effectiveness of the opposition. Subjecting the "near abroad" to force is far less demanding than opposing the U.S. Army or NATO, especially when military force is applied selectively and is used along with economic and other coercive measures for political effect. Although Ukraine has been endowed with impressive defense assets, most of the now-independent states of the former Soviet Union are in dire military straits. As a result, these states do not share the widespread impression that Russian military power is dead. Indeed, many worry about what may lie ahead if the recent swing toward a more aggressive Russian foreign policy gathers force.

Russian political and economic trends will direct the future. If democratic reforms continue, increasing calls for a halt to disarmament may be blunted. Yet Russia has always fielded a strong army, which plays an important integrating role in Russian society. Even Yeltsin and other reformers have been supporting the military in response to pressure from hardliners, whose own strength was bolstered in the parliamentary elections of late 1993. If a dangerous world produces even modest authoritarianism and a neo-imperial foreign policy, the effect will be to strengthen the role of military power in Russia's strategic calculus. If fascism were to gain power and promote a xenophobic foreign policy aimed at coercively reuniting the former Soviet Union and intimidating other nations, the effect would be even more pronounced.

In all cases, the health of the Russian economy will have a strong bearing on Russia's military. A perpetually weak economy will prevent military recovery. Free-market reforms will promote such recovery by making more resources available for it. Thus, the combination of a right-wing authoritarian government, an imperial foreign policy, and a robust capitalist economy would be most likely to restore Russian military power.

Even in the tenuous atmosphere of today, senior Russian officers are laying plans for military stabilization and eventual recovery. Marshal Pavel Grachev's new statement on military doctrine asserts that a powerful military posture will be needed to fulfill Russia's security requirements. Grachev makes clear that the military will serve the federal state and constitution, and that its primary intent is to protect Russia's borders and internal social order. But his new doctrine also acknowledges that military force can be used beyond Russia's borders in support of national interests.[5]

Grachev's vision, moreover, calls for highly modern forces, equipped with state-of-the-art weapons and designed to carry out strategies

---

[5]See Marshal Pavel Grachev, *Main Provisions of the Military Doctrine of the Russian Federation*, Moscow: Russian Ministry of Defense, 1993.

and tactics similar to those of the West's best forces. His doctrine suggests that the Russian military has learned from Desert Storm to discard the old emphasis on massive forces and plodding operations in favor of greater emphasis on airpower, smaller forces, mobile operations, high technology, precision-strike weapons, combined arms, and sophisticated maneuvers that blend firepower and maneuver. In essence, Grachev intends to replace the bludgeon with the rapier. Some of these changes are evolutionary departures from the doctrine of the Cold War. To a degree, the Russian military may be planning to mimic U.S. thinking on force size, weapons, and doctrine. To the extent that it succeeds, it will build an impressive posture—equal to that of any enemy force it might encounter. Success in this endeavor will definitely allow Russia's forces to project power beyond their borders. (See Chapters Seven and Eight.)

Grachev's doctrine lays down unclear strategic concepts for guiding this military rebirth. But it clearly anticipates an "all-azimuth" focus; that is, Russia intends to be able to defend against threats from all directions but is agnostic about the relative importance of each threat. Russian commentators often point to threats from the south, evidently responding to the prospect of localized violence in the Caucasus and Central Asia. China is a far more likely source of an organized invasion of Russia, and a threat from Japan is another possibility. Although Grachev proclaims that NATO is not viewed as an adversary, Russian planners evidently are privately examining contingencies for a NATO invasion of their soil. In any event, Grachev embraces the idea of being prepared for large-scale operations. Apparently his plans call for the capability to conduct multidivisional campaigns of "field army" level, with as many as three field armies in operation at any one time.

Decisions have not yet been made on the size and disposition of the defense posture needed to carry out this doctrine. Manpower guidelines have called for no more than 1 percent of the population to be in military service, which equates to an active force of 1.5 million. Yet Russian commentators sometimes discuss lower or higher numbers, ranging between 1.25 and 2.0 million. One idea evidently calls for the core of the posture to be a highly ready "mobile command" with two echelons of forces. If adopted, immediate-reaction forces—available within a few days—would be provided by 5 airborne divisions, 1–2 other divisions, and specialized units. Rapid-reaction forces, to be available somewhat later, would include three army corps of 12 divisions and 3–4 air armies. This mobile command therefore would field about 20 divisions and 850 combat aircraft and would be Russia's main instrument for continental operations. A large air defense force would protect Russia's airspace with fighters and surface-to-air missiles. Reduced but still-sizable naval fleets in the North Sea, the Baltic Sea, the Black Sea, and the Far East would defend Russia's seacoast.

These active-duty forces would be backed up by mobilizable reserves, which could swell the size of the army if activated. Assuming about 20 divisions are kept at high readiness, Russian spokesmen have envisioned lower-readiness reserves of an additional 20–30 divisions. Thus, Russia would have a total mobilizable army of 40–50 divisions, most of them heavily equipped as armored and mechanized units, but also with sizable airborne, helicopter, and artillery forces. Basing arrangements for these forces are unclear. Most likely, existing facilities and geographic requirements would interact to call for a scattered pattern whereby about 50 percent of the units are based west of the Urals and the remainder are based in the Siberian Far East.

A key issue is the maximum number of forces that could be made available for operations outside Russian territory if conflict occurs there. Taking into account the need to protect borders and maintain internal control, we estimate that about 50 percent of the posture could be deployed: about 20–25 divisions and 1600 combat aircraft. If so, the bulk of these units could be drawn from active forces, although some call-up of reserves would be necessary. Moreover, Russia would be required to shift some forces from the Far East to European Russia or vice versa, because neither region could be left without troops on homeland soil.

This need to mobilize reserves and to transport forces across large distances could take substantial time and likely would delay the onset of major combat operations for several weeks and months after the initial order had been given. Yet air forces could be used quickly, as could airborne troops and some other ground units. Thus, Russia will have assets for quick-breaking emergencies. Unlike during the Cold War, it will not be capable of launching a large surprise attack on its neighbors.

Will this posture be affordable? Marshal Grachev has said that about 6–7 percent of gross national product (GNP) would be required to fulfill his military plans—a fair estimate, assuming a slow-but-steady economic recovery, but far less than the 15 percent of GNP spent during the Cold War because Russia's posture will be only one-fourth as large as that of the former USSR during the 1980s. However, 6–7 percent is more than the 2–3 percent funding levels envisioned for most Western defense establishments, and it could tax an economy struggling to recover. Some Russian civilian experts have discussed defense spending of no more than 4–5 percent GNP, but it is hard to see how the envisioned posture could be sustained at this level if economic recovery is anything short of robust.

Perhaps the Russian military will wield the political influence needed to gain support for adequate budgets. Nonetheless, the act of recovery will take time. Some observers suggest that fully 10–15 years will be needed. A more reasonable estimate is that many essential steps could be accomplished within 3–5 years of the time that an intensive effort is launched, because bases, infrastructure, and most weapons are already available. The pacing elements are manpower levels, training, readiness, and maintenance. Constraints in these areas cannot be surmounted overnight, but the process will be accomplished more quickly than if more-difficult changes were needed. When this effort will get fully under way is uncertain and is subject to the vagaries of Russian politics. But in all likelihood, Russian forces will slowly improve in the years ahead; by the turn of the century, Russia will be well on the road to becoming a military power to again be reckoned with.

The conventional balance in the former Soviet Union will be defined in terms of how Russian forces compare with those of the newly independent states of the "near abroad." Table 6.1 provides a crude gauge for this comparison. It measures forces in terms of ground division-equivalents in firepower (GDEFs) and air division-equivalents in firepower (ADEFs), assuming that 162 aircraft are roughly equal to a heavy ground division. These two metrics are then combined to yield total division-equivalents in firepower (TDEFs), thus providing a single indicator of joint combat power.

Table 6.1 postulates a Russian projection force of 25 GDEFs and 1000 combat aircraft (9.3 ADEFs), thus yielding a score of 34.3 TDEFs.

Table 6.1

Force Levels in the "Near Abroad"

State	GDEFs	ADEFs	TDEFs
Russia	25.0	9.3	34.3
Baltic States			
Estonia	0.6	0.5	1.1
Latvia	0.6	0.5	1.1
Lithuania	2.0	0.2	2.2
East Central Europe			
Belarus	6.0	1.5	7.5
Ukraine	13.0	3.7	16.7
Moldova	1.0	0	1.0
Caucasus			
Georgia	3.0	1.0	4.0
Armenia	3.0	0	4.0
Azerbaijan	3.0	0.5	3.5
Central Asia			
Kazakhstan	3.6	1.1	4.7
Turkmenistan	2.4	0.3	2.7
Uzbekistan	1.2	0.9	2.1
Tajikistan	1.0	0	1.0
Kyrgystan	0.6	0.8	1.4

NOTE: GDEF = ground division-equivalent in fire-power; ADEF = air division-equivalent in firepower; and TDEF = total division-equivalent in firepower.

Forces for the other states are based on the assumption that all will conform to the Conventional Forces in Europe Treaty (CFE) mandates and keep about 60 percent of the units now on their soil. This estimate seems reasonable, given present trends. No allowance is made for qualitative differences in weapons; because all these states field similar weapons, quality is not a dominating factor.

Stability can be gauged by applying a 1.5:1 ratio to the relationship between Russia and each individual state; that is, instability will occur when Russia enjoys more than a 1.5:1 advantage, a ratio commonly employed by defense planners as a yardstick for determining when an attacking force enjoys a sufficient numerical advantage over the defender to provide confidence of victory. It is based on the premise that a 1:1 ratio is inadequate for the attacker because the defender enjoys inherent advantages (e.g., prepared positions and shorter lines of supply), thereby allowing it to fight somewhat outnumbered. When the ratio is less than 1.5:1, the defender is relatively confident of its ability to repulse an attack; as a result, there is no incentive for aggression.

Even before stability is addressed, what stands out from this table is the high level of armaments that will exist in the former Soviet Union even after CFE and expected drawdowns are fully implemented. Quite apart from Russia, the other states will deploy about 41 heavy divisions and 1782 combat aircraft: close to what NATO planned to use to defend Central Europe during the Cold War. These forces will have an immense potential for violence if employed against each other or within their own countries. This state of affairs makes the danger of interstate conflict and civil war all the more serious.

Moreover, the situation will be one of gross imbalance, owing to Russia's overwhelming superiority over its neighbors, especially in the Baltic states, the Caucasus, and Central Asia, where no single country comes close to a defensive capability against Russia. Even if neighboring states banded together, they still would not be able to defend themselves. Nor could a sizable outside intervention force readily rectify the imbalance. This situation spotlights the military vulnerability of these states not only to direct invasion but also to coercion through measures in which military power plays only a contributing role. Importantly, the economies of these states are integrated with Russia's, which leaves them even more vulnerable. Baltic independence aside, Russia's emerging efforts to reintegrate these states into the Commonwealth and under Russian suzerainty suffers from no lack of powerful levers to accomplish the task.

A less one-sided military situation would apply in East Central Europe if Belarus and Ukraine were to band together, balancing Russian forces. Such joining is unlikely, owing to Belarus' close ties with Russia, and leaves Ukraine vulnerable. In today's world, the balance between Ukraine and Russia is nearly 1:1 because of Ukraine's large forces and Russia's low military readiness. But a drawdown in Ukraine is under way as a result of economic and demographic constraints and will leave Ukraine outnumbered by about 2:1. Ukrainian forces would be capable of putting up a stiff fight and inflicting heavy losses on an invading force, but they probably would lose. Added on top is Ukraine's precarious economic situation and dependence on Russia for energy, industrial goods, and commodities. Ukraine, therefore, must also be counted as a vulnerable state, further adding to instability.

These data do not imply that Russian forces could sweep through the Commonwealth and achieve forcible reintegration in a single campaign. Nor do they imply that a combined campaign of political, economic, and military measures would succeed in a single phase. But they do illustrate that, by focusing its attentions, Russia will enjoy an advantageous position for defeating these states one by one, or a few at a time. Forcible reintegration, of course, might be more trouble than it is worth. It might not be attempted if Russia pursues a tolerant policy or if these states elect to draw close to Russia for reasons of their own. Nevertheless, coercive reunification of the Commonwealth will be a viable strategic option if Russia recovers its internal strength and pursues an imperial policy in the "near abroad."

Eurasia—East Central Europe

Table 6.1 also illustrates the negative military implications for Europe if Commonwealth reunification is achieved. Developments in the Caucasus and Central Asia might not pose a strategic threat, but control over Belarus and Ukraine would again give Russia direct access to East European states. The Visegrad countries and Romania would be especially threatened because the classical invasion corridors to them would be reopened. Moreover, high reintegration might give Russia control of the forces of these Commonwealth states. For example, if one-half of Belarus and Ukrainian forces are added to the ledger, Russia's projection power grows from 34.3 TDEFs to 45.4 TDEFs: nearly a 33 percent increase. The consequence would be even greater instability across all of East Central Europe than will exist from Russian military supremacy alone. These data thus highlight the strategic incentives for measures to help ensure that Ukraine remains an independent state for the strong buffer it provides today between Russia and the democratizing states to the West.

Similar judgments about instability apply when Russian military power is compared with that of the individual states in East Central Europe and the Balkans. Table 6.2 displays force levels that assume

Table 6.2

Force Levels in East Central Europe

State	GDEFs	ADEFs	TDEFs
Russia	25.0	9.3	34.3
East Central Europe			
Belarus	6.0	1.5	7.5
Ukraine	13.0	3.7	16.7
Poland	7.4	3.0	10.4
Czech Republic	3.4	0.9	3.0
Slovakia	2.3	0.7	3.0
Hungary	4.7	1.2	5.9
Moldova	1.0	0	1.0
Balkans			
Romania	6.6	3.0	9.6
Bulgaria	5.8	1.6	7.4
Serbia	5.0	2.0	7.0
Croatia	2.0	0	2.0
Slovenia	1.0	0	1.0
NATO	12.0	4.0	16.0

NOTE: GDEF = ground division-equivalent in fire-power; ADEF = air division-equivalent in firepower; and TDEF = total division-equivalent in firepower.

participating states use 70 pecent of their CFE entitlement to field organized military forces. Again, the 1.5:1 standard provides a measure for instability, not only for these states in relation to Russia but also in relation to each other.

A NATO Rapid-Reaction Force of 12 divisions and 648 aircraft (4 ADEFs) is displayed to help illuminate how NATO forces could contribute to greater stability in this region. If Russia gains physical access to this region, it will preponderate numerically, not only over Ukraine and Belarus but also over all other East Central European and Balkan states—a situation that explains partly why many of the countries are eager to join NATO and benefit from its security assurance. Absent an alliance, they will be unable to defend themselves if Russia reappears as a military threat. Poland is especially exposed, owing to its long eastern border adjoining Belarus and Russian Kaliningrad, the rolling terrain, and the proximity of Warsaw to the border. Hungary and Slovakia are buffered by Ukraine against Russia, but this buffer could be lost if Ukraine is drawn back into

Russia's orbit. If NATO does not provide these countries with satis-factory assurances through the "Partnership for Peace" process, they will face a powerful incentive to form an alliance of their own.

Interestingly, the Visegrad countries together could form a functional conventional deterrent, but they would have no margin of safety, and effective operation of this alliance would require that all four small states jointly stand up to Russia. An alliance between Poland and Ukraine would provide equivalent deterrence, and the other Visegrad countries' being part of that alliance could add extra margin.   If Ukraine and Belarus are drawn back into Russia's orbit, however, the effect would be to leave the Visegrad nations not only physically ex-posed but also militarily vulnerable. These suppositions help explain the complex security politics now unfolding in this region, for absent credible alliance assurances, the East Central military situation will be unbalanced and the consequence will be greater instability.

Imbalance would stem from factors beyond Russia's advantages. For example, Ukraine will enjoy a 1.5:1 advantage or more over all five smaller nations on its western border. Slovakia will be outgunned by neighboring Poland and Hungary. Moldova will be squeezed by Romania and Ukraine. The military situation to the south also merits scrutiny. The countries of Hungary, Romania, Serbia, and Bulgaria all will be in approximate military balance with each other. Yet im-balances could be created if two or more countries form an alliance against a single state. For example, Hungary, Romania, and Serbia form a triangular geographic pattern that invites erratic alliances of two against one. A similar situation exists with Serbia, Romania, and Bulgaria, and the presence of Greece and Turkey nearby adds further potential fuel to competitive alliance dynamics. The military situa-tion in the former Yugoslavia speaks for itself, for it has helped pave the way to the bloody war there.

What do these military mathematics tell us about future security affairs in East Central Europe and the Balkans? Obviously, political-economic factors will dominate the way these countries come to re-late to each other and to Russia. Peaceful relations could be the out-come. Yet all these countries have long track records of struggling with each other over borders, ethnic minorities, status, economic resources, and other issues. At one time or another, virtually every country has waged war with its immediate neighbor, and the history of this region shows a pattern of ever-shifting alliances of convenience and treacherous conduct.[6]   Poland and the Czech Republic enjoy stable relations with each other and with neighboring Germany.   Further to the south, however, the problems of old are coming back to life.   Hungary still resents its loss of territory after World War I, and it faces the problem of a large Hungarian population living in neighboring Slovakia, Romania, and Ukraine.   The Vojvodina area is a breeding ground for ethnic conflict among Serbia, Hungary, and Romania.   The Bosnian tragedy illustrates what might come next, for the entire southern Balkans remains the tinderbox of history.

Summary: The Military Mathematics of Imbalance

The consequences are hard to predict.   What can be concluded is that peaceful democracy will be hard-pressed to survive in an atmosphere of high political tension and deep-seated security anxieties. This is especially the case in countries where democracy is encountering difficulty in establishing itself, but it also is potentially true in countries where recent experience has been more encouraging.   In essence, tension and insecurity invite the return of authoritarian regimes.   By fanning the flames of ethnic hatreds and promoting militarism, authoritarian regimes would be likely to further destabilize the region politically, as has already happened in Serbia and may occur elsewhere.

Overshadowing this turbulent setting is the dark side of Russia's strength and future foreign policy.   In a dangerous world, a malevolent Russia may intrude into this region by encouraging ethnic nationalist hatreds and interstate rivalry as a way to pursue its own expansionist agenda.   Military force could be one instrument of choice in an extremity.   This situation poses the risk not only of Russian meddling and East Central European explosiveness, but the additional risk that Germany, its own political-economic power growing but its faith in NATO diminishing, might enter the fray to secure its eastern flank.   The plausible result could be a mounting political

---

[6]For an overview of these struggles, see F. Stephen Larrabee, *East European Security After the Cold War*, Santa Monica, Calif.: RAND, MR-254-USDP, 1993.

confrontation between Germany and Russia that unravels Europe in the ways it has unravelled before.

The military mathematics of imbalance are relevant precisely because the political situation in this region is inherently so unstable. Power vacuums and military imbalances have contributed to this region's undoing before, and they could do so again. It is here that NATO military power enters the equation. Absent a weighty NATO security role, virtually all countries will be vulnerable. The effect could be to touch off competitive military dynamics that further destabilize an already-volatile situation. Conversely, a powerful NATO presence would alter the military mathematics in the direction of stability, thus lessening the potential for a destructive political explosion and providing a climate in which democracy and peaceful relations can grow.

A NATO projection capability of the magnitude illustrated in Table 6.2 could profoundly calm and reassure all countries in East Central Europe and the Balkans that, if NATO elects to intervene, they will not be vulnerable to their immediate neighbors. Equally important, this NATO force, when joined with the forces of host nations, could powerfully deter Russian military coercion. In particular, Poland would be protected and the vital North Central Plain—the access route to Germany—would be secured. Hungary and Slovakia also would be far better protected, and even Ukraine could draw comfort from NATO. The best way to accomplish this goal would be to bring the most strategically important of these countries into NATO by granting them full membership. Yet membership is meaningless without the military forces needed to carry out security guarantees. Regardless of how NATO acts politically to ensure security and promote democracy to the east, an adequate military projection capability will be a *sine qua non* of its continuation.

CONVENTIONAL-FORCE TRENDS IN ASIA

In today's world, military analysis of Asia focuses mostly on the dangerous confrontation in Korea. In tomorrow's world, Korea will remain important, but the North-South standoff may give way to a reunified Korea, thus bringing about an entirely new geostrategic setting on the peninsula. Irrespective of Korea's future, regional security dynamics in Northeast Asia will be shaped by a larger development: the military relationship among China, Russia, and Japan. Events there will have a ripple effect southward, but the emerging defense policies of other, increasingly prosperous countries will play influential roles as well. An optimistic scenario is that political equilibrium and military balance may be achieved across all of Asia; indeed, a collective security community might emerge. But if old, traditional rivalries reappear to help contribute to a dangerous Asia, the consequence may be not only heightened political tension but also widespread military competition in a multipolar setting.

Korea

At first glance, the military standoff in Korea appears similar to that of two decades ago. In reality, the situation is even more dangerous not only because of the growing threat of nuclear proliferation by North Korea but also because of the DPRK's successful efforts to build an imposing conventional threat. Today's North Korean army totals 40 division-equivalents configured to carry out an offensive strategy (see Table 6.3). Primarily an infantry force configured for Korea's rugged terrain, it is highly ready, deployed well forward, and bolstered by a host of special-purpose units (e.g., commando and river-crossing units). This posture also includes 3000 tanks, 4000 AIFVs/APCs (armored infantry fighting vehicles or armored personnel carriers), 6800 artillery tubes, and 2400 multiple rocket launchers (MRLs)—equipment that is mostly older-generation but well-maintained, serviceable, and of similar vintage to South Korean technology. This combined-arms posture further enhances the DPRK's invasion options. The DPRK air force is composed of 730 mostly older-model combat aircraft but also comprises over 50 Russia-built modern aircraft (e.g., MiG-29s). This posture is intended for air defense but also possesses a limited ground attack capability. The DPRK navy is small and configured primarily for coastal defense; it has a limited capacity for amphibious operations. For all these reasons, North Korea poses a serious offensive threat even if it does not acquire a nuclear arsenal.

Yet South Korea deploys offsetting assets of its own. The ROK Army (ROKA) totals 27 division-equivalents (counting marines) plus large mobilizable reserves that mostly provide rear-area security but can

Table 6.3

Conventional Forces in Korea: 1993

Component	North Korea	South Korea
Division-equivalents	40	27
Tanks	3000	1800
AIFVs/APCs	4000	2550
Artillery tubes/MRLs	9200	4630
Combat aircraft	732	403
Major surface combatants	3	4
Submarines	26	4
Patrol and coastal combatants	379	179

be used to replace casualties to front-line units (Table 6.3). Upgraded in recent years, the ROKA now includes 1800 tanks, 2550 AIFVs/APCs, and 4600 artillery tubes. Although outgunned by North Korea by 1.5:1 or more, the ROKA benefits from well-developed positions on highly defensible terrain. Also, it protects a frontage of only 200 kilometers on the demilitarized zone (DMZ), and it faces a small number of invasion corridors that are narrow and well known. This advantageous situation enables the ROKA to deploy a robust combination of forward defenses and operational reserves, and to focus on predictable axes of attack. The ROK's air force is small, with only 400 combat aircraft; its navy deploys 38 destroyers and frigates plus 80 patrol vessels and is intended for coastal defense. The air force and navy are kept small in response to the assumption that wartime requirements will be fulfilled by large U.S. reinforcements.

Key to assessing the Korean military situation is the wartime contribution of American forces. The U.S. peacetime presence would swell from 1 Army division and 72 combat aircraft to about 6 Army/Marine divisions, 10 USAF fighter wings and 100 bombers, and 4–5 Navy carriers. The effect would be to transform numerical imbalance into balance while giving U.S.–ROK forces major advantages in technology, long-range firepower, and operational sophistication. If the DPRK were to attack, it would suffer major losses in the early battles; it then would face the prospect of crushing defeat from an overpowering U.S.–ROK counterattack. Although prudent analysis cannot rule out an ROKA defeat before large U.S. reinforcements arrive, the principal risk is not that South Korea would be overrun and permanently lost but that the huge capital city of Seoul, critical to the ROK's vitality and located only about 25 miles from the DMZ, might be lost or heavily damaged by an initial surprise assault. Indeed, long-range enemy artillery tubes could pummel Seoul without leaving their current fortified positions. This loss alone would be a staggering reversal.

The current situation can best be labelled "precarious deterrence" made all the more tenuous by doubt that rational calculations will govern North Korean policies. If the near-term dangers can be surmounted, the long-term picture should brighten considerably. The principal reason is that isolated North Korea already is economically incapacitated and will not gain any semblance of prosperity as long as it remains strangled by a totalitarian government, a command economy, and dark-ages policies. Unless the DPRK is given life-saving transfusions of aid from outside powers, its economy will remain stagnant and, eventually, its military power will dwindle as well, or at least not keep pace with that of other countries. The likelihood of outside salvation is low, for both Russia and China seem to have lost faith in their former vassal.

Meanwhile, South Korea is democratizing and continues its remarkable drive toward great economic strength. As it acquires modern technology and a robust defense industry, South Korea's larger population (twice that of the DPRK) and vastly stronger economy will come to dominate the military confrontation. In the years ahead, South Korea can be expected to pull closer to North Korea in military power, and eventually it might gain outright supremacy.

An increasingly probable scenario is that North Korea will collapse and that unification will occur. Unification plausibly could take place slowly, in stages, with confederation as an initial stage. Europe's experience, however, suggests that unification will come quickly because the totalitarian DPRK regime is swept aside, thereby allowing the ROK government to take control of the entire peninsula. Whether achieved slowly or overnight, this outcome would confront the ROK with a monumental rebuilding task exceeding that faced by recently unified Germany's eastern states. This outcome also would fundamentally transform the military situation in ways requiring adoption of an entirely new defense concept. The old task of defending along the DMZ would give way to the new task of protecting

Korea's revised borders. Casting a wary eye on China, Russia, and Japan, a unified Korea would set about the task of reconfiguring its military posture for all-azimuth defense in an era whose stability would depend on overall trends in Asia, not on developments on the peninsula itself.

This profound upheaval would confront the U.S.–ROK security alliance with a challenge similar to that faced by NATO at the Cold War's end. Because unification would have swept away the original military threat, the future would depend on whether there are compelling reasons to preserve the alliance in altered form with new missions. A tranquil situation across Asia might lead to the withdrawal of U.S. forces and the downgrading of the alliance to a loose security accord, one aimed at preserving the option of military reconstitution if events ever warrant that step. By contrast, a tense Asia might lead to a reinvigorated alliance aimed at defending northern Korean borders now threatened by China or Russia. Alternatively, a revamped U.S.–ROK alliance might acquire a larger regional role, one aimed at promoting peacetime stability and at providing a capacity for joint power projection in crises. Regardless of the option selected, major political and military retooling would be needed.

Russia

The critical triangular relationship among Russia, China, and Japan will be shaped by the security and defense policies of these three countries and by how those policies interact. Currently, all three countries are self-absorbed to the point of not pursuing outward-looking security agendas. Yet this stance, and the resultant lack of political conflict among the three, is historically abnormal. If a dangerous Asia takes shape, a primary cause will be some combination of resurgent aggression by Japan and Russia, coupled with the emergence of a powerful China determined to play an influential regional role. As discussed in Chapter Four, this development could give rise to heightened political conflict among these three powers. It also could give rise to altered military strategies and force postures. Currently, all three countries embrace military strategies focused primarily on defense of their borders. The mixture of outward-looking security policies and rivalry with neighbors could lead all three countries to alter this approach in favor of military strategies and force postures that project power outward. Especially if the intent is not only defensive but also to broaden each country's political influence and access to coercive options, the result could be a new and dangerous form of multipolar military rivalry in Asia.

Today, in its Far East military district, Russia deploys a large military posture of 25 divisions, 1000 combat aircraft, 100 naval bombers, 63 submarines, and 54 major surface combatants. During the Cold War, this posture was sufficient to make Russia a major Asian military power. China feared an attack across its northern borders, Japan worried about an attack on Hokkaido, and U.S. forces expected major combat against Russian forces in the event of an all-out global war. In the years ahead, this Russian posture will be reduced appreciably: A 50 percent cut is conceivable. Yet sizable forces will remain, they will be slowly modernized, and they could be reinforced in the event of a war. For these reasons, Russia will remain an Asian power to be reckoned with, albeit in less threatening terms than in the past.

China

China's military evolution will be the key variable in shaping future Asian security dynamics. During the Cold War, China deployed a massive but unready and ill-equipped military establishment that seemingly was more focused on internal control than on outside events. In recent years, China has embarked upon an effort to reduce this establishment and reorganize it around a more modern doctrine. As a result, China today has a smaller army of about 100 divisions deployed rather uniformly across its landmass, but with sizable strength along China's northern borders with Russia. It is still primarily an infantry force for homeland defense, but it includes 10 armored divisions, 8000 tanks, and nearly 20,000 artillery tubes. China's air force is composed of about 4000 combat aircraft, nearly all of which perform air defense missions. Its navy is structured for coastal security and includes 54 surface combatants (destroyers and frigates), 44 tactical submarines, and nearly 900 small patrol craft. This entire posture, however, is in the middle of an important transition, and the future is unclear.

Today's China can defend its territory but still relies more on massive forces than on high technology and sophisticated concepts. Assuming China's vigorous economic growth continues, we predict that the years ahead are likely to witness acquisition of a more professional military with better equipment, which will result in a shift toward modern combined-arms operations, including a capacity for joint air-ground maneuvers.

Although China's landmass would be better defended, the overriding issue is whether this modernization effort will be accompanied by a growing interest and capability for power projection beyond China's borders. This issue will be decided by China's strategic horizons, but the military effects of greater power projection can be outlined. Emergence of a modern but still-large army, backed by an air force capable of attack missions, would pose a direct threat to Asian land-mass countries around China's periphery: Russia, Korea, Southeast Asia, and India. For all its seriousness, this situation would merely intensify what already is a worry for these countries. China's deployment of a blue-water navy that can operate away from China's coastline is the additional development that could fundamentally transform Asian security affairs. China today is pursuing a vigorous naval expansion, but its ultimate objectives are uncertain. Better coastal defense is one priority, yet emerging trends suggest that China is parting company with its traditional image of being a purely continental power. If a blue-water navy is built, China would pose a new threat to Asia's vital sea lines of communication and trade routes. China also might directly menace many offshore countries, including Japan, Taiwan, Malaysia, and Indonesia.

None of these transformations in continental and maritime forces could be achieved easily. All would require years of effort and great expense, and they would have to be accompanied by larger logistics support structures, modern communications and intelligence, new facilities, and access to overseas bases. Not only because of their intrinsic character but also because of the reactions triggered in other countries by these transformations, the outcome would be to help create a more dangerous Asia.

Japan

Particularly affected would be Japan, a country that may be led to develop power-projection capabilities to counter China's transformation and to go beyond it. Prior to its defeat in World War II, Japan possessed a large navy, army, and air force capable of operating in strength across all of Asia. Conquest by U.S. forces brought about complete disarmament, followed later by a Cold War effort to build a conventional posture able to defend Japan but not to project power beyond its shores. Late in the Cold War, Japan agreed to protect nearby sea-lanes to a distance of 1000 kilometers from its shores; this change aside, Japan's military strategy continues to focus on home-land defense. As a result, Japan today deploys an army of 13 small divisions with only 1210 tanks, an air force of only 440 combat air-craft, and a modest navy of 6 destroyers, 58 frigates, and 13 tactical submarines. In addition to its lack of large forces, any Japanese interest in power projection is constrained by the absence of logistics support, bases, and overseas facilities. For these reasons, Japan to-day can protect itself from external aggression, but it lacks the physical capacity to do much else.

Whether Japan will alter its military strategy by adopting a focus on greater power projection remains to be seen. What can be said is that the sheer size and highly industrialized nature of its economy would enable Japan to double or triple defense spending and still spend no more of GNP than do most European countries. Political interest in investments of this magnitude does not exist in today's climate. However, one important fact remains: Japan is a vulnerable island country that depends heavily on outside economic resources and markets. Interest could emerge through some combination of rising Japanese nationalism, reduced confidence in U.S. security guarantees, and a perception of greater threats to Japanese interests in Asia. If it does, Japan would be able to afford the higher defense budgets needed both to defend the homeland and to deploy sizable forces for power projection. Development of a larger navy and air force would be the most probable course of action, but a well-equipped expeditionary army is not beyond the realm of possibility. As with China, this development could not occur overnight; if favor-able political conditions arise, it could unfold over one or two decades.

Northeast Asian Military Competition

If stiff maritime competition among Russia, China, and Japan is to take shape in the years ahead, it will be a result of efforts by all three nations to upgrade their current naval power. Of the three, only Russia is today associated with large naval deployments outside its home waters, and these deployments have recently declined. Even it lacks the full array of air defense and ongoing replenishment assets for major projection missions, especially in wartime. None of these countries will acquire the large carrier task forces, sophisticated air defense/ASW (anti-submarine warfare) systems, and amphibious capabilities of the U.S. Navy. Yet today, these three countries already deploy a total of 172 surface combatants and 120 submarines in Pacific waters: a sizable amount by any standard. Both China and Russia may acquire 1–2 small carriers in the coming decades; if faced with compelling strategic incentives, Japan plausibly might move in this direction as well. Short of this step, large wartime deployments to distant oceans will not be possible. Use of land-based aircraft and cruise missiles, coupled with current-day surface combatants and submarines, however, allows for projection to a distance of about 1000 kilometers from homeland coastlines. This capability alone would enable China to exert control over the western sea approaches to the offshore states, stretching from the Philippines to Japan. A 1000-kilometer arc would also result in overlapping zones of operations in Northeast Asian waters for all three navies.

If all these events transpire, Northeast Asia thus will witness a growing concentration of heavily armed forces equipped with modern technology in the coming two decades. Even defensive strategies aimed at coastal protection and control of commercial sea-lanes could set the stage for vigorous military competition with powerful political overtones. If Russia, China, and Japan pursue offensive strategies and power-projection assets, the incentives for competition would be all the greater.

Whereas the Cold War primarily took the form of a Russian threat to China and Japan, the future could see two-way threats flowing from different directions. Russia might still threaten both countries, but a powerful China could threaten Russian territory as well as the sea lines of communication to Japan. A powerful Japan could pose naval and air threats to the coastlines of China and Russia, and to the Pacific sea-lanes of both countries. During peacetime, the naval forces of all three countries could compete with each other in the Sea of Japan, the Yellow Sea, and the East China Sea. Caught in the middle would be Korea. If unified, however, Korea itself could emerge as a major regional power.

Perhaps this dangerous situation will produce political equilibrium and military balance. Conceivably, all four countries will emerge strong enough to defend themselves but not sufficiently powerful to create incentives to use coercive power against each other. An equally probable outcome is continuing efforts to achieve a margin of supremacy amid a rapidly changing technological scene that might make at least temporary supremacy a viable goal. If the political atmosphere is one of tension brought about by aggresive foreign policy rivalries, the prospect of these four major military powers' competing with each other does not bode well for stability.

Emergence of tense military competition in Northeast Asia, coupled with adoption of influence-seeking agendas by China and Japan, would have a profound ripple effect across all of Asia. Magnifying the effect would be the growing economic strength of other countries, which even today allows many to contemplate a steady military buildup. Taiwan already is well armed, but Malaysia, Singapore, and Indonesia are small military powers defining the critical straits joining the Pacific and Indian Oceans. Reacting to the uncertainty of the post–Cold War era and their own growing economic strength, all three countries are bolstering their military establishments and are showing signs of acquiring power-projection assets of their own. Emergence of potential threats from China and Japan probably would further stimulate these agendas. The outcome would be greater capacities for self-defense, but it also could take the form of growing military competition among these three countries.

Southeast Asia

A similar worried forecast applies to the Southeast Asia landmass, where Thailand and Vietnam today are roughly in balance but look on China and Japan with long-range wariness. Neither of these countries possesses the developed economy that permits a rapid military buildup, but both could be expected to take steps to safeguard themselves against a more threatening environment. For that matter, so would India, whose own aspirations may lead to stronger forces for regional power projection in the years ahead. For all three countries to bolster their forces could heighten tensions across the entire region, not only because of any threat posed by China and Japan but also because these countries, by taking such steps, would threaten each other as well as other neighbors.

Summary: Asia in a Dangerous World

In a dangerous world, Asia thus could face a combination of renewed rivalry among the major powers and tensions among multiple lesser powers. These two trends could make Asia not only politically turbulent but also vulnerable to enhanced military competition that could acquire political momentum of its own. An interactive sequence of increasing political tensions and enhanced military competitiveness could have negative consequences, spreading across all of Asia. Northeast Asia could witness a mounting political-military standoff among Russia, China, and Japan, a confrontation that would be played out not only on the Korean peninsula but also in nearby waters, where the naval forces of all three countries could fall into a competitive triangle involving struggle over control of strategic sealanes. The effects could easily spread to Southeast Asia, a region where local powers might fall into competitive political-military rivalry for reasons of their own.

This dismal forecast of a geostrategic arc of crisis stretching from Northeast Asia to India may be at the outer limits of probability. But because something similar happened before, spanning from 1900 to 1940, a repetition is far from implausible in a dangerous world. Uncontrolled security dynamics of this sort played a major role in creating the conditions that brought about World War II in the Pacific. Many Asian observers fear a repeat of this history if security events are not carefully managed.

The risk of such an Asian future is all the greater because, in contrast to Europe, Asia lacks equivalent collective security guarantees and multilateral alliances. Most Asian countries, consequently, must plan their future defense postures on a unilateral basis, the result of which, ironically, is a strategic situation especially susceptible to the onset of nationalism and multipolar rivalries. An equally probable result is that military imbalances stemming from major disparities in the distribution of economic power will be imposed. Perhaps new security alliances would form, providing the needed stability. But such an outcome did not occur when Asia experienced similar problems before, and it is far from a given in the years ahead.

To an uncertain but important degree, the outcome would be affected by U.S. policies aimed at maintaining a balance of power. Throughout the Cold War, the United States, by its formidable military presence, lent great stability to Asia. But this presence is now declining in response to the Cold War's end, to termination of basing arrangements in the Philippines, and to cutbacks in the U.S. defense posture. If a dangerous Asia evolves, military balance and political stability will depend even more heavily than today on the ability of the United States to retain a still-sizable presence—especially in Northeast Asia and somewhat in Southeast Asia. Absent this presence, a dangerous Asia is likely to witness an even greater propensity for unsettling national agendas, intensified military competition, new security alliances, and other manifestations of spreading instability. With a U.S. military presence targeted at reassuring allies, dissuading potential adversaries, and fostering overall balance, the dangers could still be serious but, at least, more controllable.

CONVENTIONAL-FORCE TRENDS IN THE MIDDLE EAST AND THE PERSIAN GULF

Similar to Asia, the Middle East and the Persian Gulf have the potential to be regions of stiff military competition and an imbalance of power in the years ahead, but for reasons different from those prevailing in Asia. The situation in Asia is one in which a large number of increasingly wealthy countries will be deciding whether to expand their currently limited military postures in anticipation of future political stress. In the Middle East and Persian Gulf, great political tensions already exist. Marked by pre-modern societies and economies, most of the countries are poverty-stricken and lacking outlooks for prosperity anytime soon. Yet many already possess large military postures configured for offensive operations. The central issue is whether they will bolster these arsenals by acquiring modern weapon systems. To the extent that they do, the result will be a region of even greater military competitiveness and potential imbalance than exists today.

Middle East

As Table 6.4 shows, the Middle East arc of political conflict stretching from Algeria to Turkey already is an armed camp. Together, this arc's seven countries host a total of 87 divisions, 19,760 tanks, 41,760 AIFVs/APCs, 12,000 artillery tubes, and 2554 combat aircraft. Most navies are small and focused on coastal defense: The current capacity for maritime competition in the Mediterranean thus is small. Yet the potential for massive ground and air violence is huge, as has been demonstrated by the sequence of four Arab-Israeli wars between 1947 and 1973 and by the always-tense, often-violent, military standoff since then.

Barring a political settlement that brings enduring peace to the region, these force levels are unlikely to change a great deal in the years ahead. They are shaped by a combination of factors that remain relatively constant from one decade to the next: demography, economics, geography, threat perceptions, and military strategy. As a result, virtually all countries will retain options not only for defending themselves but also for coercing their neighbors.

The principal change likely will be a slow, qualitative upgrade brought about by normal replacement of obsolescent systems and affordable modernization. The prospect of significant improvement in Middle East forces is created by access to new technologies: intelligence and communications systems, longer-range missiles and indirect-fire weapons, better air defenses, better logistics support,

Table 6.4

Conventional Forces in the Middle East: 1993

Component	Algeria	Libya	Egypt	Israel	Jordan	Syria	Turkey
Division-equivalents	7	7	16	18	4	13	22
Tanks	1000	2130	3100	3900	1130	4600	3900
AIFVs/APCs	1400	2200	3700	5400	1100	4200	4000
Artillery/MRLs	750	1720	1300	1520	468	2300	4230
Submarines	2	6	4	3	0	3	12
Surface combatants	3	3	5	0	0	2	20
Patrol craft	23	45	39	61	3	30	47
Combat aircraft	242	409	492	662	113	63	573

improved ground attack platforms, and sophisticated sensors and munitions. Whether access to new technologies will bring about a commensurate revolution in doctrine and operations is uncertain. Apart from Israel's, the military establishments of countries in this region do not enjoy reputations for readiness, leadership, morale, sound organization, or battlefield skill. Therefore, they would be unlikely to resort routinely to large-scale offensive campaigns. As much as anything else, this state of affairs has kept the Middle East from being even more explosive than it already is. Yet many Arab countries are slowly undergoing economic and social modernization, changes that could bring about slow-but-steady improvements in military expertise. To the extent this is the case, the outcome could be a greater propensity to military conflict and systematic violence.

In the years ahead, violence is most likely to take the form of ethnic and religious strife in the West Bank, Gaza, and Lebanon. Unstable Arab governments may experience growing internal turmoil, and terrorist attacks against Western Europe and the United States may increase. This localized violence aside, three strategic issues will govern the future:

- The military policies of Algeria, Libya, and Egypt

- The Israeli-Arab military balance

- Turkey's security on its southern flank.

Military Policies of Algeria, Libya, and Egypt. Algeria, Libya, and Egypt are important because they border the Mediterranean sea lines of communication; in addition, Egypt controls access to the Suez Canal, a vital artery to the oil-rich Persian Gulf. Libya already is under the sway of Muammar Qaddafi, and Algeria recently has shown signs of drifting in the direction of Islamic fundamentalism. Egypt today is led by a pro-Western government, but because its society is Islamic, a fundamentalist upheaval is conceivable. If radical Islam were to take hold in all three countries, the North African strategic equation would be transformed, and for reasons that go well beyond the obvious potential for terrorism.

Today, the air, naval, and missile assets of Algeria and Libya are limited, and Egypt's defenses are not pointed northward. But if a drift toward Islamic fundamentalism were to be accompanied by an upgrading and aligning of these three countries' military postures, the three could pose a serious threat to Western control of the Mediterranean as well as the Suez Canal. The outcome could be intensified security competition between NATO and these Arab powers in the Mediterranean, and the regular potential not only for small incidents but also for major military conflict. This prospect by no means is a high-probability event, but it is well within the scope of plausibility in a dangerous world.

Israeli-Arab Military Balance. Today, Israel retains its military supremacy over its Arab neighbors while making diplomatic progress toward easing Arab-Israeli political animosity. Yet this region remains one of deep religious and cultural hatreds. Israel's military supremacy can be attributed primarily to qualitative advantages that can be transient. In population, Israel is outnumbered 13:1 by its immediate Arab neighbors. In military quantity, it trails by a ratio of 2–3:1. Provided Egypt remains at peace with Israel, these numerical advantages are far less serious. Indeed, Israel's military posture is as large as that of its principal rival, Syria. But if Egypt were to fall back into the camp of Arab radicalism, Israel would be reconfronted with the multifront threat from far-larger Arab forces that it faced from 1947 to 1979. If successfully achieved, Arab efforts to close the qualitative gap would then acquire greater menace and could become a forerunner of renewed Arab-Israeli military conflicts. Again, this development is not a high-probability event, but it is not beyond the realm of possibility. If it occurs, Israel might be left more dependent on the United States than it is today.

Security on Turkey's Southern Flank. In a dangerous world of radical Arab fundamentalism, another military hot spot could arise in the form of a threat to Turkey's southern flank. Today, Turkey's forces are large but are not ready and equipped with modern weapons. Turkey's southern border is an unstable ethnic mix, and the region contains water resources that are vital to heavily armed Iraq and Syria. Turbulent Iran also adjoins the Turkish border. Out of this situation plausibly could come a military conflict if Syria, Iraq, and Iran band together to coerce Turkey. This prospect is a serious concern for the West because Turkey is a member of NATO and, therefore, would call for Alliance military help if it is attacked. Large-scale combat operations in southern Turkey would confront NATO with military challenges wholly unlike those faced in the Cold War. NATO today does not possess the infrastructure and transport assets needed to quickly project large forces to this region of Turkey.[7]

Persian Gulf

If the Middle East requires a slide into political extremism to create the conditions for warfare, the same does not apply to the Persian Gulf. Today, Iraq and Iran provide the strategic ambitions for conflict. The risk of violence and warfare is further magnified by the serious imbalance of military power prevailing in the Persian Gulf and by the precarious domestic stability of the Arab sheikdoms there. The result is a region of simmering tensions that could explode in several different ways. Perhaps the situation will stabilize in the years ahead, but the equal risk is that it will worsen from military changes that capitalize on unsettling political, economic, and social trends.

For all their violence, the wars of the past decade have brought temporary military stability to the Persian Gulf. As of the late 1970s, pro-Western Iran had become the region's dominant military power, owing to major U.S. security assistance. The Islamic revolution had the effect of shattering not only Iran's pro-Western demeanor but also its professional defense establishment. Then came the long Iraq-Iran War that inflicted huge casualties on Iran, bled its military arsenal dry, and blunted its expansionist policies. In the aftermath, Iraq emerged dominant, with a battle-tested army, a suite of modern Soviet-built weapons, and a large posture of nearly 60 divisions, 600 aircraft, and modest naval forces for coastal defense. Now able to ignore Iran, Iraq promptly set about to refocus its military strategy on asserting influence over Kuwait and Saudi Arabia. Invasion of Kuwait in late 1990, however, was followed shortly thereafter by a shattering defeat at the hands of the U.S.–led Coalition that wrecked Saddam Hussein's visions of a greater Iraq.

In addition to being expelled from Kuwait, Iraq was left with a battered military posture only a fraction of its original size. Beyond this, its doctrine, weapons, and organization had been exposed as wholly

---

[7]For more detail, see Richard L. Kugler, *NATO Military Strategy for the Post–Cold War Era*, Santa Monica, Calif.: RAND, R-4217-AF, 1992.

inadequate against a powerful Western force. Its air defenses had proven ineffective, those of its combat aircraft that got off the ground were successful only in escaping to Iran, and its small navy was destroyed. Unable to withstand joint air-ground assaults by the Coalition, Iraq's vaunted army had been outflanked and decimated in only 100 hours of combat. The massive Coalition air campaign had also destroyed much of Iraq's logistics support system, military infrastructure, and defense industry. The effect was to leave Iraq with only enough forces to preserve internal control. Saddam Hussein's dictatorial regime survived, but Iraq was finished as a near-term military threat to anyone.

The past three years have seen initial steps by both Iraq and Iran to recover their military strength. The pace has been slowed by their own weak economies and Western diplomatic opposition, yet progress is being made. Neither country is likely to regain the status of a heavily armed regional power anytime soon, but the long term may be another story. The rate of improvement and the ultimate destinations for both countries are major question marks.

Iraq seems likely to maintain its current ground posture of about 30 divisions. It can be expected to marginally enlarge its current air force of 320 combat aircraft and to rebuild its navy. Eventually, it will reconstitute its military infrastructure and defense industry. Iran likely will retain its army of 12 divisions, and it will somewhat expand its air force of 262 combat aircraft and its navy of 3 destroyers, 5 frigates, and 33 coastal combatants. A noteworthy development is its recent efforts to begin building a submarine force that can interdict passage along Gulf waters. If this forecast proves accurate, these force levels, although smaller than in earlier years, will be large enough to allow both countries to contemplate expansionist visions at the expense of the far weaker powers that occupy the Gulf.

Iraq and Iran will be able to pursue expansionism only if they can avoid falling again into bitter rivalry with each other. These two countries are rivals for a host of strategic, cultural, and religious reasons. Notwithstanding Saddam Hussein's brutal regime, Iraqi society is fairly modern, whereas Iran remains locked in Islamic traditionalism. Gulf suzerainty by one presumably can be accomplished only at the expense of the other. Yet both share common enemies in the Western powers and the traditional Arab monarchies on the

Gulf's western shore. If aided by the appearance of more cooperative governments in Baghdad and Tehran, this commonality plausibly could become translated into an ability to coordinate their strategies or, at least, into an agreement not to stand in each other's way. If so, both Iraq and Iran could eventually rebound from their current weakened conditions to again threaten Persian Gulf stability.

An important issue will be whether Iraq and Iran succeed in building modern military postures that can compete with those of Western opponents. As Desert Storm showed, large forces are little help if qualitative differences result in weak air defenses and gross disparities in maneuverability, firepower, and survivability. If Iraq and Iran are to overcome their current disadvantages, they will need to register major gains in professional leadership, training, readiness, technological sophistication, logistics support, cross-country mobility, intelligence and communications, and modern doctrine and tactics. Such gains are neither inexpensive nor easily acquired. Yet over several years, progress can be made slowly, and it can have a cumulative effect. Neither Iraq nor Iran is likely to equal U.S. forces in quality, but they may be able to narrow the current huge gap.

A nightmarish scenario is that Iraq, emboldened by military reconstitution, might again invade Kuwait and not repeat its earlier mistake of stopping at Saudi Arabia's border. An Iraq invasion force of 20–25 divisions would be smaller than the 45 divisions that plunged into Kuwait in 1990. But if they are well prepared and move fast, they could be more militarily effective. A second, murkier scenario is that of internal turbulence in Saudi Arabia and other Arab sheikdoms that permits Iraqi or Iranian intrusion under quasi-legitimate auspices. A third possibility is that Iran might employ its improving air and naval forces to impose a blockade on the Persian Gulf, thereby greatly reducing Western access to Gulf oil. If Iraq and Iran were able to coordinate their actions in these endeavors, they would pose an even greater threat.

The risks ahead will be magnified because all the Arab sheikdoms are small and weakly armed, and they are led by governments that preside over unsettled societies. Militarily, the strongest country is Saudi Arabia. Its forces today number only 4 division-equivalents, 293 combat aircraft, 8 frigates, and 12 patrol craft. Kuwait deploys only 1 division, 72 combat aircraft, and 2 patrol craft. Among them, the four other tiny Arab sheikdoms deploy only about 1 division, 94 combat aircraft, and 30 patrol combatants. These forces provide each country with assets for internal control and a modicum of protection from external invasion, but they are far from adequate for defending against a large threat—and they are unlikely to grow in the years ahead. Although the Arab sheikdoms are more vigilant in the aftermath of Desert Storm, as yet they have neither formed a firm collective security pact nor shown a capacity to closely coordinate their defense strategies. The effect is to leave them still vulnerable to invasion, and still dependent on the United States for support.

The strategic situation confronting the United States thus is unlikely to improve noticeably in the years ahead, and it might worsen. The United States still has vital interests at stake because the West depends on Persian Gulf oil. In contrast to Europe and Asia, the United States will lack a powerful regional alliance capable of helping to defend those interests. Iraq and Iran have been temporarily quashed, but their diminished status is not necessarily permanent. The current equilibrium may give way to threatening military imbalance, political instability, and renewed strategic vulnerability. This state of affairs, at least, is how a dangerous world may manifest itself in the Persian Gulf. The effect will be to enhance the importance of maintaining a capacity to rapidly project strong U.S. power to the Persian Gulf.

THE COMPOSITE PICTURE

This chapter's portrayal of the future military environment in a dangerous world has highlighted several trends that may manifest themselves in the coming era. The threat of widespread nuclear proliferation is especially worrisome, but conventional-force trends may bring unsettling consequences of their own. These developments should be analyzed for their individual features, but they should also be seen as a composite whole, for they will not unfold in isolation. All the key regions of Europe/Eurasia, Asia, and the Middle East/Persian Gulf could be affected by nuclear and conventional trends working together. The consequence could be high levels of armaments, stressful rivalries, and major military imbalances that will manifest themselves regionally but could have a destabilizing global impact.

A dangerous political world could beget a dangerous military world, and the two could reinforce each other, engendering further negative trends.   Whereas the future does not seem likely to produce the threat of global military conflict that impelled the Cold War, it could produce an upsurge of regional conflicts that combine to create the equivalent of global turbulence.   Moreover, the peacetime rivalries, intense crises, and wartime struggles that lie ahead may be very different from those of today.   For this reason alone, the U.S. military future merits close scrutiny.   The next chapter proposes a military strategy for handling the difference, and Chapter Eight offers an approach to U.S. force planning that can accommodate the variety of political and military scenarios set forth in Chapters Four through Six.

Chapter Seven

MILITARY STRATEGY FOR TOMORROW

If a strong defense posture is needed in today's world, it will be doubly important in a dangerous world of tomorrow. Compared to today, peace will be more tenuous, crises more difficult, and wars more frequent. Owing to this grim prospect, military power will acquire greater importance for many countries, including the United States, as Chapter Six has discussed at length. Because of its worldwide involvements, the United States will require substantial military power not only to wage war as a last resort but also to manage crises and to help carry out an activist national security policy in peacetime. Military power thus will play a crucial role as an instrument of diplomacy and security management in a turbulent multipolar world. Today's world may allow the United States to treat military power largely as a sword to be kept sheathed and drawn only in an emergency. But if a dangerous world appears, the United States definitely will not have this luxury tomorrow.

For U.S. military power to be useful in war and peace, it will have to be guided by a sound military strategy. Because tomorrow's world may bear little resemblance to today's, future U.S. strategy might be quite different from the one now embraced. The term *military strategy* would itself have to be defined in enlightened ways. In some quarters, this term is still defined narrowly, as a device to choreograph military operations so that opponents are outwitted in wartime. In a dangerous world, *military strategy* would have to be defined in more comprehensive terms: as a conceptual scheme for relating military means to political and strategic ends in peacetime as well as in wartime. Strategy's wartime role would remain important, but a far larger and more encompassing set of criteria would be applied to determining its characteristics and assessing its performance.

U.S. military strategy would reacquire the scope and importance of its strategy during the Cold War. However, future U.S. strategy will bear little resemblance to the strategy of the Cold War. The future task will be to employ military power in a fluid setting of multipolarity, ambiguity, many different kinds of conflict, and a highly complex U.S. international agenda. Equally important, tomorrow's strategy for a dangerous world will pursue a broader agenda than today's, and it will be guided by different precepts, goals, commitments, requirements, and calculations. An era of strategy change thus may lie ahead. Indeed, the prospect of seasonal changes in global politics may require the United States to periodically shift its strategy in response to newly emerging situations, to become a nation of many different strategies according to the challenges confronting it.

CURRENT U.S. DEFENSE POLICY

Current U.S. defense policy provides a basis for gauging the strategy departures that may lie ahead. The approach endorsed by Les Aspin's *Report of the Bottom-Up Review* lays down sensible security precepts for dealing with today's world, and it also provides an adaptable framework. Nonetheless, the prospect of major international changes in the years ahead implies that this strategy should be regarded as temporary until the future becomes clear. If the world moves toward communal peace, a less vigilant and ready strategy will be needed. But if the global system slides into instability—for reasons that include, but also go far beyond, the failure of market democracy in Russia—even greater vigilance could be required. Precisely how a new strategy might be constructed would depend heavily on the exact features of a dangerous world.

As characterized by the Bottom-Up Review, the new defense strategy is based on the concepts of "Engagement, Prevention, and Partnership." *Engagement* is to be the primary vehicle for protecting traditional, vital U.S. interests, for avoiding the risks of global instability and imbalance, and for shaping the international environment. *Prevention* aims at forestalling dangers by promoting market democracy, economic growth, and peaceful resolution of disputes.

Partnership refers to the goal of maintaining close ties with existing friends and building cooperative relations with former adversaries.

This strategy deems the building of a coalition of democracies as central to its purposes, calling on the United States to remain a leading partner in existing alliances in Europe, East Asia, the Near East, and Southwest Asia. These alliances, however, are to be updated to meet the new conditions ahead. Critical to this adaptation is to be an effort to sustain U.S. leadership at lower cost by crafting fair burden-sharing arrangements. The Bottom-Up Report points out that these alliances provide a security framework within which collaborative economic relations can take place. It also asserts that if major U.S. security contributions are to continue being made, the allies will need to be sensitive to U.S. interests in trade policy, technology transfer, and multinational security operations.

This defense strategy is focused on managing the four dangers that Aspin cites, which are reiterated as follows:

- The spread of nuclear, biological, and chemical weapons

- Aggression by major regional powers or ethnic and religious conflict

- Potential failure of democratic reform in the former Soviet Union and elsewhere

- Potential failure to build a strong and growing U.S. economy.

It emphasizes dealing with nuclear proliferation and a variety of regional conflicts, from major regional contingencies (MRCs) to lesser conflicts requiring peace enforcement and other intervention operations. For major conflicts, it outlines a four-phase approach to U.S. combat operations:

1. Halt the invasion by promptly deploying U.S. combat forces capable of arriving early with sizable combat power.

2. Build up U.S. combat power in the theater while reducing the enemy's power through attrition-inflicting missions by air, land, and sea forces.

3. Decisively defeat the enemy through large-scale joint and combined operations by attacking its centers of gravity, retaking oc-

cupied territory, destroying its war-making potential, and achieving other military objectives.

4. Provide for post-war stability by stationing appropriate forces in the theater of operations.

The Bottom-Up Report uses two roughly concurrent MRCs in the Persian Gulf and Korea as a basis for sizing U.S. combat forces. For each conflict, it proposes an illustrative "building-block" commitment of 4–5 Army divisions, 4–5 Marine brigades, 10 U.S. Air Force (USAF) fighter wings, 100 USAF heavy bombers, 4–5 Navy Carrier Battle Groups (CVBGs), and special operations forces. Reserve component (RC) forces are to augment forces if additional requirements arise. The effect is to create a need for the total force posture endorsed by the Bottom-Up Report, which is to include 10 active Army divisions plus 37 RC brigades at staggered levels of readiness, 3 Marine Expeditionary Forces (MEFs), 20 USAF wings (active and reserve), 11 U.S. Navy (USN) carriers, about 50 attack submarines, and 346 ships.

Compared with the "Regional Defense Strategy" inherited from the Bush Administration, the Clinton defense policy represents continuity rather than a revolutionary departure, for the changes it makes are relatively small. Apart from modest program cutbacks and somewhat greater emphasis on counterproliferation, the previous approach to nuclear deterrence remains largely unchanged. Equally important, the new policy reflects the old strategy's call for a highly ready and modern force posture capable of fighting two major regional conflicts. It also carries forth the military Decisive Force Doctrine, which calls for joint operations to swiftly attain clear objectives at low cost. It places somewhat greater emphasis on airpower as the principal vehicle for rapid projection and initial combat operations, but it makes clear that strong naval and ground forces are needed to carry out all stages of major campaigns. It endorses reliance on combined multilateral operations, but, as with the Bush strategy, it makes clear that the United States must remain capable of unilateral military action.[1]

---

[1]See Secretary of Defense Dick Cheney, *DoD Annual Report for FY1993*, Washington, D.C.: U.S. GPO, 1992.

The chief difference lies in the new policy's call for a smaller conventional posture, but only 10–15 percent smaller than the Bush Administration's Base Force. The new posture will maintain a similar mix of ground, air, and naval forces, but relies more heavily on RC forces to meet requirements not covered by the active posture. The readiness of 15 Army RC brigades is to be increased for this purpose. The Clinton policy de-emphasizes overseas presence by endorsing plans for troop cuts in Europe and Asia. Yet troop strength in each theater is to be kept at a relatively high level of 100,000, thereby providing capabilities for quick reaction and infrastructures for rapid reinforcement. The new policy also calls for increased prepositioning in the Persian Gulf and programs to upgrade strategic airlift and sealift for power projection.

Owing to budget reductions, the Clinton policy calls for slower modernization and defers acquisition of a few expensive tactical air programs. Yet it continues to emphasize the importance of high technology, a strong industrial base, and the need for qualitative superiority over future opponents. It calls for modest changes in service roles and missions aimed at reducing redundancy, yet it largely perpetuates the distribution of labor inherited from the Cold War. The overall effect is a defense strategy similar to that of Bush but with modestly smaller, slightly altered, and less expensive forces.

MORE VIGILANT STRATEGY NEEDED FOR DANGEROUS WORLD

If a more dangerous world arrives, the United States will need to replace the Clinton approach with a more vigilant and ready military strategy attuned to a wider set of troubles and security missions. Because the new strategy will be determined by the exact ways in which danger is manifested, the three key variables analyzed in Chapter Four will influence the outcome: Heightened regional tensions would mandate intensified efforts to deal with the kind of troubles that occupy today's strategy; the emergence of traditional geostrategic rivalry with Russia and China would compel a fundamental departure from U.S. strategy by focusing on new security missions that are a largely peripheral concern for today's strategy; weakened cohesion within the Western Alliance would deprive the United States of important resources that undergird today's strategy and, therefore, would bring about a shift toward greater unilateralism.

The following analysis reflects the strategic scenarios deemed most worthy of scrutiny in Chapter Four. It thus excludes worst-case events as well as bizarre changes in international politics, all of which are too improbable to be analyzed in any depth. Were they to occur, the changes to U.S. military strategy would be even greater than those discussed below.

Strategic Scenario 3

The strategy changes facing the United States would be least sweeping in the event that a dangerous world takes the shape of heightened regional tensions but harmonious relations with Russia and China and a still-cohesive Western Alliance. The United States would not have to worry about opposition from Russia and China as it turns to address growing regional troubles, and it would benefit from strong help provided by its Allies. The easiest departure would be that of altering U.S. strategy to address an upsurge of regional strife in only the Persian Gulf and Northeast Asia, the two regions that U.S. strategy focuses on today. For example, the emergence of greater military threats by Iraq and North Korea could compel the United States to strengthen its peacetime force deployments and reinforcement capabilities for both regions. Yet it would not mandate adoption of entirely different security missions from those of today. The appearance of entirely different military threats and political strife in these two regions would compel greater changes, but continuity would be maintained because U.S. strategy would still be focused primarily on the Persian Gulf and Korea.

Strategic Scenario 1

The United States would face a more demanding challenge if heightened tensions in these two regions are accompanied by a similar upsurge of regional strife in Europe. Such strife could be brought about by the spread of ethnic conflict across the Balkans and the unfolding of destabilizing security dynamics in East Central Europe. Whereas today Europe does not figure centrally in U.S. force sizing, a new strategy would have to be adopted in which intensified security initiatives are launched in Europe without an accompanying downturn in Asia and the Middle East/Persian Gulf. The demands of this new strategy would be more unwieldy than those of today because the United States would be juggling three regional "balls" instead of two. Regardless of the number of challenges involved, heightened regional tensions would allow U.S. strategy to focus on goals similar to those that animate today's strategy.

By contrast, the outbreak of geostrategic rivalry with Russia and China would require a major shifting of strategy gears because a new set of goals and priorities would have to be embraced. Whereas today's strategy does not require a major emphasis on defense preparations in response to these two major powers, rivalry with them would require such planning. It would also virtually put an end to prospects for using the United Nations as a vehicle to carry out major military operations beyond peacekeeping. In most cases, Russia and/or China would use their veto power to block UN intervention in ways that damage their interests. In a dangerous world, the likelihood of NSC agreement would be small for most crises.

Military multilateralism therefore would be carried out primarily through U.S. alliances. At a minimum, the United States would be compelled to work with its European and Asian allies to ensure that a military balance of power is maintained vis-à-vis Russia and China. Even greater preparations would be needed if Russia and China were to fashion offense-oriented strategies and force postures that posed an immediate threat to their neighbors and U.S. interests—all the more so if Russian and Chinese foreign policies acquired an aggressive and imperial cast. The extreme case of violent confrontation with Russia and China is unlikely; if it occurs, the United States could find itself facing political challenges reminiscent of those of the past.

Strategic Scenario 2

As was argued in Chapter Four, the task of balancing Russian and Chinese military power amid a setting of muted political rivalry is the most probable case in a dangerous world. While this task would compel a wholesale shift in U.S. military strategy, such a shift might not be especially onerous if this were the only task to be performed. A far more difficult situation would be that of turning to address rivalry with Russia and China at a time when tensions in two or even all three other principal regions were themselves mounting. This would be the case even if the Western Alliance remains cohesive and is upgraded to meet the new situation, for the United States would be required to play a leadership role. It would not be compelled to carry all the new burdens; however, at a minimum, it would be required to carry its fair share of burdens, which would be weightier than those of today. The task would be further complicated because, whereas today Russia and China do not interfere heavily with U.S. regional policies, they might do so in this variant of a dangerous world. Even short of this, U.S. military strategy would be called upon to juggle five "balls" at once: three similar to those of today, but the other two, quite different.

The new U.S. strategy would no longer be merely "regional," yet it would not be "global" in the sense that this term was used during the Cold War, because the United States would not face the daunting threat of coordinated worldwide aggression led by a superpower Soviet Union. Yet U.S. strategy would be compelled to deal with a multiplicity of regions, dangers, and commitments scattered across the globe. Today's risk of concurrent regional conflicts would increase in intensity with the growing likelihood that adversaries could coordinate their actions. Moreover, regional conflicts would have a greater propensity to escalate if Russia or China were potentially involved. For all these reasons, U.S. military strategy would be at least "quasi-global."

Strategic Scenario 4

A far worse situation would prevail if these downturns are accompanied by a weakening in the cohesion of the Western Alliance. Such weakening would be serious enough if the only problems faced are the regional tensions of today's world. It would be more serious yet if regional tensions are intense and widespread, and still more serious if they are accompanied by Western rivalry with Russia and China. The likelihood of less effective alliances decreases in the face of mounting regional troubles and major-power rivalries, for the natural reaction of Alliance partners would be to band together. Yet, this outcome is not implausible. One potential path is that harmonious relations with Russia and China might result in the loosening of Alliance bonds even as regional troubles mount. Another path would be Alliance erosion in response to internal economic frictions, especially if those frictions increase before regional strife intensifies and relations with Russia and China degrade.

Even if U.S. alliances remain effective for border-defense missions, their failure to adapt to new security challenges beyond borders could leave the United States lacking the partners it needs for dealing with the problems of a dangerous world. At a minimum, the United States could be compelled to deal with mounting regional strife in the absence of close allies; at worst, it could face both regional strife and rivalry with Russia and China without them.

In both cases, the current emphasis on multilateral planning, combined operations, and a well-prepared overseas infrastructure would have to be downgraded. Allies might be available in some contingencies, but their contributions would be offered on an ad hoc basis and could not be relied on in advance. As a result, U.S. military strategy would have to become far more unilateral than it is today, relying primarily on power projection from the continental United States (CONUS) and preparing a largely expeditionary force. Whereas the presence of strong alliances would promote the current U.S. force mix, a shift toward greater reliance on naval strength and strategic mobility forces would logically accompany the absence of alliances. The United States would revisit conditions of the 1930s, when it faced a darkening international scene in the absence of overseas alliances.

CHARACTERISTICS OF U.S. MILITARY STRATEGY

Precepts for conventional defense will themselves undergo an important transformation in this dangerous world. The effects of the altered precepts on U.S. force planning are discussed in Chapter Eight. Here we treat the effect on overarching U.S. conventional strategy.

Peacetime Shaping Function

U.S. military strategy would be key to translating military power into an effective policy instrument in peace, crisis, and war. Therfore, its characteristics merit fuller elaboration. In U.S. strategy for this dangerous world, the so-called shaping function of peacetime would rise from today's modest role to a position of preeminent importance. As originally coined by former Secretary of Defense Cheney, the *shaping function* referred largely to the act of coping with local regional troubles while preserving the greater "strategic depth" in time and space won by the U.S. Cold War victory. In a dangerous world, much of this depth would have been lost as a result of already-serious problems that would be more than narrowly regional. Accordingly, the principal and all-important goal of the shaping function would be to help shore up a tottering international security system and to prevent wholesale collapse from occurring.[2]

U.S. military strategy would be required to help perform the shaping function in five ways:

- Projecting an image of U.S. power and resolve onto the turbulent world scene

- Maintaining control of vital sea-lanes for commercial, military, and strategic reasons

- Preserving the solid security foundation and bonding political ties that allow U.S. alliances to function effectively in economic cooperation, diplomatic coordination, and combined military planning

- Managing rivalry with Russia and China in stability-enhancing ways, e.g., by contributing to a dissuading balance of power while not provoking political confrontation

- Stabilizing turbulent regional strife by reassuring friends, warning enemies, and providing the means for activist U.S. intervention when necessary.

In performing the shaping function in these ways, U.S. military strategy would be geared to more laborious tasks than today's because it would confront powerful global dynamics that threaten to counter its effects. The fluidity of international politics and the complications of U.S. policy would render difficult those attempts to project a strong image of U.S. constancy and purpose. Lacking a clear external threat

---

[2]Ibid.

and exposed to internal economic frictions, U.S. alliances would be less easily held together.   The act of dissuading Russia and China would be complicated by simultaneous U.S. efforts to achieve political equilibrium with them.   U.S. efforts to project influence into turbulent regions would be made difficult because the seething tension of such regions would lead many actors to oppose American policy.

Defense Planning

The traditional domain of defense planning is to determine how military forces will be used in crisis and in war.   Tomorrow's world will be similar to today's in that U.S. strategy planners will not need to worry about an all-out global conflict of Cold War proportions. Future wars likely will continue being regional and limited in their goals and scope.   In many other ways, however, the future will be very different.   The thinking involved in reestablishing the two principal subcomponents of military strategy—nuclear strategy and conventional strategy—must be innovative.   The emergence of geostrategic rivalry with Russia might seem to presage the end of the Strategic Arms Reduction Talks process and the onset of a new nuclear arms race.   Although this could be the outcome, both the United States and Russia grasp that the Cold War's unwanted nuclear dangers grew out of their intense ideological confrontation and unchecked military competition.   Even in a situation of geostrategic rivalry, they will retain a capacity to cooperate, including in arms control talks.   Both the United States and Russia will have an incentive to reduce nuclear threats to their survival, and neither side will be compelled to depend heavily on nuclear weapons to deter conventional attack.   For these reasons, a new arms race may be avoided and, plausibly, the two countries might be able to push the START negotiations into additional reductions.

Provided U.S.–Russian cooperation is feasible, strategic nuclear forces can be retired to the background in their relationship.   During the Cold War, both nations deployed these weapons not only to deter attack but also to enhance their political status and underwrite their foreign policies.   The process began in the 1950s when NATO adopted a nuclear strategy of massive retaliation to help compensate for its weak conventional forces in Central Europe.   In the late 1960s, NATO switched gears by adopting the strategy of flexible response, which sought to reduce dependence on such weapons and to en-hance prospects for controlling escalation. But the former Soviet Union stimulated the arms race by embarking on a huge nuclear buildup aimed at matching and surpassing that of the United States and NATO. By the late 1970s, the result was a standoff in which each side boasted a massive arsenal of about 2000 launchers and 14,000 nuclear warheads, plus large inventories of tactical weapons in Central Europe.

This situation was additionally dangerous because of built-in incen-tives to escalation: The most worrisome risk was not that an inter-continental nuclear war might spring out of the blue but that a re-gional event might spiral upward into a higher-level conflict. Even a purely local conflict in a peripheral area posed the risk that fighting could spread to Central Europe. Conflict there threatened to lead to a tactical nuclear exchange that might begin small but spin out of control, inflicting devastating damage on both countries. Thus, the balance of terror was truly delicate even though both sides deployed strategic nuclear postures that were invulnerable to surprise attack.

Both countries will possess ample conventional forces to pursue their security agendas, and their political conflicts will be limited, not all-out. Therefore, it is hard to imagine a situation in which either side would want to run the risk of using nuclear weapons against each other, although both countries might be willing to treat such weapons as instruments of defensive last resort for only the most dire of emergencies. If so, the effects will be beneficial for reasons that go well beyond the lessening of old dangers. The Cold War nuclear standoff was manageable because the security order was bipolar, thereby allowing the United States and the former Soviet Union to control events. The future will be more multipolar, thereby weaken-ing those two countries' control over crises, emphasizing that certain risks should not be run at all.

Complete disarmament will be infeasible because both countries will want a still-sizable nuclear posture to provide deterrence, to meet commitments to allies, and to balance the inventories of other nu-clear powers. Yet if the START process moves beyond current con-cepts, new questions will appear on the agenda: Will the precepts of assured destruction, multiple options, and graduated escalation still be appropriate? If not, what new precepts should be adopted? Will

U.S. nuclear strategy still contain plans to destroy enemy urban areas in a world in which all-out war seems improbable? Will the United States still worry about disarming first strikes and counterforce exchanges? If not, what targets will it plan to strike and why?

The intellectual armory of nuclear precepts that has been inherited from the Cold War seems so unrelated to the strategic conditions ahead that it qualifies only as a dusty museum piece. Yet if this armory is to be cast aside, what is to take its place? Will the United States be left with a nuclear posture in search of a strategic rationale? If a rationale can be found, what will be the irreducible requirements for offensive systems in a multipolar era? What employment doctrines will be needed to achieve deterrence, attain wartime objectives, and provide flexibility? Will a triad posture still be needed, or will two legs suffice—or even one leg? To decrease the risk of accidental launch and to promote greater mutual confidence, to what extent can readiness be reduced and collaboration increased? How can retired launchers and warheads best be safely disposed of? Should the United States offer Russia and other CIS republics financial help in this endeavor?

All these questions will beg answers until a new nuclear strategy can be fashioned. However, the START process has already reduced force levels from those of the Cold War to about 1000 launchers and 3000–3500 warheads when START II is implemented. Observers are contemplating reductions to a few hundred launchers and 1000–2000 warheads, which may reflect what ultimately is achievable under START. If so, both countries will remain nuclear superpowers, but their force levels will be vastly smaller than today's. Equally important, nuclear forces will play diminished roles in their military strategies. Indeed, the future might even witness the displacement of nuclear deterrence itself as a centerpiece precept. For both countries, military strategy may come to regard nuclear forces for intercontinental attack as playing a limited backup role of "dissuasion": i.e., not posing a heavy-handed threat of immediate retaliation but rather sending a less strident warning not to transgress (see Chapter Six). Yet if still-large forces will be retained, a rationale will need to be found for determining how they should be structured and used. The quest for a coherent nuclear strategy thus will mutate in new directions but will not end.

The threat of widespread proliferation could elevate the role of deterrence and nuclear forces in U.S. military strategy (and that in Russia), especially if nuclear weapons are acquired by rogue states that threaten the interests and survival of the United States and Russia. In addition to somewhat enlarging offensive targeting requirements, proliferation could lead the two countries to alter the Anti–Ballistic Missile (ABM) Treaty to provide leeway for at least a thin screen of ballistic missile defenses to cover their homelands. Nuclear defense could also be required by their forces deployed on foreign soil, and the territory of threatened allies.

For U.S. strategy, proliferation also could necessitate efforts to strengthen extended nuclear deterrence coverage of Allies and to offer this coverage to other countries that currently do not require it. Obvious candidates are South Korea and friendly Persian Gulf states, but the requirement might not end there if proliferation is rampant: Countries in Eastern Europe could be threatened by new nuclear powers or by a Russian army that has come to embrace tactical nuclear war as a substitute for the large conventional forces of yesterday. Along with extended deterrence would have to come intensified measures to build counterproliferation assets that could be used to efficiently strike targets in rogue nuclear states. Owing to the looming prospect of regional nuclear crises, tactical nuclear doctrines and forces could make a comeback.

The re-emergence of extended deterrence thus could move U.S. military strategy away from increasingly emphasizing purely conventional defense toward promoting at least partial nuclear reconstitution. The effects on U.S. defense plans could be profound. Because extended deterrence normally is not credible unless U.S. forces are present, overseas deployments could easily increase, and U.S. units might be dispatched to entirely new locations. If tactical air forces are insufficient to meet requirements, nuclear weapons might reappear in the inventories of U.S. ground and naval forces. Equally important, new operational concepts might have to be fashioned to guide the use of nuclear forces in regional crises.

During the Cold War, the United States had the luxury of knowing that tactical nuclear weapons would be used only to defend vital terrain against a massive Soviet invasion and in response to a failure of NATO's conventional defenses. Escalation could be planned in flexible ways, and the prospect of a Central European war seemed to offer some hope that escalation could be controlled. For all its dangers, this situation imparted a helpful measure of clarity. Unfortunately, a proliferated world might offer the opposite of clarity: an entirely new and exceedingly complex environment whose components are not well understood.

Many troubling questions come to the fore: In what situations should conventional military force be employed to destroy an emerging nuclear threat? Under what circumstances would nuclear weapons by used—only as a last resort or in anticipation of an opponent's first use? How would escalation be conducted? What if the geography being defended is not truly vital, U.S. adversaries are not rational, and conventional defense alternatives have not been exhausted? What if a nuclear crisis occurs among third parties, thus posing no immediate threat to U.S. interests or those of close allies, but creating the risk of a larger crisis or merely setting a dreadful precedent? The answers are not apparent, but the questions suggest that the past may not be prologue.

One important change is that Europe seems destined to make a comeback as a theater for conventional operations in a dangerous world, a development that will owe to mounting local conflicts but also to the need to counterbalance Russian military power. Whereas today's U.S. conventional strategy is focused intently on only two theaters—the Middle East/Persian Gulf and Korea—in tomorrow's dangerous world it will need to address three theaters. This is an important development because the European political-military environment is very different from that in the other two regions. The effect will be to push upward the demands placed on U.S. military planning and resources.

Changing Geographic Perimeters

Another important change is that the geographic perimeters of U.S. conventional strategy seem destined to expand outward in these three theaters, and especially in Europe. Most probably, NATO membership will be enlarged to include other countries, and those countries will qualify for protection under the NATO treaty's collective defense clause of Article 5. NATO could find itself planning for the defense of Poland, Hungary, and the Czech Republic, as well as that of the EFTA nations. Even short of expanded membership, the "Partnership for Peace" proposal offers the equivalent of Article 4 guarantees to full participants, and NATO forces will need to become capable of carrying out these commitments. NATO's informal perimeter could extend as far east as the Baltic states and Ukraine and as far south as the Balkans. Although the pace of change may be slow, NATO is moving eastward, and U.S. conventional strategy will need to move along with it.

A less dramatic but still significant change seems in store for the Middle East/Persian Gulf: the need to contend with growing military threats from Iraq and Iran, which may result in periodic combat operations on their borders and even in their territory. After all, the last two years have witnessed frequent U.S. military excursions into Iraq to help enforce UN sanctions and assert the U.S. Persian Gulf security agenda. Barring major political transformations in Iraq and Iran, the U.S. defense perimeter in the Persian Gulf seems likely to remain constant: protection of Kuwait, Saudi Arabia, and the other Gulf sheikdoms. In the Middle East, military threats from radical Islamic states could pull U.S. and NATO conventional strategy southward into the Mediterranean Sea and North Africa, and eastward to Turkey.

A similar extension of defense perimeters may also lie ahead in Asia, especially if Korea unifies, a change that would push the ROK's borders north to the Yalu River. Another key development could be the emergence of a large zone of naval competition in western Pacific waters if China, Japan, and Russia endeavor to pursue outward-looking security policies through the vehicle of blue-water maritime power. Finally, Southeast Asia could become a region of growing conventional rivalry in ways that pull U.S. air and naval forces into this region, at least periodically. If all these developments take place, U.S. conventional strategy could face a much wider geographic scope in Asia than exists today.

The extension of defense perimeters into turbulent regions will underscore the continuing importance of an overseas military presence in U.S. strategy and prevent wholesale reversion to power projection from North America. A strong overseas presence will be needed to project U.S. influence, to reassure Allies and conduct training with their forces, to signal resolve to adversaries, and to provide a capacity for immediate responses to quick-breaking emergencies. This presence would take the form of Army and Air Force command staffs, combat forces, support units, and reinforcement infrastructure. It also would require U.S. Navy fleets in the Atlantic, Mediterranean, and Pacific, coupled with a maritime presence in Persian Gulf waters. Troop requirements in key regions might be higher than are planned today, but, at a minimum, they certainly would be no lower. Thus, the United States would retain large troop deployments in Europe and Asia, and at least a modest detachment in the Persian Gulf.

Power Projection

A sizable overseas presence nonetheless would have to be backed up by a strong capacity for power projection from CONUS, because major reinforcement would be critical to fighting any large-scale war. Projection forces would be provided not only by combat and support units but also by strategic mobility assets. The U.S. airlift force might be similar to that of today, but the already-large sealift force would have to be better organized and more responsive for the faster deployment rates mandated by a dangerous world. Thus, overseas presence and power projection would work together in U.S. strategy. The former would provide the foundation that makes outside reinforcement physically viable and politically credible. The latter would provide the backup punch needed to win wars quickly and decisively. Overseas presence would provide outposts in the three critical theaters, and power-projection forces in CONUS would provide a large strategic reserve that could be sent in any direction, to wherever conflicts might occur.

Limited Wars

Precisely what military conflicts lie ahead is uncertain, but what can be said is that most will take the form of "limited wars": conflicts that will be constrained in geographic space, time, and objectives. To control escalation, force employment will often be inhibited. Combat missions will aim to defeat enemy forces, but the larger goal of battlefield supremacy will be to shape post-conflict political arrangements. It therefore follows that a centerpiece of U.S. military strategy should be a well-honed capacity to tailor military operations to serve political purposes.

During the Cold War, linear defense of nearby borders was the dominant strategy of the Western Alliance. In a dangerous world, borders will still be defended, but some will not be located nearby and many will not be protected linearly. Forces will have to be projected long distances to reach new borders, and operations often will be decidedly nonlinear, employing a combination of deep-strike air campaigns, mobile ground maneuvers, and supporting naval operations. Still other conflicts will not take the form of border defense at all. The goal may be to drive enemy forces out of occupied territory, to liberate cities, to seize economic assets, or simply to send an intimidating message to adversaries. The past three years already have seen U.S. operations of this type in the Persian Gulf; in the years ahead, such operations may spread to other regions.

The capacity to conduct both defensive and offensive operations, therefore, must be stressed in U.S. conventional strategy. Various campaign plans for both purposes, ranging from modest in scope to quite ambitious, must be included in those operations. In some cases, U.S. forces may be acting alone; in others, close allies will be at the United States' side under an integrated command and the task will be to execute a well-choreographed operational plan. In still other situations, U.S. forces will operate with traditional allies but under ad hoc command arrangements on behalf of improvised plans. Or traditional allies might stand aside but entirely new partners, with whom the United States has little experience, will arrive on the scene to work closely with U.S. forces. A very wide range of wartime conditions thus may be encountered, far wider than during the Cold War: The Persian Gulf conflict may be a forerunner of things to come. As a result, the premium for U.S. strategy and forces will be on achieving great flexibility and adaptiveness.

Desert Storm as Model

The Decisive Force Doctrine will remain the preferred model of choice for guiding U.S. force employment. Desert Storm shows the advantages of fighting wars in ways that flow from well-conceived military strategy, and the disastrous Vietnam experience illuminates the perils of doing otherwise. Yet if "decisive force" is interpreted to mean the wielding of a huge military hammer to quickly destroy the enemy irrespective of the political circumstances, it will not be a feasible or appropriate doctrine in all cases. Lower-level conflicts will take the form of brief intrusions for political effect, along with peacekeeping and peace enforcement to carry out shaky accords. Even mid-intensity conflicts may require the application of the rapier, not the bludgeon. All these conflicts may require operations very different from those pursued in Desert Storm.

The real lesson of Desert Storm is that political goals, military strategy, and combat operations were woven seamlessly. It is this model that should be emulated, not rigid reliance on a single military plan.

Regardless of their political coloration, future conflicts will increasingly be waged with modern weapons by all participants—friends and adversaries. For this reason, U.S. conventional strategy will need to remain anchored on sophisticated doctrinal concepts of the type demonstrated in Desert Storm. If anything, airpower probably will grow in importance, but ground maneuver doctrine and modern maritime operations will remain important as well. The current emphasis on joint operations thus will need to be retained and strengthened, as will the U.S. capacity to conduct combined operations with Allies. NATO today provides the best example of successful combined operations. When political conditions permit, its model should be emulated by U.S. alliances in the Persian Gulf and Asia.

Owing to its clarity and simplicity, the Cold War eased the task of planning U.S. forces to support U.S. conventional strategy. The years ahead will not be similarly easy. A dangerous world might produce tangible enemies in ways that help alleviate the present difficulty of planning U.S. forces under ambiguous conditions. Equally plausibly, however, a dangerous world may be even more difficult for force planning than it is now. The United States might find itself facing a global system composed of numerous countries that are neither friend nor foe—countries that are not sufficiently threatening to justify planning against but that overnight could endanger U.S. interests if their policies or regimes change. Iraq's behavior in 1990 may presage the future: Prior to Saddam Hussein's sudden aggression against Kuwait, the United States had no immediate military quarrel with that nation, which overnight switched policies and became an enemy.

Forms of Conflict

Conflicts will be hard to predict years in advance. When they do occur, they may be fought in multiple locations, some of them surprising and out of the way. As will be analyzed in greater depth in Chapter Eight, future wars may take many different military forms. Major regional conflicts will remain possible, but smaller lesser regional contingencies (LRCs) might occur. Nor can the possibility be dismissed that wars larger than MRCs might be fought if Russia and China reappear as rivals, or if two or more medium-sized powers band together. What form would a Persian Gulf war take, for example, if Iraq and Iran were to resolve their differences and join together in a common front?

This wide variation means that sometimes large forces will be needed, but, on other occasions, small commitments will do. Sometimes combat operations will be over quickly, but, on other occasions, they may drag on. Sometimes airpower will be the dominant solution; other times, ground forces or naval forces will lead the way. Sometimes events will unfold slowly; other times, they will erupt with breakneck speed. Sometimes surrounding conditions—geography and politics—will be ideal; other times, they will be less than perfect and may even be dreadful. In a fluid world of this sort, the incentives to anchor U.S. force planning on strategic missions and generic conflicts rather than on concrete enemies and threat-based contingencies will be even greater than those of today.

CONVENTIONAL STRATEGY AND FORCES IN A DANGEROUS WORLD

What will be the relationship between conventional strategy and forces in a dangerous world? Because military strategy today is not a hotly debated item, the public discussion is dominated by three issues that fall more into the realm of force sizing than this relationship:

- Whether overseas-presence requirements can be satisfied by postures of 100,000 troops each in Europe and Asia, along with a small presence in the Persian Gulf

- Whether U.S. plans and programs should be based on the capacity to wage two concurrent MRCs in the Persian Gulf and Korea

- Whether MRC requirements can be fulfilled by the building-block postures laid down by the Bottom-Up Review.

For the immediate future, these issues will remain critical. Over the long term, however, a much broader set of issues may come to the fore. The problem goes far beyond the mere fact that conflicts other than MRCs might have to be fought in these two regions. A more fundamental problem is that U.S. military strategy may change, and more than once. Today, the United States is still focused on the task of carrying out a single dominant strategy. Tomorrow, it may have to plan its forces much as one plans a wardrobe: so that they can carry out several different strategies, each of them to be worn briefly, then taken off in favor of a new strategy "outfit" when the political weather changes.

Today's geostrategic situation leads our military strategy to focus on the Persian Gulf and Korea, to juggle two "balls." But even if the sole problem is that of regional strife and conflict with medium-sized powers, tomorrow's situation could be very different in ways mandating major shifts in strategy, causing more "balls" to be juggled. And as the number of "balls" to be juggled changes, so will the number of "jugglers," as Table 7.1 illustrates. The ability of U.S. military strategy to accommodate a fast-changing, dangerous world will be strengthened if U.S. political foundations remain solid—a situation that cannot be ensured because the cohesion of U.S. alliances might wax and wane in equally perplexing and unpredictable ways, as discussed in Chapter Six. NATO might weaken temporarily and then rebound, but the United States' Asian and Persian Gulf alliances might then deteriorate. About the time that the situations in Asia and the Persian Gulf improve, NATO might start faltering again. This prospect would be less worrisome if the United States could be confident that its Allies will grow stronger when the local external situation becomes more tense, and will weaken only when stability favors it. But this happy prospect is far from ensured. If U.S. nightmares come true, its alliances might weaken at the moment they are

Table 7.1

Examples of Changing Situations and Strategy Shifts

- If Korea unifies, worry about an MRC there could quickly disappear. Yet the military situation in the Persian Gulf might worsen, and North Africa could explode into virulent hostility toward the West. Concurrently, East Central Europe and the Balkans could sink into a morass of chronic instability and war. The United States would be compelled to undertake a wholesale shift in strategy by de-emphasizing Northeast Asia, stepping up efforts in the Middle East/Persian Gulf, and focusing intently on Europe.

- A few years later, the pendulum could swing in yet another direction. The Middle East/Persian Gulf might cool down, but Europe might heat up and serious political tension might emerge in Southeast Asia. The effect would be another disruptive shift in regional strategy.

- A shift could come if political dynamics culminate in all three regions' sinking into tense instability.

- Overlaid atop this ever-evolving regional scene may come abrupt changes in U.S. relations with Russia and China. Today, Russia is relatively weak and dormant, but in a few years it might emerge as a serious geopolitical rival in Europe. The succeeding years might see relations with Russia slowly improve. However, a more powerful China might emerge by causing trouble in Asia.

- Alternatively, both Russia and China might become U.S. rivals at the same time and remain so for many years, causing fundamental alterations of U.S. strategy to take into account major-power rivalry amid a setting of regional tensions. Yet the exact strategy to be adopted would depend on the specific constellation of relations with Russia and China. Rivalry with Russia is one thing, rivalry with China is something else, and rivalry with both, something else again. At varying times in the future, U.S. strategy may have to reflect all three situations.

---

most needed and rebound to strength when the danger has passed, only to again shrink into impotence when danger reappears. This is not a logical outcome, but nightmares are not logical, and sometimes they come true.

Whereas scenarios can help bring conceptual order to policymakers' thinking about the future, they cannot bring order to the future itself. In the final analysis, policymakers face great uncertainty not only because the world ahead may be very different from today's, but also because it might change many times over, at high speed. One geostrategic structure might appear for a time and then vanish, to be replaced by something quite different, which in turn departs in favor of yet a third international security system. For this reason, the United States might become a nation of several different military strategies over the coming two decades, each having quite dissimilar characteristics from its predecessor and its successor. The great up-heaval of 1991–1992 confronted the United States with the unsettling prospect of major strategy change for the first time in many decades—a situation the country may have to get used to if a dangerous world emerges and does not remain static.

The methodology associated with conventional-force planning—designing a single strategy intended to remain in place for many years, then carefully tailoring force posture to support that strategy—may be infeasible in a dangerous world, because forces can change only slowly: far slower than strategy can shift and may have to shift. For this reason, the United States may be compelled to employ the reverse methodology of shaping forces first and strategy second. If so, the military will be best advised to devise an all-purpose force posture that can be made to fit several different strategies without inordinate hammering and tinkering.

Only in-depth analysis, which is beyond the scope of this study, can shed light on the desired shape of an all-purpose posture capable of carrying out multiple strategies. What can be said is that this posture will need to be flexible enough to respond to ever-shifting demands; capable of doing several different things well, even at the expense of doing nothing perfectly; diverse and endowed with many different assets; and capable of performing a broad range of missions with varying combinations of strength, for it is this capability that determines whether multiple strategies can be carried out.

The requirement for flexibility will argue against any single-dimension posture that is optimized for one response, such as the postures in Table 7.2. The inability of a single-dimension posture to provide flexibility, however, is no guarantee that a multidimensional posture will provide the kind of flexibility that is needed: coherence in all situations. If proper flexibility is to be attained, it will come only through careful planning, not the indiscriminate scattering of resources that can produce incoherence. In theory, money can buy flexibility by enabling deployment of a large posture that provides myriad assets, each sizable enough to meet the requirements of the day. Yet even in the best of times, when budgetary resources are ample, across-the-board adequacy is seldom achievable. When resources are scarce, painful trade-offs must be made, and there is no guarantee that the choices made will automatically be the right

Table 7.2

Single-Dimension Postures

- An air-dominated posture may be crippled if the situation unexpectedly demands ground forces.

- A ground posture designed for mechanized warfare may prove badly suited if infantry missions must be performed, and vice versa.

- A posture designed for continental operations may prove deficient if maritime operations are demanded but the United States no longer has a large navy.

- A posture designed for power projection may be rendered impotent if the situation requires overseas presence and allows for no substitutes.

- A posture designed for Northeast Asia and the Persian Gulf may come up short if Europe is the region of trouble.

- A posture composed of only ready-but-small active forces and no reserves might be capable of deploying quickly, yet it may be left unprepared for a situation that requires larger forces and the time to mobilize them.

- A mobility posture dominated by air transports may enable light forces to be deployed quickly to distant locations; the absence of cargo ships, however, might prevent the timely backup of these quick-reaction forces with heavy forces.

- A posture equipped with modern weapons may be capable of performing brilliantly at first; however, if it lacks sustaining stocks and logistics support, it may run out of energy at the moment the war gathers force.

ones. Flexibility thus will be achievable only if an effort is made to determine how defense resources can best be invested to meet tomorrow's requirements.

What will these requirements be? Although tomorrow's needs are unclear, what can be said is that wartime requirements for a dangerous world almost certainly will be no less than they are today, and indeed they may be higher. If sufficient forces are required to fight two MRCs today, at least the same standard will apply tomorrow, when the likelihood of regional wars will be equal or greater, as will the risk that the United States' enemies in two different regions might coordinate their aggressions. Moreover, individual regional opponents might field larger and better-armed forces, thereby elevating U.S. needs for individual MRCs. The posture endorsed by the Bottom-Up Review arguably can meet current MRC requirements; but, short of drawing heavily upon low-readiness RC forces, it provides little margin for safety for handling larger threats. Nor does it deal with the risk that a dangerous world might produce a worse situation than two concurrent MRCs: e.g., one or two additional small conflicts elsewhere that might require at least modest commitments.

The prospect of a dangerous world thus argues against premature cutbacks beyond those already planned, and it may create a legitimate requirement for even larger forces. If elevated requirements emerge, perhaps the downward trend in U.S. defense budgets of recent years will be reversed. Yet barring a remarkable upsurge in the U.S. economy that produces greater revenues, a major rearmament is unlikely to be launched anytime soon. For at least the next several years, a dangerous world will have to be faced with defense resources similar to those being contemplated today. Even if additional resources do become available, careful planning will still be needed: The idea of designing a flexible-yet-coherent posture to support multiple strategies is not one that comes automatically, and the task itself is not easily accomplished.

Careful planning will need to include serious analysis of whether flexibility and performance can be increased by altering the internal composition of the conventional-force posture. Employing large numbers of people and highly sophisticated technology in the most deadly of environments, military organizations are complex entities that are hard to build but easy to destroy. For this reason, they prefer evolutionary change to revolutionary transformation, testing the waters as they go. Their ideal model is that of a carefully guided, slow-but-steady march into the future. This cautious stance toward change is based on calculations more sophisticated than bureaucratic impulse. Change for its own sake should not be pursued, for if a military organization is not broken, it has no need of being fixed. Measures that produce the appearance of improvement but not the reality are illusions. As many disappointing experiences show, experimentation on behalf of ill-considered ideas will often do more harm than good. Even good ideas can cause damage if they are implemented so fast that temporary chaos is the result.

Moreover, the advantages of an existing situation are often ignored in efforts to find fault or to imagine something better. The currently planned posture of 13 active Army and Marine divisions, 20 USAF fighter wings, and 11 Navy carriers reflects an internal mix similar to that of the Cold War posture. To some, it suggests a lack of imagination and innovation: a preference for continuity for its own sake. Perhaps it can be improved by making marginal changes in one direction or another. Yet the price of increasing assets for one component is loss of assets for another. Doubtless a wholesale change would leave the United States better prepared for some challenges. But the real issue is whether wholesale change would leave it better prepared for the full range of future challenges and of strategies that might have to be carried out. When this sobering issue is considered, the attraction of radical departures diminishes. At a minimum, such departures should be subjected to stern tests of proof that take into account all the trade-offs, not just some of them.

Yet no military establishment can rest on its laurels or embrace history as an end in itself. As experience shows, failure to innovate is a well-traveled path to defeat on the battlefield. Moreover, the proper internal balance of yesterday is not necessarily the best balance for tomorrow. Sometimes flexibility can be enhanced by pursuing altered arrangements. Emergence of new doctrine and technology often creates positive incentives for change. A good example is the procurement of the Joint Surveillance and Target Attack Radar System (JSTARS) and Tactical Missiles (TACMs), which has led to greater cooperation between the Army and Air Force in orchestrating operational fires near the battlefield. Also, a change in the strategic situation often calls for pursuing new priorities and abandoning long-established but outmoded practices. If this mandate is ignored, the consequence can be a force posture locked in the past rather than pointed to the future, one that ignores opportunities to both conserve and improve.

ENHANCED JOINTNESS

Efforts are already under way to avoid redundancy by eliminating unneeded assets, to foster innovation, to alter the tri-service mix at the margins, to pursue new roles and missions, and to reshape service postures to meet new requirements. Among these measures, steps to promote the sharing of intelligence assets and training facilities promise to upgrade all three services while conserving resources. Greater collaboration between the Air Force and the Navy will help both perform critical air missions at less strain to their forces. Measures by the Army to provide artillery and armor support will enhance the ability of the Marines to perform high-intensity ground combat missions without degrading their capacity for amphibious warfare. Creative use of amphibious assault ships can help compensate for reductions in carrier time-on-station, and the same effect can be gained by using task forces of surface combatants for this purpose.

The common theme of these measures is *enhanced jointness*: the capacity of the services to work together. Within each service, steps to conserve while enhancing proficiency are also being taken. Marginal reductions in the size of USAF and USN air wings help reduce resource demands while not unduly sacrificing each unit's ability to perform combat missions. Perhaps emerging technology will allow the Army and Marines to pare back the size of their divisions and logistics support assets, thereby enabling them to field smaller, more agile, but still-effective forces. In any event, the Army and Marines already are upgrading their RC forces to help compensate for reduced active forces. Especially if a dangerous era emerges in a situation of tight constraints on defense spending, additional innovations should be pursued when analysis proves them appropriate. The outcome can be not only reduced costs but also increased effectiveness.

As it seeks to achieve a sensible blend of continuity and change in a world of multiple military strategies, the United States today stands, fortunately, on a solid military foundation for facing the future. Owing to the multiple demands of the Cold War, the conventional posture inherited from that conflict had many controversial aspects, but it did offer balance and diversity. The downsizing now under way is under attack from many quarters because it is unfolding in mostly linear ways. Yet linearity has the advantage of preserving a posture that, albeit smaller, can still do many different things. As a result, the posture being planned today provides a spectrum of assets that promote the carrying out of several different strategies, or at least can be rendered capable of doing so through only modest adjustments. More by accident than design, the United States will have exited the old era with a force posture that proves well suited for a new, entirely different era, as Chapter Eight shows.

CONVENTIONAL-FORCE PLANNING FOR A DANGEROUS WORLD

Conventional-force planning for tomorrow begins by recognizing that the U.S. defense posture must be able to execute multiple military strategies. But it must also build a new framework for planning and analysis that is as sophisticated as the old edifice yet different in fundamental ways. The new analytical framework must marry the abstract with the concrete so that policy and strategy can be linked with specific plans and programs. The result is a coordinated defense effort that flows in preordained directions and achieves consciously elaborated goals. One reason the Cold War was won is that the United States succeeded in assembling an elaborate framework that allowed planning to focus intently on this conflict's military dynamics. A similarly powerful framework will be required for the future, but it will need to address a dangerous era's new characteristics, not those of the conflict that has been left behind.

The Department of Defense is building a new framework, which, because of its complexities, will not be complete for several years. This chapter endeavors to nudge the effort along by addressing issues that should be considered in the near future. It argues that a new planning framework should begin by capitalizing on the superior performance shown by U.S. forces in Desert Storm while not allow ing this singular event to become a basis for abandoning *prudent conservatism*: the standard that aimed at achieving a relatively high margin of confidence rather than at eliminating risk. A hallmark of sound military planning is not exaggerating one's own talents or underestimating those of the enemy.

Provided prudent conservatism guides offical planning, canonical scenarios (e.g., MRCs in the Persian Gulf and Korea) can be used to gauge U.S. military priorities, although a few canonical scenarios are unlikely to offer the all-encompassing analytical power of their Cold War predecessors, and they could produce tunnel vision if they are taken too literally. Conventional planning, therefore, must be alert to the large number of nonstandard contingencies that might arise, because their characteristics and requirements may be different from those of canonical scenarios. Indeed, the core issue may not be preparing for specific conflicts that can be foreseen but configuring U.S. forces to execute generic missions in the face of great uncertainty about where and how wars will be fought. The capacity to perform such missions may hold the key to military security in a world where conflicts may occur in surprising places.

If U.S. planning does confront the full set of dangers that may lie ahead, the United States might discover that its conventional posture is neither large enough nor strong enough to meet future requirements and institute an expansion. But there are several way stations between today's posture and any return to Cold War vigilance. Moreover, additional U.S. forces are not the only solution to rising requirements, given that U.S. allies have forces of their own that can contribute if they are properly prepared for new security missions beyond their borders. NATO comes immediately to mind, but other friends and allies could be called upon as well. Just as the Cold War was won by collective security and Coalition planning, not by the United States' acting alone, a more dangerous era will be best managed if the United States can draw on this experience to supplement its own efforts.

WILL U.S. FORCES REMAIN QUALITATIVELY SUPERIOR TO THE ENEMY?

During the Cold War, the West agonized about its ability to defend against the leviathan Warsaw Pact, but now a reverse psychology seems to be taking hold. Owing to the overwhelming dominance shown over Iraq in the Persian Gulf War, the expectation has been built up that U.S. forces can be counted on to remain superior to all enemy forces for the foreseeable future. Fueling this expectation is the judgment that new technology and modernization can preserve, or even enlarge upon, the advantages displayed in the Gulf War. A theory emerging among some analysts, therefore, holds that agile, mobile, and well-equipped U.S. forces will always be able to overwhelm future opponents, and at low cost, to boot. Along with this belief has come growing hope that bloody battles with heavy casualties can be relegated to the ash can of history.

If U.S. forces retain their current superiority over opponents, the military risks of a dangerous world will be reduced. Adversaries will be less likely to commit aggression, friends will be more eager to stand alongside, and when war occurs, the United States will always stand an excellent chance of winning. The goal of continued qualitative superiority, therefore, should animate U.S. defense planning, not only today but especially if a dangerous world emerges. If it takes care to plan its defenses carefully, the United States stands a good chance of attaining this goal, for the United States will continue to possess all the resources needed to remain the globe's leading military power.

This goal should be pursued, however, in a way that guards against backfires from damaging psychological by-products: Being superior today does not mean that superiority tomorrow already has been achieved. The military world is very competitive, and if the United States remains superior, it will be because the country recognizes that it cannot afford to rest on its laurels. To avoid overconfidence and the relaxation of diligence that it brings, the United States must avoid the temptation to discard critical military assets on the premise that they are no longer needed because it is superior, when, in fact, those very assets are what established superiority.

What Standards Should Be Employed for Force Sizing?

At issue here are the standards to be employed for sizing U.S. forces and the associated approach to be followed for determining confidence levels and risk management. During the Cold War, the analytical approach normally used was based on the standard of prudent conservatism. No effort was made to match the enemy in numbers, but sufficient forces were demanded to carry out a coherent campaign plan based on joint operations and to maintain a minimally adequate force ratio. This approach tended to create a requirement for substantial forces for most conflicts.

Some argue that this standard can be relaxed in today's world because less military margin is needed. But a dangerous world seemingly will create incentives for the resurrection of prudent conservatism. Maybe new and enduring military realities have created less-demanding requirements for sizing U.S. forces. Nevertheless, a dangerous world will be dangerous not only for political reasons but also for military reasons.

A dangerous world also creates incentives for not interpreting the determinants of superiority so narrowly that the wrong choices are made in allocating U.S. defense resources. The belief in qualitative superiority has major implications not only for how expectations are set for the performance of U.S. forces but also for how defense requirements and priorities are defined. The new theory emphasizes modernization and readiness as the highest priority, and it downgrades sustainability on the premise that long wars no longer will be fought. By postulating that future wars will be won through quality, this theory also relaxes traditional standards for overpowering mass and thereby levies a requirement for smaller numbers of combat units. Further, it calls for an altered force mix with more air wings and fewer divisions and ships.

In essence, this theory proposes to fight future wars according to the Persian Gulf model, emphasizing those force components that allegedly were most important in that victory. However, by building posture according to a single model, those components carry with them the risk of creating an unbalanced force that can follow a single path to superiority but cannot divert to other paths when the future requires. In the end, the task of maintaining superior U.S. forces may turn out to be more complicated than merely embracing one temporarily glittering theory and following its dictates.

The theory of qualitative superiority originated in the early 1980s, when recognition was growing that the United States was lucky to have won World War II by brute force alone, and that overreliance on this approach was responsible for the Vietnam setback. Greater emphasis was attached to building qualitative excellence in strategy, doctrine, tactics, weapons, and other areas. This excellence, however, was to be built atop the traditional approach, not substituted for it. Owing to the Persian Gulf victory, taking a giant step forward and actually substituting it is being considered.

Is this theory so on target that it should be allowed to guide defense policy? To question this theory is to doubt computer simulation models that portray how lethal U.S. weapons can sweep the battlefield clean of enemy troops. Yet any computer simulation, by definition, is a tautology because it measures reality in terms of its own properties. It does not conduct an independent investigation of reality but, instead, relies on the data and judgments that are fed into it by humans. The real issue is whether those inputs are valid, but their validity cannot be gauged by consulting the computers. The fact that a computer simulation predicts victory does not *guarantee* a happy outcome. If the simulation and its human creators exaggerate the effects of U.S. weapons, misgauge the determinants of combat power, or misinterpret battlefield dynamics, they may be creating an illusion that will be dashed when reality intervenes.

Indeed, past computer simulations may have created such illusions because they drew their inspiration from the tenuous military balance in Central Europe and, even there, may have underestimated NATO's ability to blunt a Warsaw Pact invasion. When the Persian Gulf war occurred, many predictions consequently inflated Iraq's ability to put up a stiff defense and misjudged U.S. prowess. If simulations erred in the past, why not in the future, especially since war is so hard to predict? But underestimation of U.S. prowess in the past is no guarantee of similar misjudgment in the future; just as easily, overestimation can be the result. Computer simulations will tell what they are told to reveal. Everything depends on the accuracy of the data and postulates fed into them. If they are fed information that misgauges relative military capabilities one way or the other, they will offer no safeguard against illusions.

Hope for a future of unchallenged supremacy rests on projecting that the ongoing technological revolution will produce a new generation of wonder weapons that will keep the United States years ahead of any enemy. Perhaps so. Yet can planners be confident that these weapons will work as advertised and that they will even be purchased in the face of tough budget constraints? Can the United States be certain that all its enemies will fall further behind, rather than close the gap? It was only a few years ago that optimistic predictions about the current generation of high-technology weapons were dismissed as salesmanship on the part of those wanting to sell and buy them. Conventional wisdom held that U.S. weapons were not much better than those of the opposition and, in any event, could be expected to perform less well than advertised by sales brochures. The doubting Thomases were proven too doubtful by Desert Storm. But does this experience mean that all skepticism should be cast aside? Is the Luddite mentality best offset by becoming cheerleaders for high technology, or is a middle-ground position best?

Common sense suggests that degree matters in assessing U.S. qualitative superiority. What seems sensible is the idea that, owing to their quality, U.S. combat units will have greater combat capability than enemy counterparts on a one-for-one basis. Less sensible is the assertion that this edge will always enable U.S. forces to gain total battlefield victories at little cost, regardless of extenuating circumstances. Even less sensible is the idea that this edge allows for a reduction of forces well below normal levels while sacrificing nothing important in decisiveness of outcome. Common sense is no substitute for in-depth technical analysis, but when unsubstantiated claims fly in the face of common sense, they should not be accepted at face value.

The Lessons of Desert Storm

What matters is the bottom line: performance on the modern battlefield. What also matters is the distinction between fact and fiction and between theory and reality. By drawing on history and a scrutinizing appraisal of the Persian Gulf conflict, some insights can be gained on whether this war offers a generalizable model for the future. The central message of the following observations is that, for all its appealing features and useful lessons, Desert Storm may fall short of a general model: Easy victories cannot always be expected in the wars ahead, and caution must be exercised in accepting the ideas of deploying far fewer forces than was previously thought proper and of sacrificing flexibility by building a posture that is optimized for a single kind of war.

Contradicted Historical Precedents. By a wide margin, the new thinking runs counter to the judgments and lessons of the past, before Desert Storm. Although the past is not always prologue, it provides sobering reasons for caution about embracing one war that contradicts a lengthy history of different experiences. Throughout its long military history, the United States seldom based its defense strategy on the presumption of overpowering qualitative superiority, or on the hope that victory would come on the cheap. Indeed, U.S. troops often have entered battle worried about their ability to match the enemy in quality, and even to win. This underdog mentality led U.S. commanders to assemble large forces and to prepare themselves in every feasible way, often playing a key role in helping American forces perform well and gain victory. Prudence often helped U.S. forces take advantage of opponents who thought that their own forces were better than American troops.

In the Revolutionary War, George Washington was under no illusions about the superiority of Continental troops over British regulars; nor did Andrew Jackson entertain fantasies at the Battle of New Orleans in the War of 1812. Prudent realism helped both generals craft strategies that led to victory. In the Civil War, General Ulysses S. Grant was well aware of the fighting prowess of Confederate soldiers and confident that defeat of General Robert E. Lee could be achieved only if the North was willing to pay a high price. He therefore assembled a large Army of the Potomac backed by imposing logistics support and staying power, then slogged his way to Appomattox, crushing Lee in the process.

In World War I, General John Joseph Pershing understood that he would be fighting a strong German army, and he arrived in Europe with a large American expeditionary force to help tilt the balance. Similar prudence was applied in World War II. General Dwight D. Eisenhower was given 65 U.S./Allied divisions and a massive air force to carry out his victorious drive into Germany. In the Pacific, Admiral Chester Nimitz and General Douglas MacArthur were provided large ground, air, and naval forces to defeat Japan. Both campaigns were guided by coherent strategy, but the principal means was brute force rather than adroit skill and high technology. Although emphasis in World War II was placed on keeping casualties as low as possible, neither the European nor Pacific campaign was launched in the expectation that victory would come cheap. In the end, casualties were lower than might have been the case, but awareness of the difficulties helped prepare the U.S. government and people to stay the course. As a result, unconditional surrender was pursued even though temporary setbacks were encountered along the way.

In these conflicts, U.S. forces seldom fell victim to overconfidence; when they did, the outcome often was unpleasant. At the onset of the U.S. Civil War, Union forces felt that the Confederates could be easily defeated, and they suffered one bruising setback after another until greater realism about Confederate strengths took hold. Early in World War II, U.S. forces were ill prepared and suffered the consequences. Pearl Harbor is a monument to underestimation of the enemy. The early South Pacific maritime battles saw serious reversals because U.S. naval forces were not competitive with those of the Japanese. On the other side of the globe, the U.S. Army's initial encounter with Germans at Kasserine Pass in North Africa was a disaster. These setbacks were overcome, but only after U.S. forces came to realize the full magnitude of the task ahead.

When American forces were successful, overconfidence on the enemy's part often helped them. In the Revolutionary War, the British overrated the ability of their professional army to defeat what was regarded as an armed and unruly mob. In the Civil War, Lee launched his ill-fated attack at Gettysburg in misplaced confidence that Confederate soldiers were better than their Union opponents. In World War II, both Japan and Germany dismissed American military prowess and therefore provoked the United States to demonstrate its massive industrial might. In the Gulf War, Saddam Hussein evidently doubted that the United States possessed the will or ability to defeat his large and experienced army.

The painful experiences of Korea and Vietnam did nothing to dispel ingrained U.S. caution and the conservative planning that flows from it. If anything, they reinforced the notion that, if U.S. forces are to win, mass and firepower will continue to be needed, along with skill and technology. As a result, General H. Norman Schwarzkopf was sent to the Persian Gulf with a large joint force. When his orders were changed from defense to offense, he requested even larger forces, and additional units were sent. Most observers, including U.S. commanders, anticipated a battle in which success would be achieved, but at a high price. The unexpected result was a victory so overpowering and cheap that it has now raised questions about rethinking the doctrine of massive forces and firepower.

Indeed, the Gulf victory was overwhelming in ways that not only surpassed the expectations of most seasoned observers but also set historical records. Never before has so large and well-equipped an enemy force been defeated so quickly at so little cost. Not serendipitous, this victory owes to the imposing mastery of modern warfare achieved by U.S. forces during the 1980s. Yet as defense analyst Jeffrey Record has written, Desert Storm may have been the mother of anomalies, not a fixed blueprint for the future.[1]

Desert Storm was undertaken during a period when U.S. forces were very strong, and it was waged against an opposing force that had failed to keep pace with modern times. U.S. superiority in the Persian Gulf resulted from other qualitative advantages, and these also can be fleeting. U.S. forces were better trained and led, had higher morale, were well-equipped and -supported, had a sophisticated doctrine, knew how to fight a modern war, and benefited from a coherent strategy. Iraqi forces were deficient in nearly all these areas: a combination that would have proved fatal even if U.S. technology was not so superior. A disparity this great is unlikely to occur again anytime soon. Even if U.S. forces retain their sharp edge, future opponents will learn from Desert Storm's harsh lessons. Even if they lack the money to buy new weapons, they will realize that major improvements can be made in many other areas on the cheap, and they can be expected to make such improvements. As a result, they might not be the easy pushover that the Iraq Army was. Despite its experience in the long Iran-Iraq War, a conflict reminiscent of World War I's trench warfare, the Iraqi force was fighting out of its league by a wide margin, especially the Iraq Air Force, which now found itself fighting the world's best air force. Moreover, Iraq's forces were victimized by a poor military strategy that not only played to American strengths but also ceded to U.S. forces almost every advantage in the books. In essence, Iraq led with its jaw against a heavyweight with a knockout punch.

After sweeping through Kuwait, Iraqi forces halted at Saudi Arabia's borders and idly stayed there, thus giving U.S. forces almost six months to build up. When Desert Storm began, Iraq's air defenses were exposed as ineffective, but the Iraq Army remained passive rather than forcing battle, thereby allowing Coalition air forces to

---

[1]Jeffrey Record, *Hollow Victory: A Contrary View of the Gulf War*, Washington, D.C.: Brassey's (U.S.), 1993.

pummel it with impunity for more than a full month. Owing not only to superior technology but also to the desert terrain and mostly clear weather, U.S. air attacks were effective, inflicting heavy destruction on Iraqi targets on the battlefield and in the rear. To compound matters, Iraqi ground commanders chose to fight a stationary linear defense in depth, with their right flank exposed. This strategy gave the Desert Storm ground force a golden opportunity to launch a devastating flanking attack against poorly coordinated opposition. For these reasons, the Coalition's total victory is understandable but also unique.

Will future opponents display the same devastating combination of inferior forces and bad strategy? Although the answer will be determined only when the next wars are fought, the globe is littered with potential opponents whose military reputations far surpass that of Iraq. Also, history shows many cases in which losers did far better, and winners less well, the next time around. For example, Europe's most famous military commanders achieved their greatest victories early in their careers, when they surprised their opponents with new approaches to war aimed at achieving annihilating victories. Later, their performance slackened when opponents deciphered their tricks and learned how to counter them. This pattern was true for Gustavus Adolphus, the Duke of Marlborough, Frederick the Great, and Napoleon. It also was true for the celebrated German *Wehrmacht* of World War II, which triumphed early but then suffered defeat to opponents who learned how to wage combined-arms operations and maneuver battles of their own. Because wars repeat themselves about as often as lightning strikes in the same place, premature generalization may well be a sure formula for wrong judgments.

Had Technological Advantage. What can be said is that U.S. superiority in the Persian Gulf War can be attributed partly to technological advantages that can be fleeting, in the critical areas of communications and intelligence, air defense suppression, highly accurate munitions, lethal artillery fires, and armor/anti-armor penetration. In all these areas, the decisive edge enjoyed by U.S. forces was a product of two decades of fast-paced technological competition in which the advantage flowed back and forth between the West and its opponents. In 1991, U.S. technology held the lead. Had the war been fought five years earlier, a different situation might have prevailed.

Because even marginal changes in technology can cause major shifts in the competitive balance, the situation some years from now might also be different. Much will depend not only on the maturation of U.S. technology but also on how potential enemies improve their weapons.

Employed Airpower Decisively. Victory in the Persian Gulf also was a product of airpower's delivering on its long-awaited promise to become a decisive military instrument on its own. The experience suggests that, in many future conflicts, airpower can be employed to equal advantage. Yet, here again, the uniqueness of the Gulf War argues against transforming this conclusion into a sweeping generalization for all conflicts. It also argues against downgrading estimates of requirements for other types of forces and in favor of joint operations. Airpower had a field day in Desert Storm because the conditions were ideal. Its performance could have been less stellar had Iraqi air defenses been better, the terrain less open, the weather less suitable, and the ground war launched earlier—in which case Desert Storm could have taken the form of a more traditional campaign in which airpower played a less dominant role amid a setting of coequal joint operations.

Integrated Naval and Ground Forces. Moreover, the important roles played by naval and ground forces in Desert Storm are often overlooked but should not be underestimated. Although naval forces contributed to Desert Storm, they were not instrumental because Iraq had a paltry navy and Iran chose to stay out. Control of the oceans was needed to carry out the massive seaborne buildup that took place before Desert Storm was launched. Yet no other nation attempted to interdict this effort, which passed through the Mediterranean and the Suez Canal and Red Sea. Future conflicts might be different, and strong U.S. naval forces will be needed to guard against them.

As for ground forces, they provided the forward screen that prevented the Iraq Army from invading Saudi Arabia as Desert Shield was completed and the air campaign was launched. The threat of an early ground attack compelled Iraqi ground forces to assume a deployed defensive posture, thereby making them more vulnerable to U.S. air attacks against exposed combat forces and logistics networks. The Iraq Army emerged from the air war battered, but a thunderous Coalition ground campaign was needed to eject it from Kuwait. This campaign was launched by fully 17 U.S. and Allied division-equivalents, a large force that was needed to mount the combination of a central thrust and a flanking maneuver that prevented the Iraq Army from concentrating, thus exposing it to the *coup de grâce*. Because of the complex maneuvers that had to be launched, a smaller ground force probably could not have accomplished this campaign. In any event, a less prolonged and overpowering initial air campaign would have made the need for large ground forces all the more compelling.

Carried Out Decisive Force Structure. The Persian Gulf victory was achieved also because the United States was able to carry out the Decisive Force Doctrine to the letter. Yet, here also, the uniqueness of this conflict raises questions about whether similar favorable circumstances will arise anytime soon. Aiding in the successful implementation of the Decisive Force Doctrine was the fact that the United States and its many Coalition partners were able to agree upon their political goals. The result was that combined operations on behalf of a common approach became possible. Once this political framework had been set, Coalition military leaders were able to fashion a coherent military strategy, with confidence that politics would not interfere to change military operations in midstream. The geography of the conflict also aided clear military thinking. Coalition military strategy was able to fasten on the dominant objective of ejecting Iraqi forces from Kuwait and was able to tailor campaign plans accordingly. The Euphrates River provided a natural point at which to stop the ground attack, and, once all Iraqi forces had left, a clean disengagement could begin. Desert Storm thus was a near-perfect laboratory for the Decisive Force Doctrine and Coalition warfare.

Bosnia: A Recent Example of Less Favorable Conditions

The Bosnian war is an illustration of how less favorable conditions can apply. The potential for such conflicts should not be lost in assessing how future wars will be waged. In cases where Decisive Force's planning must be set aside, victory will be harder to come by than in Desert Storm.

Desert Storm, therefore, cannot be relied upon to repeat itself any-time soon. This sobering prospect does not mean that the United States should abandon the quest for military superiority purchased by qualitative superiority or cease analysis of alternative require-ments and force mixes. But this prospect does imply that reliance on the Desert Storm model should not become an assumption of plan-ning that leads to relaxed standards, false expectations, and flawed choices.

Cautions

The need for sobriety and perspective cautions against the belief that all future wars can be won on the cheap, especially with forces that are less than adequate. Since World War II, the United States has fought three major regional wars, in all of which it began by hoping that modest forces would suffice and ended by sending a joint force composed of a full field army of 10 divisions and comparably large air and naval forces. One of these conflicts was won quickly, but the other two were long, drawn-out affairs that did not end in decisive victory. As it contemplates the future, U.S. defense planning should remember all three conflicts, not just Desert Storm, for three cases are often a far better statistical predictor than one.

The need for prudence also cautions against the kind of cavalier overconfidence that led Napoleon to assume that Wellington would be a pushover. In earlier years, Napoleon had defeated every army in Europe and was finally driven from power only after several nations joined and marched into France. Wellington, however, had been an exception to the rule. Indeed, Napoleon became outraged when the upstart British commander not only dared to stand up to invincible French forces led by Napoleon's brother on the Iberian peninsula but defeated them, as well. In itself, the incident was a local setback, but it helped inspire confidence elsewhere that Napoleon was beat-able and thus played a role in mobilizing the coalition that swept into France. Banished to Elba, Napoleon was left thirsting for revenge, confident that he could crush Wellington if the two ever met on the battlefield.[2]

---

[2]See David Chandler, *The Campaigns of Napoleon*, New York: McMillan Publishing Company, 1966.

The outbreak of war in 1815, after Napoleon returned to power from Elba, provided the French leader an opportunity to settle the score. Only days before Waterloo, Napoleon had inflicted a crushing defeat on the Prussian Army, which was thought to be better than the British Army. As Waterloo got under way, Napoleon felt that he had a 90 percent chance of winning. But he squandered the opportunity in a series of badly coordinated attacks. As he prepared to launch his final fatal thrust against Wellington's center, he defied logic by predicting at least a 50 percent chance for total victory. As exhausted French troops slammed into Wellington's impenetrable line, a Prussian contingent arrived on the battlefield. Shocked and demoralized, *La Grande Armée* unravelled and Wellington launched a bold counterattack that routed Napoleon and sent him into exile. Whereas Napoleon's reputation as a military winner had been based on 20 years of many successful battles, not on one engagement, it was lost in a flash, a victim of the fortunes of war. Had Napoleon been more aware of *La Grande Armée's* own weaknesses and Britain's prowess, he might have fought better and Waterloo might have ended differently. Ditto other armies that wrongly thought a successful past meant victory in the future. For this reason, military realism needs to be a central part of U.S. planning for the future. Desert Storm's success was a product of thorough preparation anchored on sound planning carried out flexibly so that it responded to the situation at hand. But it is not a fixed blueprint for the future or a reason for unfettered optimism that discounts the military dangers ahead. This is the enduring lesson of that conflict.

CANONICAL VERSUS NONSTANDARD SCENARIOS

In addition to accurately measuring its ability to win wars, the United States will need to think deeply about which wars it will be required to fight. Deciding which future conflicts should be studied will influence the forces built and weapons procured, and therefore the wars that can be fought. Making such decisions will not be easy, for wars are hard to predict years in advance and the analytical resources (i.e., staff planners) to study all potential candidates in depth will be lacking. Strategy planners, therefore, will have to pick and choose, yet must not draw the circle too tight.[3]

Current practice calls for intensive study of a small number of canonical scenarios that are deemed worth worrying about and are representative of the larger class of potential conflicts. A *canonical scenario* imparts intellectual focus to defense planning by specifying—in time, place, and features—a future wartime conflict that might be encountered. It typically includes an estimate of adversary and allied force levels, mobilization and reinforcement rates, strategy and doctrine on both sides, and other key data. These details provide the concrete information needed to make decisions about force requirements and program priorities, and they help provide insights on how forces might actually be used if the scenarios come true.

The primary purpose of canonical scenarios is to empower the defense effort, not imprison it. The principal risk is that these scenarios will be used to purchase in-depth focus on a few events at the expense of grasping a wider set of challenges, that they will propel planning in the wrong direction. Canonical scenarios are invaluable aids to planning and programming, provided they illuminate the wars that actually will be fought. They cannot be held to the impossible standard of clairvoyance, but they do need to get the future roughly right: to put defense planning in the proper ballpark and provide guidelines on the game to be played. The danger is that they will produce intellectual misconceptions about what lies ahead because the real wars of the future may take a quite different form. The risk is not that operational planning will be left impotent, for U.S. military commanders can quickly adjust their plans for force deployment and employment. Instead, the risk is that these scenarios will propel programming in the wrong directions, thereby leaving commanders with inadequate forces to carry out even well-conceived operational plans.

Canonical scenarios first rose to prominence during the Cold War. They had a constructive effect, but they also left a mixed legacy (see Appendix B). The canonical scenarios of the Cold War have now

---

[3]See Paul Davis and Lou Finch, *Defense Planning for the Post–Cold War Era: Giving Meaning to Flexibility, Adaptiveness, and Robustness of Capability*, Santa Monica, Calif.: RAND, MR-322-JS, 1993.

been cast aside; replacing them have been the new canonical scenarios of concurrent MRCs in the Persian Gulf and Korea. Although these MRCs are accompanied by several LRCs that also are to be studied, the MRCs will principally drive U.S. force planning and programming. These two MRCs have been equipped with all the specific features of their Cold War predecessors and thereby stand poised to guide the Department of Defense into the future.

The core issues are as follows: Do these canonical scenarios illuminate the full array of military conflicts ahead? Or do they illuminate only a few challenges, leaving force planners uninformed about a host of others and vulnerable to them? Do their details reflect how regional wars in the Persian Gulf and Korea actually will take shape? Equally important, are these MRCs representative to the point where U.S. forces designed to fight them will be prepared for all other conflicts? If the United States maintains a posture large enough to fight two concurrent MRCs, will it be able to confidently treat all other conflicts as lesser included cases? Or will it be left to worry that its forces will lack the wherewithal to deal with other conflicts that might occur?

Because a dangerous world offers little comparable clarity to that of the Cold War and great potential for unwelcome surprises, there is less reason to be confident of today's canonical scenarios. Indeed, there is concern that becoming too preoccupied with these scenarios will result in a distorted vision that does not see what may lie ahead. To reduce the risk of such vision, horizons can be expanded by adding a few "nonstandard scenarios" to U.S. planning—scenarios of other regions, against different enemies, and driven by dissimilar military dynamics. Nonstandard scenarios may not be amenable to in-depth study comparable to that of canonial scenarios, but an understanding of their basic features may prevent vulnerability to unpleasant surprises. We discuss such scenarios after discussing the force needs for canonical MRCs.

FORCE NEEDS FOR CANONICAL MRCs

A strength of today's canonical MRCs is their call for strong U.S. military forces, which bars wholesale disarmament. They do so by postulating low-warning and roughly concurrent enemy attacks aimed at overrunning Kuwait/Saudi Arabia and South Korea. The

Persian Gulf scenario envisions an Iraqi attack with 20–25 divisions and 500 combat aircraft. The Korea scenario contemplates a DPRK attack by 30–35 divisions and 700 combat aircraft. Both attacks are so large that they could not be handled by Allied forces alone but require the speedy deployment of large U.S. reinforcements.

Sizable mobility assets—airlift and sealift—would be needed to deploy U.S. combat forces to these theaters expeditiously. Once these forces have arrived, the situations in both theaters would mandate a U.S. military response as envisioned by the Decisive Force Doctrine. In the Persian Gulf, large combat operations would be conducted to stop the enemy attack, then to launch a sweeping counterattack, akin to Desert Storm, to eject the enemy, destroy its forces, and attain political objectives. In Korea, U.S. and ROK forces initially would have to mount a stiff defense to block the North Korean advance. They then would have to launch a counteroffensive to restore the DMZ, destroy enemy formations, and achieve related goals. Following success in both theaters, U.S. forces would withdraw, leaving behind postures as required for peacetime conditions.

The U.S. forces required for these MRCs is a matter of debate. In releasing results of its Bottom-Up Review in September 1993, the Defense Department proposed an MRC building block of 4–5 Army divisions, 4–5 Marine brigades, 10 USAF fighter wings, 100 USAF heavy bombers, 4–5 Navy CVBGs, and special operations forces. This posture, DoD asserted, will be adequate to deal with either MRC. The Pentagon thus implied that, if both MRCs are to be fought concurrently, about 10 Army divisions, 3 Marine divisions, 20 USAF fighter wings, and 10 carriers will be needed, accounting for all the forces (minus Army Reserve Component brigades and 1 Navy carrier) in the new conventional posture recommended by the Bottom-Up Review. As a result, this total justifies the decision to reduce the Base Force by about 15 percent, but to reject further cuts as unsafe.

The MRC building block offers a good tool for orientation, yet it does not resolve the debate about its creation as a justification for other decisions, for the simple reason that requirements for these MRCs are not reducible to single-point estimates: The future adversary threat is a variable, not a constant; smaller threats lead to lesser requirements. But the converse is also true: The nature of the military operation to be conducted also has a major effect on requirements.

A counteroffensive mandates larger forces than defense, yet defense and offense often interact. A successful initial defense normally results in lower requirements for a follow-on counteroffensive; again, the converse is also true. Finally, confidence levels influence force needs: Greater margins of safety mandate ever-larger forces. Continuing analysis will be needed as the future military balance unfolds in both regions, and such an analysis should take into account the full set of factors that enter into force sizing.

Persian Gulf MRC

If the Defense Department has erred in calculating force needs for the Persian Gulf MRC, the error may lie on the side of underestimating requirements, not inflating them. A recent RAND analysis entitled *The New Calculus*[4] concluded that a building-block posture could defeat an Iraqi thrust southward, but it was careful to point out that many battlefield dynamics would have to work in favor of U.S. forces. Rapidly deploying USAF units would have to be equipped with modern munitions that will be available only in future years. Air bases in Saudi Arabia would have to be stocked with enough fuel, munitions, and supplies to permit full-scale air operations to begin immediately. *The New Calculus* assumed readily suppressible Iraqi air defenses and a ground threat of only 20 divisions, 10 of which were lightly equipped, motorized infantry units and thus easily bombarded from the air. It further assumed that the Iraqi advance would proceed at less than lightning speed, thereby allowing USAF units time to deploy, and that Iraq would fail to suppress U.S. air bases. Under these conditions, U.S. Air Force and Navy air operations were accurately assessed as enabling a successful counterattack by only 4–6 Army and/or Marine divisions, provided those divisions could be deployed fast enough to carry out the task. But do these assumptions reflect the future?

If Iraq were again to attack but with a smaller force, it might first take care to rectify the weaknesses shown in the Gulf conflict by deploying a joint posture that could strike boldly and swiftly. It might strive to deploy a Desert Storm force of its own by assembling a better air

---

[4]See Christopher Bowie et al., *The New Calculus: Analyzing Airpower's Changing Role in Joint Theater Campaigns*, Santa Monica, Calif.: RAND, MR-149-AF, 1993.

defense, ground posture, and deep-strike force. It also might try to create a political atmosphere that leaves the United States confused and hesitant, not poised for a powerful response. Whether it could achieve these goals is uncertain; accurate intelligence estimates will be key to assessing future U.S. force requirements.

Sensitivity analysis is needed to assess how requirements could be affected if the Iraq attack is strong and fast-moving.[5] Kuwait would easily be overrun, but Saudi Arabia would be far less so. Because no major Saudi cities are located near the northern borders with Iraq and Kuwait, a defense in depth is possible. Owing to Saudi Arabia's huge size, Iraqi forces would be compelled to march long distances in several directions to seize key targets—cities, air bases and ports— needed to prevent U.S. forces from deploying in strength. Distances from the Iraqi border are as follows: 500 kilometers (km) to Riyadh, 750 km to the Red Sea, 800 km to the largest oil fields, 1250 km to the Straits of Hormuz, and 1250 km to Oman. These distances alone would prevent Saudi Arabia from being conquered overnight, even if its sparse population permits occupation with relatively small forces.

How fast could occupation be accomplished? If indigenous Saudi forces are well-deployed and fight hard, they could slow an Iraqi advance, thereby giving U.S. forces time to deploy. Yet an effective Saudi defense is not guaranteed, for surprise and political confusion could leave the Saudis caught off guard. In this event, Iraqi forces might advance quickly. Even against light-but-organized opposition, a modern mechanized army can attain advance rates of 100 km per day. Against no opposition, rates of 250 km per day are feasible. Thus, the time needed to occupy Saudi Arabia is a variable. Several weeks could be required, but if Iraqi forces are well prepared and lucky, the act could be largely accomplished in a matter of days. After all, Germany's *blitzkrieg* across northern France in 1940 was achieved in only 17 days, and it was done in the face of organized resistance from one of the world's largest and best-prepared armies.

Prompt deployment of U.S. air forces would be critical to slowing the advance, yet USAF deployment rates are also a variable. If ample strategic warning is available and acted upon, deployment could be

---

[5]A *sensitivity analysis* is a careful examination of alternatives to key assumptions to determine whether they would change the simulation's conclusions.

fully accomplished before an attack is launched. Surprise, however, could compel a mad rush to deploy before the situation is beyond repair—a situation similar to the tense early days of Desert Shield. Small U.S. forces already deployed nearby could react almost immediately, and initial USAF reinforcements from CONUS would arrive within a few days. But even if air bases and stocks are available, deployment of fully 10 wings could take one month or longer. In the meantime, U.S. interdiction strikes would be conducted with available assets, but Iraqi air opposition could interfere if only to compel a time-consuming U.S. effort to achieve air superiority. The amount of delay and damage inflicted by U.S. air forces on an Iraqi ground invasion thus is also a variable, one subject to great uncertainty.

Clearly, an air strategy is the best means to blunt an Iraqi *blitzkrieg* long enough to allow other forces to converge on the scene. Yet a successful air campaign aimed at destroying Iraqi forces is not ensured to the point where only small ground and naval forces must be sent. At issue is the adequacy of a full, reinforced ground posture that, even counting Allied units, would still leave U.S. forces outnumbered by 2:1 or more, fighting on open terrain that invites mobile operations by both sides.

U.S. weapons will be superior enough to provide the major advantages in relative attrition rates that allow for U.S. forces to fight outnumbered to some degree and still win. Nonetheless, a 2:1 margin is at the high end of plausible defense if airpower is anything less than truly dominant—all the more so if the ground balance might begin at 10:1 and decline to 2:1 only as U.S. reinforcements are slowly deployed. U.S. airpower could inflict enough damage on the Iraq Army to ease the situation if it is given 2–3 weeks to operate before the ground battle begins. But what would happen if the next war does not permit a lengthy preparatory air campaign?

The nature of the U.S.–Allied ground defense campaign would have a bearing on the adequacy of the planned force and buildup rate. In the unlikely event that a forward linear defense is mounted, a U.S. posture of only 5–6 divisions (along with 3–4 Allied divisions) would be affected by force-to-space relationships and thereby could be hard-pressed to form an adequate line to contain an Iraqi thrust. Much would depend on the Iraq Army's ability to move off existing roads and advance across the open terrain. In the likely event of a mobile defense, force requirements could be elevated by the need to perform pinning maneuvers, frontal assaults, and flanking operations. Mobile defense is far from a cure-all if the enemy is skilled at maneuver. As for the counteroffensive that would be needed to restore Allied borders, the goal could be accomplished with small forces if the task is to drive back a battered Iraq Army only a short distance. But if the task is to fight a fresh enemy, larger U.S. forces should be required—all the more so if the distance to be covered is hundreds of kilometers.

The Bottom-Up Review noted that additional U.S. forces might have to be sent to compensate for possible failures in the initial defense, to mount a decisive counteroffensive, or to accomplish ambitious war objectives. The report did not call for more air or naval forces, but it did suggest that two additional Army divisions might be needed, thereby raising the Persian Gulf ground force from 5–6 divisions to 7–9 divisions. This is an important caveat, for it elevates potential U.S. force needs closer to what was needed for Desert Storm, and to what was deployed in Korea and Vietnam: wars in which airpower could not play a dominant role.

Korean MRC

If the building-block posture might prove too small for the Persian Gulf MRC, the opposite appraisal applies to a Korean MRC. Again, many variables must be considered. But in the likely event that ROK forces acquit themselves well, a smaller U.S. force of 2–3 divisions, 7–10 fighter wings, and 2–3 carriers might be adequate. The requirement for a full commitment of the building-block posture stems from the potential need to help conduct a more aggressive counterattack to restore ROK borders and attain other objectives. But force needs for this counterattack would depend on the amount of territory lost in the original invasion, the number of North Korean casualties, and the ability of ROK ground forces to conduct the operation on their own. Because the Korean peninsula is so narrow and the ROK Army is large, space constraints alone might limit the need for U.S. reinforcements. Why send large ground forces if they cannot find enough shoulder space to enter the battle?

Summary

The DoD analysis seems reasonably on target in the aggregate. If there are grounds for quarreling with it, they would be that it underestimates Persian Gulf needs but overestimates needs for Korea. The effect is to cancel both reasons for complaint as a basis for criticizing the size of the overall U.S. force posture. Thus, marginal reductions in the Base Force will not compromise a two-MRC strategy, provided U.S. forces are well prepared; further reductions could invalidate this strategy. Yet this judgment does not obscure the possibility that even if these canonical scenarios occur, the U.S. forces needed to fight each of them might be different from the estimates of today.

FORCE NEEDS FOR OTHER CONFLICTS

The larger issue is whether these two MRCs are an appropriate basis for planning in ways that will leave the United States prepared for nonstandard contingencies. These two MRCs compel the United States to maintain enough forces to ensure that if one major war breaks out, a decisive response can be mounted without fear of weakening deterrence of aggression elsewhere. The combination of short-warning attacks and distant locations creates a requirement for high-mobility forces and well-developed deployment plans. Together, the two MRCs wisely create a requirement for a diverse posture, especially for ground forces, because the Persian Gulf MRC calls for heavy armored and/or mechanized units whereas the Korea MRC mandates lighter infantry and airmobile formations. For both theaters, required campaign plans call attention to the need for joint and combined operations, and for both defensive and offensive actions. Modern doctrine would have to be employed in both cases, anchored on a coordinated combination of firepower and maneuver carried out by ready, well-trained, well-led, and fully supported forces that are armed with high-technology weapons. Surface appearances thus suggest that, if U.S. forces can deal with these two MRCs, they should be capable of responding to a broad range of challenges, including very different situations.

Flexibility

Yet adequate flexibility is not guaranteed. History shows many cases in which military forces that were well prepared for one type of conflict experienced reversals when war came in a new guise. If the U.S. experiences in Korea and Vietnam do not illustrate this point, then the brutal lesson learned by France in May 1940 should. At the time, the French Army was regarded as the world's best, but it had spent 20 years preparing for a canonical scenario of its own: a repeat of World War I. When the German Army crafted a nonstandard scenario through attack by *blitzkrieg*, the French Army proved incapable of reacting and was swept off the battlefield in less than one month.[6]

One risk is that, in preparing a well-choreographed response for these MRCs, U.S. forces might be hard-pressed to shift course if events in these two conflicts mandate a different response. A larger risk is that war might break out elsewhere: in an entirely different place, against a different enemy, and requiring very different U.S. deployment and campaign plans. If confronted by nonstandard challenges, could U.S. forces deploy fast enough and then carry out the operational campaigns needed for success? The answer can be known only if nonstandard situations are studied.

Deep Thinking

The need for deep thinking—the capacity to look critically at underlying premises, postulates, and precepts—is manifest because the uncertainty ahead inhibits U.S. ability to foresee which nations will appear on the scene as enemies. What can be said is that Iraq and North Korea are not destined to be the United States' only military rivals. Planners need to remember that, when U.S. preparations for the Persian Gulf were launched in the late 1970s, Iraq was not regarded as the most dangerous adversary. The experience in Southwest Asia illustrates the important lesson that politics can change faster than U.S. military forces can be altered. Today's enemies can be tomorrow's friends, but the converse also is true for nations whose internal politics or external interests can produce a sudden about-face. Iran, once deemed a permanent friend, almost overnight became an implacable enemy when the Shah departed and the Ayatollah Khomeini arrived.

---

[6]See B. H. Liddell-Hart, *Strategy*, New York: Signet, 1967.

New adversaries can build imposing military forces that permit more ambitious operations than might be feasible today. Force improvement cannot occur overnight; building modern forces that can compete with Western troops and weapons is costly and time-consuming. But especially if outside assistance is provided, buildups can take place and perhaps faster than is commonly expected. In the 1930s Germany went from being disarmed to becoming the world's strongest military power—in only six years.

Much will depend on the resources, skill, and determination of future adversaries. Nations formerly regarded as military lightweights can achieve at least middleweight status, and perhaps more, in the space of several years. In the interim, their efforts can be observed, but the act of discerning their intentions and ultimate ambitions often is not easily accomplished—especially for nations whose original agenda is unthreatening and becomes menacing only after military power is built up. History shows many cases in which newly potent adversaries suddenly appeared on the scene, to the surprise of observers who failed to peer through a veil of ambiguity to see trends that were obvious only in the aftermath.

Different physical circumstances might be encountered that do not offer favorable terrain, a well-developed military infrastructure, prepositioned assets, host-nation support, and Allied military contributions. Owing to their unique features, Saudi Arabia and South Korea are easy to defend once U.S. forces have been deployed. Other countries might be harder to protect, and even difficult to reach with sizable U.S. forces—doubly so if the timelines of war do not permit the 6-month U.S. buildup that was possible in the Persian Gulf War.

Future conflicts might be waged in response to political dynamics that are very different from those postulated by these two MRCs. Whereas these MRCs postulate aggressive enemy attacks aimed at conquering friendly nations, other conflicts might witness aggression aimed at different goals: e.g., seizure of nearby urban areas, destruction of lives and property, or imposition of a new government. Coalition political dynamics also could be quite different. Whereas these two MRCs postulate the support of many friendly governments, other conflicts might witness neutrality or even opposition. Moreover, U.S. goals might be something other than the rapid destruction of invading enemy forces and restoration of Allied borders.

The dynamics could call for military operations dissimilar to those planned for the two canonical MRCs.

Future conflicts might be waged against adversaries that pose quite different military threats than are posed by Iraq and North Korea. Some adversaries might be less well-armed, but others may field larger and better equipped forces. These forces might also be better trained and led, and guided by modern doctrines equivalent to those of Western forces. Whereas Iraq and North Korea today pose primarily ground threats, future adversaries might deploy strong air and naval forces that will have to be engaged. Indeed, some conflicts might be fought in the air and at sea, with little ground combat. Equally troublesome, some adversaries might arrive on the battlefield with nuclear forces and other weapons of mass destruction that could be employed against U.S. forces.

Compared to today's situation, a dangerous world poses a much wider expanse of geographic settings for war, as well as greater uncertainty about all elements of planning: enemy threats, Allied contributions, buildup schedules, and U.S. ambitions. These important changes magnify the risks of relying on a small set of canonical scenarios. For example, the two MRCs do not even consider Europe as a potential site of major regional war. If this assumption proves invalid, major operations may be launched well east of NATO's borders in Europe, in Central Asia, anywhere in Asia aside from Korea, or anywhere in the Middle East/Southwest Asia apart from Saudi Arabia. Will the United States be able to respond flexibly if it plans only on the basis of its canonical scenarios? The answer to this question illuminates the case for paying careful attention to other scenarios that, while "nonstandard," might be altogether too real.

NONSTANDARD SCENARIOS FOR THE FUTURE

Recognizing that World Wars I and II were both implausible scenarios before they occurred, this section offers a few possible nonstandard scenarios. Drawing on the material developed earlier in this report, the following analysis is intended to be illustrative. What it offers is an opportunity to break out of current plans by imagining different conflicts that, in one way or another, might be feasible in the coming two decades.

This analysis speculates only about military conflict in the critical theaters of Europe, the Middle East and Persian Gulf, and Asia. It thus will ignore entire regions that could become focal points of conflict: South and Central Asia, Sub-Saharan Africa, and Latin America. But coverage of only these theaters will be sufficient to illuminate the central point: the need for broad intellectual horizons, and for flexibility and adaptiveness, in U.S. defense planning.

Conventional Conflicts

War in Europe. Because war in Europe is not a canonical MRC, this theater is a good place to start. Absent war with Russia, small powers in East Central Europe and the Balkans are unlikely to band together to create the large enemy force—over 20 divisions and 500 combat aircraft—needed for any single conflict to qualify as an MRC. Yet if regional strains intensify, conflicts far larger than LRCs are possible, for the nine nations there will deploy large total forces. Apart from Serbia, no other nation there qualifies today as an adversary of the United States, but many harbor profound distaste for each other. The possibilities for confrontation are many, and the result could be a new form of warfare: something between an MRC and an LRC.

Although peacekeeping in East Central Europe or the Balkans is the mission most likely to be performed by Western forces, a situation might arise in which major peacemaking/enforcement operations, or even large combat interventions, must be initiated.[7] For concurrent conflicts, overall requirements could be for as many as 10–12 divisions and 650–800 combat aircraft. The NATO Allies could contribute, but even so, U.S. contributions might be as high as 2–4 divisions, 150–300 combat aircraft, and naval forces. This is less than an MRC requirement but sizable nonetheless.

The complex politics of the many situations to be encountered create myriad different possibilities for the employment of U.S. forces. U.S. forces might be used to keep the peace in Bosnia, to pressure Serbia, to protect Romania's borders, to quell imperial conduct by Hungary, or to defend Poland against Ukraine. U.S. forces might cooperate

---

[7]Future strategic missions are discussed in the"Toward Mission-Based Force Planning" section of this chapter.

with Russian troops to bring stability to the Baltic states, the Caucasus, or South Central Asia. All these situations could require military operations very different from the neat-and-clean planning followed in Desert Storm. Indeed, politics and diplomacy likely would dominate military strategy far more intrusively than in the Gulf War. Even if forces were committed on behalf of clear policy goals, these goals might change in midstream in response to new conditions, thereby causing military strategy to shift, perhaps several times over. If so, the prospect would be for a very complicated relationship between politics and war.

War with Russia. If democracy were to fail in Russia and that nation were to return to imperial conduct, the prospect of war with it could again have to be factored into U.S. defense planning. This conflict would be an MRC and beyond, for Russia probably would field an army of 50 divisions and equivalent air forces, about one-half of which could be committed. The size of the adversary force could increase further if other Commonwealth nations joined the fray. The need to deal with an imposing enemy force would be far from the only troublesome issue confronting U.S. defense planning; weighty political issues also would enter the calculus. For example, Where would the war be fought: in Poland, Ukraine, or the Baltic states? What political goals would be pursued? What would be the overall diplomatic context? The answers would have profound implications for force planning, and different answers could drive planning in many different directions.

Indeed, war in Poland alone could be fought in many different ways. Western forces might be committed early, in the middle of an impending crisis, or late, after fighting already had begun. The politics of this intervention could be clear, or very muddy, marked by uncertainty about the goals and calculations of many different participants. NATO might respond as a unified alliance through its integrated command, but, alternatively, an ad hoc operation, with only a few nations participating, might have to be launched outside the integrated command. The intervention might have to conducted on the fly, with only Germany providing an infrastructure and forces. Bases and reception facilities might be available in Poland, but, alternatively, they might already have been overrun by Russian forces.

Western forces might be called upon to defend Warsaw and the Bug River, to halt a Russian drive midway through Poland, to launch a counterattack from western Poland aimed at restoring that country's borders, or even to march into Belarus. The operation might be launched with air forces alone, with large air forces and some ground units, or with large ground formations. The ground campaign might take the form of a linear defense, a defensive maneuver battle, a flanking counterattack, a sweeping counteroffensive, or all of these in sequence. The war might be over quickly or drag on for weeks and months. The many possibilities are quite different from what ensued in Desert Storm.

War in the Middle East/Persian Gulf. If regional tensions were to be exacerbated in the Middle East and Persian Gulf, an equally wide range of possibilities might have to be addressed. For the near future, small-scale operations will remain the order of the day: e.g., enforcement of the no-fly zone over Iraq, coupled with antiproliferation and humanitarian missions. In the more distant future, a wide variety of MRCs are possible, some like Desert Storm, but others, quite different. For example, a repeat Iraqi invasion might take the form of outright aggression, but it might be undertaken amid complex political conditions: e.g., a domestic upheaval in Saudi Arabia in which a revolutionary movement seizes power and calls for Iraqi help.

Iraq might not be the only adversary nation encountered in this region. Indeed, Iran is now improving its forces under a still-zealous regime and might transform itself into a well-armed enemy intent on imperial conduct. How would Iran react to another U.S. intervention aimed at inflicting military defeat on Iraq? Would it remain neutral or might it try to confound the intervention, perhaps by using its air and naval forces to block the Straits of Hormuz and the Persian Gulf? If Iran did insert itself in these ways, U.S. force operations would need to change away from the Desert Shield/Desert Storm model. Indeed, how would a war with Iran alone unfold? In all likelihood, it would be an air and sea war, with U.S. operations deployed heavily from Saudi Arabia and other Gulf sheikdoms. But it might include a forced U.S. landing on Iranian soil followed by a major campaign into that nation.

Future conflicts in this region are not limited to the Persian Gulf. For example, Israel might be attacked in ways calling for larger U.S. interventions than in the past. Although force commitments probably would not be large for defending Israel, they could be larger if Turkey were to be attacked by a coalition of radical Arab partners: e.g., Syria and Iraq. In this case, large U.S. air and naval forces, with major logistics support, would be needed by Turkey. If the Turkish Army proved unable to stop the advance and restore lost territory, sizable U.S. and NATO ground forces might have to be committed. In this event, a military operation akin to Desert Storm could be conducted, but the geographical and logistics conditions would be quite different.

What will happen if Islamic fundamentalism sweeps over the Middle East and North Africa and produces a united coalition of radical Arab governments all angry at the West? The idea that another Muslim invasion of Europe could be launched—akin to that faced by Charles Martel at Tours—is far-fetched. Yet jihad can be conducted in other ways. In addition to spreading terrorism across Europe, Arab nations might assemble the air, missile, and naval forces needed for a contest with the Western powers over control of the Mediterranean, the Suez Canal, and the Red Sea. The result could be long-running air and naval clashes that would entangle not only West European forces but also U.S. forces. This conflict would not be an MRC. But to U.S. forces, it might seem that way, and current MRC plans would provide few solutions.

Conflict in Asia. Similar judgments apply to future security affairs and conventional military conflict in Asia. For the past 20 years, the threat of war with China has not been taken seriously in U.S. defense planning. But China is now undertaking a military buildup. If that nation were to embark on an imperial course in an atmosphere of intensifying political confrontation, an entirely different situation could unfold. Exactly how would a renewed Chinese military threat be manifested? Although traditional examples are threats to Korea, Taiwan, and Southeast Asia, the new era might prove to be untraditional. China might pose a nuclear missile threat to Japan; indeed, if relations with Russia also were to sour, Japan might find itself besieged by new threats from both countries. Another imminent possibility is that China might develop the larger and better-equipped navy that would allow for maritime power projection into the western Pacific. In this event, naval combat might prove to be a core feature of new U.S. defense planning in Asia.

The possibilities would multiply many times over if Japan were to follow the course of expanding its maritime power-projection capabilities. Especially in this event, major-power naval rivalry might spread outward from Northeast Asia by expanding into Southeast Asia, the Malacca Straits, and, eventually, linking to the turbulent situation in South Asia. Along with distantly deployed naval forces could come networks of new military bases across the region for projecting air and ground power. Inevitably, the southeast nations would be affected, and new security alliances would form, perhaps in ways destabilizing to the entire region. The result could be military conflicts that bear little relationship to current canonical scenarios. None of these outcomes is foreordained or even probable, but with Asia changing so rapidly in such profound ways, they are not beyond the realm of the possible.

Regional Nuclear Scenarios

The looming prospect of regional nuclear crises adds yet another dimension to the upheavals potentially ahead for U.S. planning. How would the United States act in regional nuclear crises in the Persian Gulf and Korea? Although the answer is not obvious, current plans might have to be radically altered, for any automatic deployment of large forces might serve only to grant enemies a target-rich environment. For both MRCs, new plans would have to be crafted to deal with conventional and nuclear threats.[8] Beyond these two regions, nuclear crises might appear elsewhere, and the possibilities are mind-numbing, as the summary in Table 8.1 illustrates.

Even if the threat of destabilizing actions by Japan, Germany, and other responsible nations are discounted, the need to prepare for regional nuclear crises caused by rogue states is growing. These preparations go far beyond the narrow province of defense planning, but they do include such planning. To the extent that U.S. combat operations might be undertaken, the prospect of regional nuclear crises will resurrect concerns of the past. During the Cold War, de-

---

[8]See Millot et al., *"The Day After . . . " Study,* 1993.

Table 8.1

Possible Nuclear Crises Outside the Persian Gulf and Korea

- The United States in a nuclear confrontation between Russia and Ukraine that threatens all of Europe

- A tactical nuclear standoff between nations in East Central Europe or the Balkans that had acquired these weapons

- A crisis in the Middle East or North Africa

- A crisis in South Asia or one that spreads to Central Asia and entangles Russia and China

- Many subcases in Asia that do not originate in Korea

- Japan and Germany, pressured by mounting insecurity and diminished confidence in U.S. deterrent coverage, cross the nuclear threshold, fundamentally altering the global security system

fense planning in Europe viewed conventional and tactical nuclear operations as interconnected. This interconnection would have to be recaptured in new plans, but the old concepts of flexible response, graduated escalation, and massive retaliation will no longer be appropriate.

Summary of Contingencies

Reflecting canonical scenarios and their subvariations, along with nonstandard contingencies, Table 8.2 displays the potential future conflicts discussed here. It does not identify all the possibilities but illustrates the wide spectrum of events that might lie ahead.

This is a long list, one full of new and different types of military conflict along with standard varieties. Few of these conflicts are high-probability events. But in a dangerous world, all of them would be possible. The question is: How can the United States best prepare itself? Will reliance on canonical scenarios still be the solution? Or will the situation demand planning that is less preoccupied with the details of a few conflicts and more concerned with a very wide range of potential events?

Table 8.2

Future Contingencies Involving U.S. Military Forces

Conventional Contingencies in Europe
- Peacekeeping and crisis management in East Central Europe, the Balkans, and the former USSR
- Medium-sized warfare in East Central Europe and the Balkans
- Defense of new NATO members and cooperation with other partners
- MRC versus Russia in Poland
  — At Bug, Vistula, or western Poland
  — Linear defense, mobile defense, or counteroffensive

Conventional Contingencies in the Persian Gulf and Middle East

- MRC in Saudi Arabia and Kuwait
  — Forward defense
  — Intervention after Saudi Arabia is partly overrun
  — Re-invasion after Saudi Arabia is conquered
- War with Iran
- Defense of Israel
- Defense of Turkey
- Conflict in North Africa and the Mediterranean

Conventional Contingencies in Asia

- MRC in Korea
  — Defense of DMZ
  — Recapture of Seoul
  — Re-invasion of conquered ROK
  — Conquest of North Korea
- Defense of unified Korea
- Defense of Japan
- Defense of Taiwan
- Maritime conflict with China
- Maritime conflict in Southeast Asia (e.g., Spratley Islands)
- Intervention in South Asia

Regional Nuclear Crises

- In Europe
- In Asia
- In Middle East/Persian Gulf

TOWARD MISSION-BASED FORCE PLANNING

A Continuing Role for Canonical Scenarios

Canonical MRCs should continue to play an important role, and planning should begin with them. But it should not end with them.

If the United States prepares to fight in Southwest Asia and Korea so that it is left unprepared to conduct major military operations elsewhere, it may find itself ill prepared for the conflicts that actually will occur. For this reason, the years ahead mandate far greater attention to nonstandard scenarios. If these appraisals are purchased at the expense of finely tuned canonical analyses, planning may be better for the trade-off. As someone once said, "It is better to be approximately correct than precisely wrong."

Today's canonical scenarios have risen to prominence because, in the absence of anything better, they help to establish a credible rationale for U.S. defense policy in the coming era. Because key decisions for force levels and weapon systems often hang in the balance, these scenarios are in danger of being interpreted in a literal manner that belies the uncertain analytical foundations upon which they are based. This development is unhealthy, for it exaggerates the role that contingency analysis can be expected to play. All scenarios, canonical or otherwise, are merely aids to judgment, not a fixed blueprint for predicting the future nor a singular basis for charting the U.S. defense program.

The need for national military preparedness stems from reasons far more fundamental than the transient mechanics of contingency analysis. Because the United States will remain a superpower with overseas interests to protect, it will need strong military forces to underwrite its purposes in peace, crisis, and war. As history shows, specific adversaries will come and go, but the requirement for military power will remain: a product of enduring geopolitical realities. What is required is a sense of *strategic bearing*: an awareness of the role that military power plays in maintaining the nation's international stance and the basic missions that U.S. forces will be called upon to undertake, come what may. Because older nations with vulnerable borders possess this strategic bearing, they have fewer doubts about the capabilities of their military forces. As a result, they are less dependent than the United States on contrived constructs.

Even if the United States acquires strategic bearing, it will need sophisticated defense planning. In a dangerous world, however, such planning will need to become more dynamic than it has been. The days are gone when the Department of Defense could erect an elaborate analytical framework that would endure untouched for many years. Because static thinking will no longer be feasible, basic military strategy may have to be discarded every few years, and specific plans may have to be altered even more often. Therefore, the emphasis should not be on reestablishing a timeless edifice of plans for the new era but, rather, on creating an energetic planning process that can handle regular upheavals.

The need for intellectual breadth requires that defense programming not only consider multiple scenarios but also depart from the past practice of focusing on only one way an individual contingency might evolve. Confronted by the need to come up with one construct, planners typically made "best estimates" for each variable, then added these best estimates together to create a single overall picture. The drawback of this approach can be a monolithic stereotype that ignores important variations. Also, if the act of estimation is not performed rigorously, the result can be a hodgepodge of best estimates, worst-case estimates, and favorable estimates that bears little relation to reality. The solution is analysis that considers a *scenario space*: an envelope of alternative force levels, buildup rates, military strategies, and the like. Programs would be selected on the basis of their ability to perform effectively over as much of this space as possible. This approach may eliminate the convenience of adjudicating all programs on the basis of one logic system, yet it has the virtue of helping ensure that U.S. programs will be *robust*: capable of dealing with more than one situation.

The need to prepare for the twists and turns of events also has implications for DoD's operational plans (OPLANS), which determine how forces are deployed, and for commanders in chief (CINCs) campaign plans, which determine how forces are to be employed on the battlefield. In the past, these plans often offered only one fixed blueprint for operations. In the future, as the Joint Staff and field commanders already are aware, these plans will need to be modular, based on building blocks capable of being rapidly adjusted to handle different situations. Modularity can be achieved only if scenario analysis examines a broad spectrum of events and determines the alternative responses. Analysis of individual contingencies should employ *decision trees*—decisions composed of multiple branch points—to determine the alternative paths that military operations might have to take in any single conflict.

In the quest for true flexibility, defense planning might profit from de-emphasizing the issue of the moment: whether two canonical MRCs can be conducted at the same time. *Being prepared for concurrent MRCs is important for determining the overall size of the force, but it alone does not ensure that the posture's internal mix is well conceived.* Moreover, the real issue is not fighting two major wars at once, but waging war in one region while maintaining deterrence and defense elsewhere. In today's world, the issue is one of countering aggression in the Persian Gulf while deterring an attack in Korea. Military balance has been achieved in Korea, owing to the ROK's strong forces, and deterrence there is robust even in the absence of large U.S. reinforcements. Concurrence should be considered in defense planning, but should not become so all-important that other equally important and more fundamental issues are ignored. Even today, military preparedness involves more than being able to fight two concurrent MRCs. The same may hold true tomorrow: Although most wars will probably appear one at a time, they might come in clusters, and they may well be very different from the canonical MRCs.

Handling the Full Spectrum of Military Challenges

The more fundamental issue is whether U.S. forces will be sufficiently flexible to handle the full spectrum of military challenges that might occur, even if they take place one at a time. Success in this endeavor is not automatically ensured. Even if the U.S. posture is capable of handling two MRCs, the capabilities needed for other conflicts may be different from those required for canonical events. Whether this is actually the case is a matter to be determined by careful analysis, but the issue does need to be addressed. A first-things-first approach is needed: First making sure that the United States can handle a wide array of single conflicts, then worrying about more than one conflict's erupting at a time.

To help accomplish this goal while also promoting an enhanced sense of strategic bearing, U.S. defense policy should shift away from scenario-based planning and toward mission-based planning. For all its quantitative appeal, scenario-based planning is an unreliable instrument for dealing with an era of great change. If Korea unifies and Iraq acquires a new government friendly to the United States,

today's canonical MRCs could disappear overnight. This development would not remove the need to be prepared for major regional
wars, which might occur in different places for different reasons. Yet,
unless a replacement canonical scenario were to appear, the Department of Defense would lack an intellectual basis on which to
organize its planning as well as convincing analysis to support its
case for adequate resources.

Reliance on canonical MRCs does not solve the problem of preparing
for real-but-unclear dangers when menacing enemies have not immediately presented themselves. Moreover, the capacity to fight an
MRC does not ensure that other conflicts can be waged. What if
smaller conflicts take place that demand a radically different response, and what if larger conflicts erupt that require more forces?
What is needed is a planning mechanism that enables the United
States to be prepared for the full spectrum of conflicts even while not
knowing exactly where they will occur or how they will unfold.
Mission-based planning can help achieve this goal.

Under a mission-based planning approach, defense planners would
not focus on specific threats posed by specific nations as the final
arbiter of decisions. Rather, they would identify the generic military
missions that will need to be performed so that a wide range of different situations can be dealt with. The U.S. force posture and defense program would then be designed to perform these missions.
Planners would focus on the basic categories of military responses
that might have to be launched, determining the generic assets that
would be required to implement each type of response: i.e., the level
and mix of capabilities needed to put the United States within the
parameters of each mission category. They would then design the
force posture to ensure that the capabilities required for each
mission are programmed. Scenarios would be employed to help
fine-tune the posture, but their role would be supplemental, not
primary.

Table 8.3 illustrates 12 different strategic missions that should be
taken into account in force planning. Because all 12 categories may
be encountered in three or more theaters and in several different
forms, the number of permutations is quite large. Yet if the U.S. posture is designed to ensure that it provides generic assets for performing all 12 missions at least one at a time, the United States should be

Table 8.3

**Future Strategic Missions for U.S.
Conventional Forces**

1. Peacetime stability
2. Humanitarian assistance
3. Peacekeeping
4. Counterterrorism and hostage rescue
5. Crisis management and resolution
6. Peacemaking and peace enforcement
7. Lesser regional contingencies
8. Medium-sized regional contingencies
9. Canonical MRCs
10. Nonstandard MRCs
11. Greater-than-expected MRCs
12. Regional nuclear conflict

assured that it will not be caught wholly off guard by unexpected events. By developing a posture to perform 12 different strategic missions reasonably well, the United States will enjoy greater security than if it continues developing a posture that can perform one mission perfectly in two separate regions but that ignores the 11 other missions.

Each mission differs markedly from the others, but together they do a solid job of defining in strategic terms the full range of purposes for which U.S. forces might be employed in the coming years. *Peacetime stability* refers to the role that U.S. forces, especially those deployed overseas, will play in reassuring friends, dissuading adversaries, and otherwise guiding the international system toward stability. *Humanitarian assistance* refers to the delivery of food and other supplies needed in regions suffering devastation from war or natural causes. *Peacekeeping* refers to the mission of deploying forces in noncombat situations to help maintain an existing agreement. The nature of *counterterrorism and hostage rescue* is obvious. *Crisis management and resolution* refers to the use of forces to exert political-military pressure on adversaries to achieve U.S. goals in a confrontational situation short of full-scale war. *Peacemaking and peace enforcement* refers to the use of force in combat missions to either transform an existing conflict into peace or to ensure that an existing accord continues to be carried out.

Whereas the first six categories deal with the use of military forces in the gray area between war and peace, the final six categories deal with military missions in wartime settings. *Lesser regional contingencies* and *medium-sized regional contingencies* refer to conflicts that fall short of MRCs. The category of *canonical MRCs* refers to conflicts deemed most worthy of study; *nonstandard MRCs* refers to entirely different conflicts of similar magnitude. *Greater-than-expected MRCs* refers to potential conflicts in which stronger enemy forces are employed than are projected in typical MRC planning. At the outer extreme are potential *regional nuclear conflicts* that escalate beyond conventional fighting.

In the coming years, U.S. forces will be required to perform many of these missions. Today's canonical MRCs promise a U.S. posture that can wage a repeat of the Persian Gulf War while deterring aggression in Korea. If sufficient forces are available to deal with the two canonical MRCs, in all likelihood the U.S. posture will provide combat forces with a sufficient overall size to address any single nonstandard conflict in the other categories. The real problem is that for other missions and nonstandard contingencies, specific capabilities might be lacking because they are not mandated by the canonical MRCs. For example, peacekeeping can require specialized training and equipment that are quite different from those needed for major warfighting. Crisis management/resolution, peacemaking, and peace enforcement normally require combat forces similar to those needed for warfighting, but they normally mandate employment doctrines very different from those of Decisive Force. A medium-sized regional contingency in East Central Europe or the Balkans might require logistics support forces larger, and quite different from, the support forces needed for the Persian Gulf and Korea. A regional nuclear contingency might require specialized forms of command, control, communications, and information (C3I) and air strike operations quite different from those needed for a canonical MRC. These are only a few examples of how unique capabilities might be needed for strategic missions and nonstandard contingencies that depart from the canonical MRCs, but they illustrate the basic point.

Force sizing will include planning for two canonical MRCs, but the act of developing military plans and future-looking programs should be guided by a much broader framework. Planners should begin by taking a careful look at all 12 mission categories. For each category, potential contingencies in the three identified theaters should be considered. For each theater, the robustness of solutions should be tested by examining significant deviations from expected norms. The results should then be used to gauge the adequacy of force plans and programs. The desired outcome should be a robust and flexible military posture that can perform many different kinds of operations, aided by deployment/employment plans and military doctrines that are sufficiently adaptive to respond to the situations at hand.

Assuming that overall requirements remain similar to those of today, analysis and force planning would aspire to fulfill three goals:

1. Develop a posture that can conduct two concurrent MRCs, but define the conflicts and their requirements in generic terms (e.g., a regional campaign against a threat of 25 divisions and 600 aircraft).

2. Develop a posture that can perform all 12 strategic missions one at a time, with generic levels of strength.

3. Fine-tune the posture through the use of canonical and non-standard scenarios so that flexibility is enhanced for many different specific situations.

Admittedly, analysis of this type would complicate the defense planning process. However, the goal of planning is not simplicity but comprehensiveness. Two canonical MRC scenarios buy detailed appraisals of only these events at the expense of roughly accurate assessments of a far-larger class of conflicts that might actually occur. Whereas they give the Department of Defense penetrating vision for expected conflicts, they may leave it largely blind to the surprises created by the unexpected. The outcome of considering multiple strategic missions and nonstandard scenarios would be greater confidence that the Defense Department will not be left flying blind in a dangerous-world era seemingly destined to create a fog of confusion.

WHAT IF STRONGER U.S. AND ALLIED FORCES ARE NEEDED?

If a dangerous world emerges, it might have military requirements greater than those that can be met by today's posture. Assuming a policy decision is made to spend extra funds rather than to incur added risks, the U.S. force posture would have to be strengthened. This situation, however, would not necessarily mandate a return to Cold War budgets and force levels. Between today's posture and the extreme case of a return to Cold War defenses lie a number of more moderate and less costly options.

The first step normally taken toward rearmament is preserving the existing posture while pursuing improvements to its readiness, modernization, and sustainability. A host of steps could be taken in all three improvement categories at varying expense—although their combined costs are normally less than that of a significant expansion of the posture. Yet their overall effect can be significant, sometimes greater than adding more forces, especially when the existing posture has been hollowed out by continuing funding shortfalls. By remedying these shortfalls, the existing posture can be restored, often in a time span far shorter than was needed to enlarge it.

Readiness could be increased by intensifying training, increasing operational tempo, upgrading maintenance, and buying more spare parts. Modernization could be enhanced by accelerating acquisition of new weapons and by funding additional research and development. Sustainability could be improved by buying larger reserve stocks and upgrading the manning of logistics support units. The result can be ground, air, and naval forces with far greater real combat power, capable of using their modern weapons to full advantage. Of special importance might be steps to enhance power-projection capability through development of better strategic mobility forces. Even short of buying more planes and ships, measures could be pursued to preposition more equipment stocks, add air crews to increase airlift sortie rates, enhance the availability of naval reserve cargo ships, and reduce loading time by improving port facilities. The effect can be a capacity to deploy forces to overseas conflicts faster than is now possible.

Cost-Effective Guidelines for Strengthening U.S. Forces

If the posture must be enlarged, such enlargement should be guided by a coherent plan, rather than conducted in a linear fashion. An attractive, cost-effective option would be to add USAF Reserve Component fighter wings, which cost only about two-thirds what their active counterparts cost yet have good reputations for performing their primary missions. About four RC wings can be purchased for the life-cycle cost of a single Army heavy division, yet they could be deployed overseas far faster and provide combat power similar to that division. Especially for budgets that allow for only a modest expansion, this option provides high leverage at relatively low expense: average costs for 4 RC wings would be about $3–$5 billion annually.

If an across-the-board expansion is desired at affordable expense, an appropriate strategic goal would be to acquire the added capacity to deal with a lesser regional contingency. In this event, the U.S. posture would grow from the current ability to fight two MRCs to the ability to handle these MRCs and deal with an LRC. The effect would be to upgrade U.S. strategic flexibility and reduce vulnerability to multiple contingencies. This capability could be gained by adding 2 Army divisions, 3 USAF fighter wings, and 1 Navy CVBG. Added costs would be about $12–$15 billion annually.

What could drive the U.S. defense budget and force structure back toward Cold War levels is acquiring the capacity to fight three MRCs. This step might be taken if worry grows that, in addition to defending the Persian Gulf and Korea, U.S. strategy also requires the capacity to simultaneously project a large posture to Europe. Such a posture would enable an MRC-style conflict to be fought on its own or, alternatively, U.S. forces to join with NATO forces in waging a larger-theater campaign. This step would require an added 6 Army/Marine divisions, 7–10 USAF wings, and 4–5 CVBGs. Added costs could be $40–$50 billion annually.

West European Power Projection

Although these options help illuminate how U.S. forces could be strengthened, a sensible parallel step would be to upgrade Allied forces for power-projection missions. In Europe, for example, NATO Allies continue to prepare their forces primarily for border defense. The result is a downsized post–Cold War posture that will number fully 50 mobilizable divisions and 3500 combat aircraft—nearly all to protect borders that mostly are no longer seriously threatened. The Allies today lack a capacity to project large forces to the east of NATO's borders, in Central Europe, much less to the Persian Gulf. During Desert Storm, the Allies contributed only two divisions, 200 combat aircraft, and some naval combatants. This small force represents about what they could project today.

The West European capability for power projection could be improved significantly by upgrading NATO's Rapid-Reaction Force. Originally designed for intraregional missions, this force, which includes fully 9 Allied divisions, 325 combat aircraft, and comparable naval forces, is potentially usable for operations outside NATO's borders. What constrains this force's deployability today is lack of C3I assets, mobile logistics support units, transport forces, and war reserve stocks. Improvements in these areas would be only modestly expensive (e.g., $3–$5 billion annually). Even if only one-half of these forces is available at any single time, West European forces would be able to handle some contingencies on their own, without major U.S. contributions, and to assist in other operations led by the United States.

If a dangerous world emerges in the form of new military requirements, force contributions by the West Europeans and other allies will be needed not only for military reasons but for political reasons. Otherwise, the United States will be left carrying the principal burden for new missions. In such a situation, U.S. alliances almost certainly would erode. Allies would be encouraged to refrain from taking responsibility for new problems, and the United States would lose faith in them. If rearmament becomes necessary, the task would be more difficult than charting a more complicated course for the United States alone.

Chapter Nine

CONCLUSIONS

A dangerous world may spring from today's fog of uncertainty between the optimistic vision of a cooperative world that followed from the fall of the Berlin Wall and the current international downslide. The time may be fast approaching in which the United States will be compelled to abandon today's relaxed optimism about world affairs and adopt instead a more worried, vigilant stance. This prospect is already real enough to be taken seriously.

A dangerous world will be a more traditional world than that of the Cold War. It will be a world in which there is more than one hegemonic power to be guarded against. A dangerous world may offer an insidious combination of nineteenth-century politics, twentieth-century passions, and twenty-first-century technology: an explosive mixture of multipolarity, nationalism, and advanced technology. Above all, it will be ever-changing and complex. Specific problems may arise quickly, then go away, only to be replaced by entirely different challenges. Indeed, the core features of the international system may change repeatedly as one structure gives way to another. The one constant is that, in marked contrast to the past 50 years, the chief problem will be managing several different challenges that, compounded, will make the world a troubled, complicated place in which the United States is faced with a shifting array of friends and enemies, opportunities and dangers.

A dangerous world will compel the United States to avoid the temptation to embrace the comfort of believing that the passage of the Cold War means lasting tranquility, and that global progress is predestined even if the United States does not work hard to achieve it.

The United States will not be free to assume that its global problems can be solved by making friends with former adversaries and by allowing market democracy to work its wonders. It will not be able to treat national security policy as a marginally important diversion from domestic issues and economic goals. It will not be able to view defense strategy as a wartime endeavor divorced from peacetime policy or to view military power as a distasteful instrument of last resort, a sword to be kept sheathed and drawn only if all else fails. Above all, the United States will not be able to escape history or to embrace idealism at the expense of realism, or to cast aside moral dilemmas and responsibilities. Shibboleths will have to be replaced by policy and strategy in contact with history and reality as they exist, not as some would want them to be.

FINDINGS

The specific findings of this study are as follows: U.S. national security policy should be framed around the most probable dangerous scenario ahead, which has three main components: mounting regional tensions in Europe, Asia, and the Middle East/Persian Gulf; traditional U.S. and Western geopolitical rivalry with Russia and China; and Western security alliances with an uncertain capacity to act. An appropriate U.S. policy response would be systemic containment, which would include strong measures aimed at reinvigorating U.S. alliances, maintaining equilibrium with Russia and China, and controlling regional tensions so that they do not spread outward. This containment policy would not bring about worldwide peace, but it would help preserve global stability, thereby enabling market democracy to slowly expand into new regions. By permitting the United States to juggle the troubles in five regions instead of those in the current two regions, this policy would harness geopolitical realism to help promote the cause of democratic idealism.

Accompanying this national security policy would be an activist and appropriately tailored defense agenda. U.S. defense strategy would aim not only at being prepared for crisis and war, but also at supporting U.S. global and regional peacetime goals. The U.S. force posture would be structured to pursue various manifestations of this strategy and to provide the flexibility needed to switch to alternative strategies when necessary. A new defense planning framework would be adopted that prepares for a host of operations by focusing on generic missions rather than on specific canonical contingencies, and by reacting flexibly to crises when they occur.

RECOMMENDATIONS

Regardless of whether these specific approaches are adopted, the underlying strategic framework put forth in this study is what counts. The United States should intensify its efforts to examine how national security policy and strategy should be altered in the event that a dangerous world comes about. A coherent agenda of bold action may soon be needed to help prevent the worst from transpiring and to manage the problems that cannot be prevented. In all likelihood, the policy and strategy required by a dangerous world will bear little resemblance to those of today, so the need to assess the sweeping departures that may be needed is all the more apparent.

As a result, the primary task facing the United States will be to set aside the impulse to act and, instead, to ponder thoroughly what its policy and strategy should be. This task, however, will be more fundamental than preparing an action agenda for implementation. Because the Cold War and other twentieth-century conflicts produced great clarity, they allowed the United States the luxury of acting boldly without first thinking deeply—without examining a broad spectrum of events and determining alternative responses—about the exact problems being faced, the goals to be achieved, and the means to be employed. In contrast, a dangerous world of the future will put a far greater premium on reflection because its contours will be anything but clear. Indeed, that world may be so complex that ill-considered action might cause as much damage as passivity. Before the United States can embark upon efforts to engineer a favorable outcome, it will need to forge a conceptual design of the state of affairs it is trying to achieve.

A dangerous world could take many forms. Regardless of how it unfolds, the United States will need a coherent policy and strategy anchored on sound postulates that allow for coordinated actions on behalf of a clear vision. The only effective way to deal with a dangerous world is through an engaged and activist U.S. global stance that must be supported by ample military power, a coherent but readily changeable defense strategy, and a flexible force posture.

In crafting a national security policy that translates this powerful stance into effective action, the United States should embrace an alliance-first policy aimed at global stability through systemic containment. This policy would emphasize domestic economic recovery, and would put stock in reinvigorated alliances that slowly grow outward and, above all, that can project power and security outward. In dealing with geopolitical rivalry with major states, this policy would aim for political equilibrium sustained by a military balance of power. In dealing with regional tensions, it would aim to dampen and control troubles that otherwise might propel the entire international system into chaos. It would advance the cause of global stability without expecting worldwide peace. It would put the United States in a position to safely manage what could be a turbulent era ahead and thereby pass through history's next stage in a way that allows democratic progress to slowly continue.

The United States will need to think deeply not only about what must be done but also about why. In the late nineteenth century, British Prime Minister Lord Salisbury was once asked to explain what troubled him most about being responsible for his country's foreign policy. A man in firm contact with reality who preferred to embrace problems rather than dodge them, Lord Salisbury said that the need to make fateful decisions and take drastic steps was not the most onerous task. What he found far more difficult was the need to think carefully beforehand. It was not bold action that bedeviled him but, rather, the tough intellectual gymnastics of forging conceptual order out of confusion, deciphering complex problems, weighing the issues and alternatives deliberately, *then* making reasoned choices that balance many competing concerns. History has judged Lord Salisbury and other nineteenth-century British leaders a success precisely because they proved adept at the intellectual side of national security in a complex age. Their legacy provides the United States with a model to ponder as it faces a dangerous world.[1]

---

[1]See Robert K. Massie, *Dreadnought: Britain, Germany, and the Coming of the Great War*, New York: Random House, 1991.

THE EXPERIENCE OF DEMOCRACY IN EUROPE AND ASIA

The complex road to peace and democracy in Europe can be illustrated by comparing the historical experiences of the United States and Britain with that of Germany. Both the United States and Britain are maritime nations with long-standing reputations for maintaining powerful navies. As a result, they were insulated from invasion, and this security played an important role in allowing liberal democracy to grow on their territory. Both countries had cohesive societies and also benefited from a large merchant middle class, whose belief in free-market capitalism and individual freedom encouraged democratic values. In both countries, the middle class played a large role in suppressing antidemocratic impulses normally originating from the landed aristocracy and the peasantry. The growth of their capitalist economies through industrialization and trade expansion, in turn, enlarged their middle classes and promoted satisfied societies—developments that further encouraged civic values and liberal democracy.

Thus, a combination of ideal geostrategic circumstances and favorable social structures helped pave the way for democracy to become established in both countries. Even so, the arrival of democracy did not immediately translate into benign foreign policies by the two countries. Britain remained an imperial power throughout the nineteenth century and was commonly regarded as a country in pursuit of its own interests and willing to use coercion against any rival that stood in its way. The United States was an isolationist power. However, on the North American continent, it expanded its control westward, driving out Spain, France, and Mexico and subjugating the Native American population. When the United States began to come out of its isolationism in the late 1800s, it did so as an imperial power, pushing its presence and authority into the Caribbean and the Pacific.[1]

Owing to the legacy of America's colonial subjugation by Britain, these two countries originally were not close allies even though they shared democratic forms of government. Indeed, they fell into military conflict during the Revolutionary War in the late 1700s and again in 1812. As late as the U.S Civil War of 1861–1865, the Union government feared that Britain would intervene on the side of the Confederacy to promote British commercial and geostrategic interests. After the Civil War, the two countries slowly drew closer together in response to the flourishing of mutually prosperous trade, and the fear of further military conflict faded. Alliance between them, however, came only during World War I and was initiated by the fear that militaristic Germany might assert control of the European continent: an outcome that threatened the geostrategic interests of both countries.

Throughout the nineteenth century, German philosophers demonstrated familiarity with democratic theory. But in contrast to Britain and the United States, Germany faced external and internal circumstances that did not favor democracy and prevented its becoming established there. Germany's location in Central Europe left it vulnerable to invasion from all directions. The consequent need for constant military security pushed Germany toward monarchical authoritarianism and a powerful army. German society was dominated by a landed aristocracy, and it had a conservative industrial elite and a large rural peasantry: all segments acting as bulwarks against democracy.

Authoritarian Prussia acquired some trappings of democracy from the mid-1800s onward as a parliament arose to share power with the Kaiser. Constitutional monarchy, however, did not push Germany toward a benign foreign policy: It helped, instead, infuse Germany with nationalism and hatred of democratizing France. Between 1850 and 1870, Germany unified under Prussian leadership by conducting

---

[1]See Thomas A. Bailey, *A Diplomatic History of the American People*, New York: Meredith Publishing Company, 1964. British imperial policy is assessed in Paul Johnson, *The Birth of the Modern*, New York: Harper Collins, 1991.

imperial wars against Denmark, the Austro-Hungarian Empire, and France. After 1870, Germany, its major strategic goals fulfilled, tempered its imperial conduct and sought to preserve its security through alliances with Russia, Austria, and Britain against France. It resumed imperial conduct only after 1890, when Bismarck departed and German diplomacy fell into the hands of the youthful Kaiser Wilhelm and his incompetent aides.[2]

Kaiser Wilhelm's inept-but-menacing conduct was far from the only cause of World War I, but as this conflict became a brutal stalemate that destroyed Europe, Germany was roundly blamed as the principal source. When Germany was finally defeated in 1918, the Kaiser abdicated and the Versailles peace accord, which treated Germany harshly, was forged. In the aftermath, Germany surmounted turbulent internal conditions and extremist ideologies to become a democracy under the Weimar Republic. For more than a decade afterward, it pursued a generally benign foreign policy.

The post-war European security order proved to be unstable, however, owing to the collapse of the Austro-Hungarian and Ottoman Empires, the replacement of Czarist rule in Russia with Bolshevik Communism, and economic depression brought about by protectionist policies and the failure of market capitalism to bring enduring prosperity. In this turbulent atmosphere, democracy in Germany fell to Nazism and military aggression as a response to Versailles' unfair features and great social anxiety over economic collapse and runaway inflation. Hitler came to power by democratic means, and his hallmark was strong government, a revitalized economy, a stable society, and restored prestige for Germany. The experience taught the lesson that, simply because democracy and benign foreign policy are installed for a period, they are not destined to rule forever. If they are to endure, they must be sustained by favorable supporting conditions.

Following Nazism's crushing defeat in World War II, West Germany again became a democracy, largely because of occupation by the United States, Britain, and France. Albeit a frontline state in the Cold War, it pledged itself to a benign foreign policy in cooperation with

---

[2]See Robert K. Massie, *Dreadnought: Britain, Germany, and the Coming of the Great War*, New York: Random House, 1991.

its Western democratic neighbors. Paving the way to this conversion was West Germany's entrance into NATO, a development that finally brought West Germany the military security that had been denied it for centuries and that played an important role in enabling democracy to install itself in German society. Had NATO not provided defense against the threat of Soviet communism, West Germany would have been left in a situation of chronic insecurity. The result almost certainly would have been reversion to authoritarian rule and a free-wheeling, coercive diplomacy, for these two traditional features of German conduct would have been mandated by the need to ensure security unilaterally.

Favorable geostrategic circumstances thus played a role in Germany's conversion to democracy and benign diplomacy, and the same can be said for Western Europe as a whole. Democracy arrived in the early 1800s and took hold best in countries with prosperous capitalist economies and a large middle class. But this development was far from a sufficient condition to bring about a unified community and peace. Indeed, Europe remained turbulent for nearly 150 years more, and a number of its democracies pursued imperial agendas and struggled against each other. The political cooling (i.e., relaxation of tensions) of Western Europe that took place after World War II was helped by common democratic values, but it also owed to many other factors: Nationalist passions were spent by the brutalities of World Wars I and II, which enabled some long-standing border disputes to be settled; the Common Market was established, and with it economic prosperity for these nations—a development that produced a large measure of tranquility and stabilization of democracy; equally important, the creation of NATO not only brought defense against the Soviets but also provided powerful mutual assurances—NATO meant that West European countries would be united in a common alliance and thus would never again face either a threat from each other or the need to find security through unilateral means.

A similar story can be told for Asia. Although China remains under authoritarian rule, democracy has emerged since World War II in several Asian countries, as have free-market economies and a trend toward community-building. But this process did not begin with the establishment of democracy and proceed from there to other achievements. Indeed, most Asian countries entered the post–World

War II era with traditional societies and values that produced authoritarian regimes. Democracy initially took root only in Japan, and at the insistence of occupying U.S. forces. In the rest of Asia, the projection of American military power into the region provided a sense of security against looming threats from Communist China and the Soviet Union. Once this security architecture had been established, the economic framework created by the Bretton Woods accords helped promote trade, industrialization, and rapid economic growth. As economic growth took place, authoritarian rule gave way to single-party democracies. The past few years have seen a further transition toward multiple-party democracies. The Asian experience is one in which democracy was not the cause of economic progress and community-formation but, instead, the effect.

THE U.S. HISTORICAL EXPERIENCE WITH CANONICAL SCENARIOS

The historical experience of the United States with canonical scenarios provides a mixed legacy that illustrates the strengths and limitations of such scenarios. Planning with a canonical scenario had its most powerful influence in shaping U.S. and NATO defense preparations in Central Europe. As of the early 1960s, NATO was moving toward a military strategy of flexible response anchored on enhanced conventional preparedness, but its defense posture was weak and badly out of balance.

NATO–WARSAW PACT CANONICAL SCENARIO

To help guide the needed improvements, a canonical scenario was built in the mid-1960s and was used thereafter with only modest modifications of its core postulates. This scenario envisioned a NATO–Warsaw Pact war in Central Europe, launched after only a 15–30-day period of mobilization and reinforcement, employing 90 divisions and 4000 combat aircraft, and accompanied by enemy aggression in northern and southern Europe.

This canonical scenario played a critical role in aiding NATO conventional defense planning: It helped NATO define the Warsaw Pact threat in ways that stressed the dangers facing the Alliance, the need for a sound strategy, and the feasibility of achieving tangible improvements with affordable resources. It also helped NATO embrace demanding conventional-force goals and pursue a coordinated set of improvement measures through Alliance Defense 1970 (AD-70), the

Long-Term Defense Program (LTDP), and the Conventional Defense Initiative (CDI). As a result, NATO's conventional posture grew steadily stronger, as did its capacity to conduct joint and combined operations. Because of the sustained military buildup pursued by the Warsaw Pact, NATO continued to worry about its defenses. However, a satisfactory military balance was maintained in the sense that the Soviets never gained confidence in their own ability to prevail in a war.

The effect was to preserve containment, deterrence, and Alliance cohesion in ways that not only maintained military security but also helped all of Western Europe to build the European Community and achieve growing economic prosperity under the banner of democracy. Moreover, NATO's growing defense strength helped win the Cold War by compelling the Warsaw Pact to spend ever-larger sums in its futile quest for military supremacy, thereby bankrupting communist rule. The West thus owes part of its Cold War victory in Europe to its canonical scenario and the integrated military planning that came in its wake.

In retrospect, U.S. experience with this scenario is not entirely without blemish. One sobering consideration is the extent to which this scenario became hostage to manipulation, owing to the programmatic debates that were "waged" from the early 1960s onward. The basic scenario remained intact, but its specific features were constantly being adjusted as the debates flared and abated. In one sense, this process of adjustment was appropriate for making important investment decisions. Yet there was a continuing risk that analytical coherence—indeed, intellectual contact with reality—might become lost. Precisely because canonical scenarios are used to help make tough decisions for the allocation of resources, they are not crafted in a political vacuum.

This scenario, moreover, had downsides that fortunately were not tested because war never occurred. An especially troublesome issue is how nuclear escalation would have been conducted, but equally profound issues arise from NATO's preparations for conventional war. There, intent focus on the canonical scenario was purchased at the price of little interest in nonstandard events and plans to deal with them. NATO's response to the canonical scenario was to formulate defense plans focused on building a highly ready posture of active combat units and on rapid reinforcement from CONUS through POMCUS (Prepositioning of Materiel Configured to Unit Sets) and strategic airlift. NATO therefore did not pursue options to enlarge its posture through better reserve-component ground forces and enhanced sealift—alternatives that were ruled out because they did not square with the canonical focus on a quick-breaking war. As a result, NATO was left with ground and air forces that were ready and modern but that lacked adequate size for a confident defense. Had a war occurred, however, it just as easily could have come after a more prolonged mobilization lasting weeks, not days. But NATO may have lacked the defense assets to take advantage of the opportunity.

The canonical scenario had other dubious features: In particular, it envisioned a short, violent war fought at the inner-German border, with NATO conducting a linear defense against a massive enemy assault aimed at gaining a quick, decisive victory. This scenario made sense because it squared with NATO's own strategy and with assessments of the enemy threat. But especially because war often is full of surprises, it ruled out a wide range of other conflicts that plausibly might have unfolded. To a degree, it left NATO unprepared for these outcomes.

SPECULATION ABOUT REAL-WORLD OUTCOMES

Speculation can be offered here about the effects of the canonical scenario. What if the war had settled into a prolonged confrontation lasting more than 2–3 weeks? In this event, NATO might have run out of ammunition because Allied plans assumed a short war. What if Warsaw Pact air defenses had proven highly effective? NATO's air strategy, which focused on interdiction at the expense of close air support, might have been ineffective, leaving NATO's outnumbered ground forces lacking support from the air.

What if the Warsaw Pact gained a decisive breakthrough and the outcome was decided by a swirling maneuver battle in NATO's rear areas? Although NATO shifted to a maneuver doctrine in later years, its rigid emphasis on linear defense earlier might have prevented it from winning such a battle. In its preoccupation with building a powerful forward defense that relied on firepower, moreover, NATO invested many resources in logistics assets to support the limited number of ground combat formations needed to carry out its linear array. As a result, it lacked the sizable ground operations reserves required for a rear attack. Even with the maneuver doctrine of later years, it might have had trouble defeating the enemy had major breakthroughs occurred.

More fundamental questions can be asked. What if NATO had been compelled to retreat to the Rhine River or even farther to the west? This reversal was envisioned by NATO war plans of the late 1940s, but these plans were cast aside when forward defense was adopted. Would NATO have been able to conduct the sweeping counterattack, possibly beginning with a repeat of the Normandy invasion, needed to regain lost ground? The answer is unknowable because NATO's forward defense strategy and canonical scenario prevented the question itself from being seriously addressed from the early 1950s onward.

Questions also can be raised about what NATO would have done had the battle turned out far more positively than forecasted by the pessimists. What would NATO have done if its forces had decisively crushed invading Warsaw Pact forces? Would NATO have counterattacked to liberate East Germany? Would it have gone on to liberate Czechoslovakia and Poland? Would NATO even have been able to conduct these offensive operations? The answer to this question, at least, is knowable: NATO's focus on defense kept it from shaping its strategy and posture for the offense. Indeed, the entire German Army was designed expressly to prevent it from being able to march beyond the inner-German border. Clearly, political considerations mandated a focus on defense that avoided any appearance of aggressive intent. Even so, a legitimate issue in retrospect is whether NATO tilted too far in this direction by designing a posture that was so optimized for one kind of war that it lacked the flexibility to conduct another.

For all these reasons, NATO's canonical scenario merits a balanced appraisal. Had NATO diverted its limited resources for other purposes, its ability to carry out forward defense might have been weakened in ways that had negative political effects. Nevertheless, the Alliance has reasons to be grateful that reality never tested the canonical scenario. Perhaps Eisenhower best expressed things when he said "plans are nothing, but planning is everything." That is, the purpose of the exercise is not to create a fixed blueprint that almost certainly will be cast aside at the moment of truth but to prepare for a host of outcomes requiring the flexibility to respond. Ironically, NATO's military strategy for most of the Cold War was one of flexible response. In retrospect, the issue to be contemplated is whether the canonical scenario fostered this capacity or inhibited it.

KOREAN WAR: EXAMPLE OF THE ABSENCE OF A CANONICAL SCENARIO

An example of the absence of a canonical scenario may be illustrative. Canonical scenarios have played important roles in regions outside Europe, and especially in Asia. There, the Korean War experience illustrates the drawbacks of having no canonical scenario. When North Korea attacked South Korea in June 1950, the United States was caught by surprise, with no defense plans and programs for protecting the Korean peninsula. The surprise mounted when the North Korean Army broke through South Korean defenses in the Chorwon corridor, the Republic of Korea (ROK) Army collapsed, and aggressor forces swept down the peninsula. Surprise gave way to alarm when U.S. reinforcements sent from Japan proved to be poorly armed and unready, and were themselves overpowered in a few days. Compelled to retreat, U.S. forces were soon clinging to a small foothold at Pusan. Equally bad, U.S. forces across the Pacific and in the United States were unprepared for a major war. The full-scale disarmament undertaken since World War II's end in 1945, conducted amid signs of mounting Cold War, had left an Army that, in General Omar Bradley's words, "could not fight its way out of a wet paper bag." Nor were the Marines, the Air Force, and the Navy much better off.[1]

The United States hastily mobilized and launched a reinforcement effort in which General MacArthur's counterattack at Inchon outflanked the North Koreans, and U.S. forces then drove all the way north to the Yalu River. But another planning failure occurred when the United States underestimated Communist China's determination. Again caught by surprise when massive Chinese forces crossed

---

[1]See Clay Blair, *The Forgotten War: America in Korea, 1950–1953*, New York: Doubleday, 1987.

the Yalu, U.S. units were forced into an embarrassing retreat. In the end, American forces recaptured their balance and launched a counterattack that threw back Chinese forces to the 38th parallel. Over two years of heavy losses later, the war ended in a frustrating stalemate when an armistice was signed, but at least South Korea's territorial independence had been restored. The Korean War's early days taught an important lesson about the drawbacks of not planning seriously in advance.

To a worrisome degree, this failure to plan was demonstrated again when the United States plunged into Vietnam 12 years later. To be sure, American forces were far better prepared to fight than in 1950. Indeed, the Defense Department had been preparing for a major conventional conflict in Asia since 1961, when the Kennedy Administration scrapped the then-existing nuclear strategy and embraced global flexible response. Where planning fell short was in the transparent failure of the U.S. government to concoct a sound force-employment strategy for determining how military means could achieve political ends. As a result, the United States plunged into a conflict that it was neither capable of winning nor of achieving a satisfactory political outcome for.

When the United States intervened in Southeast Asia, its military leaders had reason for confidence that their troops would overpower the enemy on the battlefield. But political constraints prevented an invasion of North Vietnam, and U.S. forces were compelled to pursue a grinding attrition war in the South. Because they were able to dictate the tempo of battle in ways that allowed them to be logistically resupplied, North Vietnamese and Viet Cong units were able to hold their own even though outgunned. The United States launched a massive air bombardment effort against North Vietnam and gradually escalated the pressure to compel the enemy to desist from its aggression in the South. But the North Vietnamese proved stubbornly resistant to gradualism, thereby debunking the theories of escalation popular at the time. To be sure, U.S. forces inflicted far greater losses on the enemy than were suffered in return, but the outcome was driven not by comparative fire-exchange rates but by relative political will. In the end, the United States suffered a bruising defeat driven not by battlefield inferiority but by poor strategy and by domestic unwillingness to accept high casualties and never-ending involvement on behalf of less-than-vital interests.

U.S. PLANNING AFTER VIETNAM

In the wake of the Vietnam debacle, the United States reoriented its military planning on Northeast Asia. Whereas China had been the principal adversary in earlier years, the Sino-Soviet rift led to relaxation of worry about Beijing's intentions. As a result, U.S. planners focused on North Korea and on the growing Soviet military buildup in Asia. Two canonical scenarios dominated planning: a surprise North Korean attack on the ROK that threatened Seoul, and Soviet military pressure against Japan, including an invasion of Hokkaido.

In response, U.S. planning concentrated on defending South Korea, protecting Japan, and controlling Pacific waters surrounding the Asian mainland. This effort was successful. The United States maintained a sizable military presence in Northeast Asia, and Japanese and ROK forces steadily gained strength. As U.S. and Allied forces grew better able to fight together on behalf of integrated military strategies, containment and deterrence grew stronger, and Alliance cohesion was solidified. Benefiting from external security and internal stability, Asian nations friendly to the United States entered a period of sustained economic growth, and the Asian security system stabilized. Although the Cold War's end was driven by events in Europe, it also was influenced by favorable trends in Asia: a monument to American political-military constancy, backed by responsive defense plans.

Even so, U.S. defense plans for Asia during the Cold War leave a troublesome controversy in their wake. Especially during the 1980s, American planners began focusing on the goal of coordinating defense strategy in Europe and Asia in the event of a global war with the Soviet Union. At issue is whether this goal was adequately achieved.

In Europe, NATO's military strategy was defensive, and to many observers, a similar defensive strategy made sense in Asia as well. Yet U.S. naval strategy flirted with the idea of horizontal escalation through offensive action as a device to bring pressure on the Soviet government in a war. This escalation was to be conducted not only in the North Atlantic but in the western Pacific as well, where Soviet installations might have been subjected to bombardment from the sea. Announcement of this strategy departure caused great consternation in Japan, where worry built that attacks on the former

USSR would cause war in Europe to spread to the Pacific, thereby exposing Japan to nuclear holocaust.

Tensions in U.S.–Japanese relations abated when efforts were launched to harmonize combined defense plans in the Pacific, but the misunderstandings never entirely were laid to rest. The end of the Cold War relegated this thorny issue to history; yet, in retrospect, lingering questions remain. In the event of Warsaw Pact aggression in Europe, would the Soviet Union have opened a second front in Asia or would it have refrained to avoid overburdening its own strategy? Granted that U.S. counterstrikes would have been needed if Soviet aggression occurred in Asia, would these strikes have made sense if the Soviets had desisted? What would have been the effect on U.S.–Japanese relations? What would have been the effect on the overall war? Would U.S. naval operations have increased the odds for a favorable outcome or would they have inflamed escalation? These questions cannot be answered in any final way. But they do help illustrate the often-unseen connections among defense plans in separate regions, connections that might continue to exist even though the Cold War threat of a global hegemony has disappeared.

PERSIAN GULF CANONICAL SCENARIO

A positive-yet-mixed legacy also arises from U.S. experience with a canonical scenario in guiding defense preparations for the Persian Gulf. Prior to the late 1970s, the United States lacked not only a canonical scenario for this region but also any semblance of serious defense preparations. Regional security was entrusted largely to the Shah of Iran's imposing defense establishment. As a result, the United States had no military command for Persian Gulf/Southwest Asia operations and allocated no forces to regional contingencies there. Furthermore, the United States lacked mobility programs to project combat forces there, logistics units to support those forces, and a host-nation military infrastructure. These deficiencies left the United States unable to rapidly deploy large forces to the region.

The collapse of the Shah's regime, the assumption to power of an unstable radical Islamic government in Iran, and the Soviet invasion of Afghanistan triggered an intense effort to remedy these deficiencies. In the wake came a canonical scenario to guide the myriad defense preparations that would be needed. The act of building this scenario was rendered difficult by regional politics in the Gulf and by an unclear picture of the future. Defense of Persian Gulf oil was deemed the dominant security goal. But two fundamental questions were difficult to answer: Exactly who was to be the enemy to be deterred and defended against? How was the defense effort to be conducted?

At the time, Iran was embroiled in internal upheaval and not looking outward and Iraq had neither the military forces nor the political orientation to pose an obvious threat to Western access to Gulf oil. The Soviet Union, on the other hand, had both the military forces and the expansionist foreign policy to pose a threat. As a result, Pentagon planners focused on that nation as a potential adversary. They further calculated that if U.S. forces could defend against a massive Soviet invasion, they could deal with almost any adversary. Accordingly, they postulated a canonical scenario involving a Soviet assault of Iran by about 25 divisions and 1200 combat aircraft, aimed at seizing Iran's oil fields and perhaps more. Later, this Persian Gulf scenario was linked to the scenario of a NATO–Warsaw Pact war in Europe. The result was an "Illustrative Planning Scenario" envisioning a Warsaw Pact invasion of Central Europe coupled with a concurrent Soviet drive deep into Iran.

In the wake came a major upsurge in U.S. defense preparations for the Persian Gulf. The Central Command (CENTCOM) was created and given the mission of preparing to project sizable combat formations to the Gulf in an emergency. A large U.S. force of ground, air, and naval units was earmarked for the region and trained for operations there. Major mobility programs were launched, including acquisition of more heavy airlift, fast sealift, and prepositioned equipment. In Europe, the NATO Allies became accustomed to the idea that Alliance facilities might have to be used to help transport large U.S. forces to the Persian Gulf, and a few Allies began preparing forces of their own for this purpose. Defense cooperation with friendly Arab nations was accelerated somewhat, and a military infrastructure capable of absorbing U.S. forces was created. Therefore, although large American forces were not permanently deployed in the Persian Gulf, the United States acquired a far better capability to intervene quickly there in a crisis. This effort deterred Soviet interest in invading the Persian Gulf.

What stands out from the experience of recent years, nonetheless, is the extent to which the crises actually faced there bore little relation to the original canonical scenario. In 1987, U.S. and Allied naval forces helped escort oil tankers through turbulent Gulf waters during the Iran-Iraq War. Then, in late 1990 and early 1991, the United States and several Allies deployed massive forces to overturn Saddam Hussein's invasion of Kuwait. In essence, the United States originally had prepared to protect Iran from the Soviet Union and instead defended Kuwait and Saudi Arabia from Iraq: a radically different conflict.

THE VALUE OF CANONICAL SCENARIOS

This experience has produced more than a little cynicism about the value of canonical scenarios. Indeed, none of the three major wars fought by U.S. forces since 1945 has taken the form predicted by these scenarios. A common criticism is that canonical scenarios have a way of forecasting wars that never occur and of failing to warn of the wars that actually do take place. If this allegation holds, the United States is left girding itself for conflicts that are not materializing while failing to take the steps to deter and prosecute the wars that are taking shape. A perfect example of flawed reliance on canonical scenarios, this argument asserts, is the Gulf War with Iraq. Owing to its obsessive concern with the Soviet Union, the United States allegedly failed to perceive a growing threat from Iraq, and, indeed, Washington's diplomacy may have signaled to Saddam Hussein that his invasion of Kuwait would not be resisted.

If carried too far, such criticism overlooks the beneficial features of these scenarios in the Persian Gulf and elsewhere. That these canonical scenarios never occurred may owe to the possibility that the United States built the military posture needed to deter them from breaking out. The very fact that war with the Soviet Union never occurred during the Cold War may be powerful testimony to the deterrence power of such scenarios, not a refutation of their value. The same applies to the tenuous situation in Korea and probably to non-Soviet adversaries in the Persian Gulf as well. Owing to the power vacuum in the Persian Gulf and the importance of oil reserves there, the most noteworthy development is not that war finally broke out in 1990 but that Kuwait and Saudi Arabia were not invaded long before then. In all likelihood, American defense activity played a role in achieving this outcome.

The role allegedly played by the canonical scenario in fostering the conditions that led to the Persian Gulf conflict needs to be kept in perspective. Canonical scenarios face not only inward but outward as well: They are intended to send a powerful deterrent message. The Carter Doctrine, proclaimed in the late 1970s, made clear that the United States would fight to protect Western access to Persian Gulf oil and to defend its allies there. Especially because of this doctrine, the canonical scenario and the programmatic measures flowing from it conveyed the clear signal that U.S. military forces were being prepared for a major conflict in the Persian Gulf—not only against the former USSR but against *any* aggressor. After all, the United States did not dismantle CENTCOM when Mikhail Gorbachev announced in 1989–1990 that he was ending the Cold War on terms laid down by the West.

This signal that the United States would defend its Gulf interests may have been officially aimed at the Soviet Union, but other nations were under no illusion that Moscow was the only target. Indeed, several Persian Gulf and Middle East nations often expressed worry that the United States was using the Soviet threat as a diplomatic cover to justify preparations for aggression against them. Saddam Hussein's decision to ignore this signal means that deterrence failed, but it does not invalidate the signal itself. Rather, it means that successful deterrence rests on more than just preparatory military measures. Foreign policy and diplomacy matter as well, and they lie well outside the province of defense planning.

U.S. defense planning, moreover, was not blind to the possibility that Iraq might commit aggression. The original scenario may have focused on the Soviet Union, but by the late 1980s, CENTCOM planners had begun to worry about Iraq and to quietly prepare a response. These efforts played a role in helping CENTCOM respond quickly when aggression occurred. Whether U.S. diplomats failed to grasp the political threat posed by Saddam Hussein is another matter, but such failure owes more to a flawed grasp of Iraqi politics than to the blinding effects of the canonical scenario. At the time the Gulf War took place, the Soviet Union was withdrawing from Europe and Afghanistan, and had not posed any overt military threat for several years. Obsession with the Soviet threat may have dimmed American awareness of other dangers in earlier times but not at the time that the events of late 1990 took place.

Critics also should remember that although the original canonical scenario may have forecasted the wrong Gulf war, it got the fundamentals right, pointing out the importance of becoming prepared to defend the Persian Gulf oil fields against major-adversary aggression. It also correctly ascertained that large U.S. force commitments would be needed: The posture sent to defeat Iraq was virtually the same posture that had been designed to defend against a Soviet attack. It accurately laid down a requirement for large mobility programs to ensure that U.S. forces could speedily deploy to the Gulf. For all these reasons, the United States may have planned for the wrong war, but, not by coincidence, it was prepared for the war that actually came.

THE BOTTOM LINE

Perhaps the most important lesson is that canonical scenarios should not be judged by the impossible standard of clairvoyance. They are analytical devices to guide planning, not exercises in crystal-ball-gazing. What matters is whether they point U.S. defense preparations in roughly the right directions and produce military measures that leave U.S. forces adequately prepared for a broad range of situations that might arise. The key to defense adequacy is flexibility and responsiveness, not the capacity to carry out a fixed blueprint. Recognition of this standard, however, does not whitewash the canonical scenarios of the past, some of which, in retrospect, have empowered the U.S. defense effort while others may have imprisoned it. The task ahead will be to ensure that future scenarios foster the needed flexibility and responsiveness, not prevent it.

BIBLIOGRAPHY

Allison, Graham, and Gregory F. Treverton, eds., *Rethinking America's Security: Beyond Cold War to New World Order*, New York: W. W. Norton and Co., 1992.

Aron, Raymond, *Peace and War: A Theory of International Relations*, Garden City, N.Y.: Doubleday, 1966.

Aspin, Les, Secretary of Defense, *Report on the Bottom-Up Review*, Washington, D.C.: Department of Defense, October 1993.

Bailey, Thomas A., *A Diplomatic History of the American People*, New York: Meredith Publishing Company, 1964.

Blair, Clay, *The Forgotten War: America in Korea, 1950–1953*, New York: Doubleday, 1987.

Bowie, Christopher, et al., *The New Calculus: Analyzing Airpower's Changing Role in Joint Theater Campaigns*, Santa Monica, Calif.: RAND, MR-149-AF, 1993.

Brzezinski, Zbigniew K., *Out of Control: Global Turmoil on the Eve of the Twenty-First Century*, New York: Scribner's, 1993.

Chace, James, *The Consequences of the Peace: The New Internationalism and American Foreign Policy*, New York: Oxford University Press, 1992.

Chandler, David, *The Campaigns of Napoleon*, New York: MacMillan Publishing Company, 1966.

Cheney, Richard (Dick), Secretary of Defense, *DoD Annual Report for FY1993*, Washington, D.C.: U.S. Government Printing Office (GPO), 1992.

Conable, Barber B., Jr., and David M. Lampton, "China: The Coming Power," *Foreign Affairs*, Winter 1992–1993.

Davis, Paul, and Lou Finch, *Defense Planning for the Post–Cold War Era: Giving Meaning to Flexibility, Adaptiveness, and Robustness of Capability*, Santa Monica, Calif.: RAND, MR-322-JS, 1993.

Ellison, Herbert J., *History of Russia*, New York: Holt, Rinehart, and Winston, 1964.

Fischer, Louis, *The Life of Lenin*, New York: Harper and Row, 1964.

Fukuyama, Francis, *The End of History and the Last Man*, New York: Avon, 1992.

Garten, Jeffrey, *A Cold Peace: America, Japan, Germany, and the Struggle for Supremacy*, New York: Times Books, 1992.

Gay, Peter, *Sigmund Freud: A Life for Our Times*, New York: Anchor Books, 1988.

Gilpin, Robert, *The Political Economy of International Relations*, Princeton, N.J.: Princeton University Press, 1987.

Grachev, Pavel, *Main Provisions of the Military Doctrine of the Russian Federation*, Moscow: Russian Ministry of Defense, 1993.

Hannah, Barbara, *Jung: His Life and Work*, Boston: Shambhala, 1991.

Hoffmann, Stanley, *Gulliver's Troubles; or, The Setting of American Foreign Policy*, New York: McGraw-Hill, 1968.

Huntington, Samuel P., *The Third Wave: Democratization in the Late Twentieth Century*, Norman, Okla.: University of Oklahoma Press, 1991.

———, "The Clash of Civilizations?" *Foreign Affairs*, Summer 1993.

International Institute for Strategic Studies, *The Military Balance*, London: Brassey's, 1992/1993.

Johnson, Paul, *The Birth of the Modern*, New York: Harper Collins, 1991.

Kennedy, Paul, *Preparing for the Twenty-First Century*, New York: Random House, 1993.

Keohane, Robert O., ed., *Neorealism and Its Critics*, New York: Columbia University Press, 1986.

Kissinger, Henry, *Diplomacy*, New York: Simon & Schuster, 1994.

Kugler, Richard L., *NATO Military Strategy for the Post–Cold War Era*, Santa Monica, Calif.: RAND, R-4217-AF, 1992.

———, *Commitment to Purpose: How Alliance Partnership Won the Cold War*, Santa Monica, Calif.: RAND, MR-190-FF/RC, 1993.

———, *U.S. Military Strategy and Force Posture for the 21st Century: Capabilities and Requirements*, Santa Monica, Calif.: RAND, MR-328-JS, 1994.

———, *U.S.–West European Cooperation in Out-of-Area Operations: Problems and Prospects*, Santa Monica, Calif.: RAND, MR-349-USDP, 1994.

Lewis, Bernard, "Rethinking the Middle East," *Foreign Affairs*, Fall 1992.

Liddell-Hart, B. H., *Strategy*, New York: Signet, 1967.

Lipset, Seymour Martin, *The Politics of Unreason*, New York: Random House, 1972.

Lukacs, John, *The End of the Twentieth Century and the End of the Modern Age*, New York: Ticknor and Fields, 1993.

Massie, Robert K., *Dreadnought: Britain, Germany, and the Coming of the Great War*, New York: Random House, 1991.

Millot, Marc Dean, Roger Molander, and Peter A. Wilson, *"The Day After..." Study: Nuclear Proliferation in the Post–Cold War World*, Volume II, *Main Report*, Santa Monica, Calif.: RAND, MR-253-AF, 1993.

Montgomery, Bernard, *A History of Warfare*, New York: William Morrow and Company, 1983.

Moore, Barrington, *Social Origins of Dictatorship and Democracy: Lord and Peasant in the Making of the Modern World*, Boston: Beacon Press, 1993.

Morgenthau, Hans J., and Kenneth Thompson, *Politics Among Nations: The Struggle for Power and Peace*, New York: McGraw-Hill, 1985.

Motyl, Alexander J., *Dilemmas of Independence: Ukraine After Totalitarianism*, New York: Council on Foreign Relations Press, 1993.

Moynihan, Daniel Patrick, *Pandaemonium: Ethnicity in International Politics*, New York: Oxford University Press, 1993.

Niebuhr, Reinhold, *Moral Man and Immoral Society*, New York: Scribner's, 1960.

Parkinson, F., *The Philosophy of International Relations: A Study in the History of Thought*, Beverly Hills, Calif.: Sage Publications, 1977.

Pfaff, William, *The Wrath of Nations: Civilization and the Furies of Nationalism*, New York: Simon & Schuster, 1993.

Prestowitz, Clyde V., Jr., *Trading Places*, New York: Basic Books, 1988.

Record, Jeffrey, *Hollow Victory: A Contrary View of the Gulf War*, Washington, D.C.: Brassey's (U.S.), 1993.

Rosenau, James N., ed., *International Politics and Foreign Policy*, New York: The Free Press, 1969.

Russett, Bruce, *Grasping the Democratic Peace: Principles for a Post–Cold War World*, Princeton, N.J.: Princeton University Press, 1993.

Schlesinger, James, *DoD Annual Report*, Washington, D.C.: U.S. GPO, various fiscal years.

Singer, Max, and Aaron Wildavsky, *The Real World Order: Zones of Peace, Zones of Turmoil*, Chatham, N.J.:   Chatham House Publishers, 1993.

Straus, Leo, and Joseph Cropsey, *History of Political Philosophy*, Chicago, Ill.: University of Chicago Press, 1988.

Thomson, David, *Europe Since Napoleon*, New York: Alfred A. Knopf, 1964.

Thurow, Lester, *Head to Head: The Coming Economic Battle Among Japan, Europe, and America*, New York: William Morrow and Company, 1992.

Ullman, Richard H., *Securing Europe*, Princeton, N.J.:   Princeton University Press, 1991.

Waltz, Kenneth N., *Theory of International Politics*, Reading, Mass.: Addison-Wesley, 1979.

Weigley, Russell F., *The Age of Battles*, Bloomington, Ind.:   Indiana University Press, 1991.

Wright, Robin, "Islam and Democracy," *Foreign Affairs*, Summer 1992.